# Defending the Undefendable III

Walter E. Block

# Defending the Undefendable III

Springer

Walter E. Block
Eminent Scholar Endowed Chair in Economics
Loyola University New Orleans, Harold E Wirth
New Orleans, LA, USA

ISBN 978-981-16-3956-2 ISBN 978-981-16-3957-9 (eBook)
https://doi.org/10.1007/978-981-16-3957-9



This Springer imprint is published by the registered company Springer Nature Singapore Pte Ltd.
The registered company address is: 152 Beach Road, #21-01/04 Gateway East, Singapore 189721, Singapore

*To Murray N. Rothbard my mentor, my friend, my teacher, my inspiration*
*To the fans of Defending I and Defending II, who offered me suggestions for this book, Defending III*

# Acknowledgement

I acknowledge my debt to Murray N. Rothbard, my mentor, my friend, my guide, my inspiration.

# Introduction

The present book is an attempt to apply libertarian principles to a whole host of activities and professions. My thesis is that as long as behavior does not violate the basic premises of this philosophy, it should be legal. And this applies, in spades, to those that are now either prohibited by law, and/or seen as problematic, even despicable, by most people. I am here attempting to deduce the legality of actions from the basic libertarian premises. Some of these behaviors are truly revolting; they constitute vices. But not all vices should be crimes. If my conclusion offends you, that these acts should be legal no matter how immoral, I will have succeeded in demonstrating that you are not a libertarian, at least not insofar as I understand that philosophy. My goal, here, is to trace the logical implications of libertarianism, no more and no less.

Before we can analyze anything from the libertarian point of view, however, we have to be clear on what this political philosophy is, in the first place. The basic premises of this philosophy are best expressed in terms of three principles.

First, is the non-aggression principle (NAP). No one may initiate violence (or the threat thereof) against anyone else. That is, anyone can do anything he wants, except he is prohibited from threatening or using violence against others. But even this must be qualified, for it is certainly permissible under libertarian law to do exactly that with the permission of the recipient of the aggression. For example, the sadist may (threaten to) beat the masochist to a pulp, provided that the latter agrees to the pummeling, even invites it. One boxer may (threaten to or actually) punch another (above the belt) because each has agreed to be "victimized" in this manner, before stepping into the ring. Indeed, no boxer would ever be allowed into the ring unless he agreed to that proviso.

The second principle is private property rights. This determines whether a given violent act is a rights violation or not. For example, at gunpoint A grabs the shoes B is wearing. Does this violate the libertarian axiom? It all depends upon who is the rightful owner of the footwear. If the shoes belong to B then this act would indeed violate the NAP. But suppose that A is the proper owner (based on homesteading of original land and resources plus voluntary exchanges such as trading, bartering, buying, selling, gifts, gambling) and B stole the shoes from A yesterday. Today, A is merely repossessing them from the thief, B. Then A's act of violence is certainly justified.

But even this does not get the core of the freedom philosophy. For suppose, now, that B is the rightful owner of the shoes, and A grabs them anyway. This is clear theft. Is this necessarily incompatible with libertarianism? No. Posit, now that the world will end unless A seizes B's property. Work with me here. Or think in terms of the movie, Dr. Strangelove or: How I Learned to Stop Worrying and Love the Bomb (1964), where unless our hero breaks into a soda machine in order to steal some coins millions of people will perish in a nuclear war. He needs these coins in order to make a phone call, which alone will obviate this tragedy. But in doing so he destroys the rightfully owned property of Coca Cola.

Does the libertarian say, "Thou shall not steal (or destroy other people's private property)"? No. This philosophy is not a suicide pact. If that were all there were to it, the sanctity of private property rights would have precluded that telephone call, and the entire world would have been destroyed in a nuclear exchange. How, then, shall we construe libertarianism, if it does not, without exception, proscribe stealing justly owned property?

The most sophisticated and accurate understanding is that libertarianism is a theory of punishment. It does not say, do not steal. It does not even demand that no one murder our fellow man (see the trolley example in philosophy), or commit other, lesser, crimes. It only mandates that if we do so, it would be justified to punish us.

Let us return to A who relieves B, at gunpoint, of the latter's rightfully owned shoes. What are we to do with A? Simply, punish him appropriately. What is the just reaction to the fictional character in the movie who shoots the Coke machine in order to get coins to use in a pay phone booth (this was before the advent of cell phones)? He did so, remember, in order to make a telephone call that will save the world from nuclear warfare. Why, penalize him appropriately of course. He should be punished to the full extent of the law, governing such robbery. At the very least he would have to pay for a new dispensing machine plus the spare change he used to make the call. In "Dr. Strangelove," another character strongly urged against engaging in this act with the horrified expression: "You can't shoot the Coke machine. Why, that's private property." Obviously, the intent of the dialogue writer was to impugn the entire notion of private property, to make this crucial institution into a suicide pact. Had he succeeded, he would have successfully undermined libertarianism which has as one of its foundational principles the sanctity of private property. And this riposte would have succeeded, against an unsophisticated notion of private property and libertarianism, but not, hopefully, against the one now being employed. Libertarianism predicated upon the NAP and private property rights based on homesteading, and legitimate title transfer is a good introductory understanding of this philosophy. But we are now engaged in discerning a more advanced understanding.

Jean Val Jean in *Les Miserables*, stole a loaf of bread. For this crime he paid a heavy price. The author of that novel directs our attention, and our pity, to the draconian nature of the penalty. And we are also asked to focus on the dire circumstances of those he fed with this loaf of bread. However, it is important to stamp out, as much as humanly possible, stealing bread or anything else for that matter. If people were commonly to relieve bakeries of their products without paying for them, the bakers would no longer be able to create this foodstuff. If that were generalized, we would all starve, not merely the poor. At the very least we would all be poverty-stricken, on the verge of starvation. That we are not stems from the fact, in great part, that stealing is properly prohibited by law. And this occurs, in turn, because there are severe penalties attached to walking out of bakeries with bread in our arms without paying. If the implicit message of *Les Miserables* were followed, and bread stealing was met with a slap on the wrist, or with no punishment at all, it would be much the worse for society as a whole as our risk of going without any bread at all will be greatly increased.

Precisely, the same fate awaits us if we denigrate the barbarism of shooting Coke machines and relieving them of their coinage. Precious few of these conveniences would still be available to us because of any such general practice. Of course, there are emergency situations. These fiction writers focus attention on them to undermine private property rights. One way to counter them is to rely on the insight that "emergency situations make bad law." But that implies a dysfunction, a bifurcation, in law. There is one set of principles for ordinary circumstances, and another, an entirely separate one, for emergencies. One difficulty with this way of looking at the matter is subjectivism: what is an emergency for one man may be an ordinary circumstance for another. Another issue is the continuum problem. Situations of this sort tend to meld into one another. Then, too, there is the difficulty of having two sets of laws for different occurrences, even if these were objectively given. The benefit of the libertarian perspective is that it becomes enmeshed in none of these traps. There is only one law. There is only one principle justifying punishment for violation of the NAP, for undermining private property rights. No one is forbidden from doing any of these things. But, if they do so, justice requires that they be punished.

The third principle of libertarianism is voluntary association: no one should be forced to associate with anyone else at all against his will. Slavery violates this (in addition to the NAP) in that the victim is compelled to associate with the master against his will. Without that, slavery would be reduced to a weird sort of voluntary sadomasochism. Rape should be banned by law because, in addition to a NAP violation, the victim is compelled to associate with the rapist involuntarily. No man of good will would disagree with these implications of this philosophy. But anti-discrimination laws, too, violate this principle. If the Christian baker does not wish to associate with the gay customer, he, too, should not be forced to do so. If the black grocer does not wish to sell to the KKK member, or the Jewish one to a member of the Nazi Party, the same applies. And the same holds true for discrimination on the basis of race, sex, age, religion, ethnicity, sexual preference, etc. Not everyone will agree to these implications, but they follow logically, inexorably, from the basic premise just as in the cases of slavery and rape.

A word about the demagogue chapter. This brilliant essay was written by Murray N. Rothbard in 1954. I include it in this book since it is so quintessentially an instance of the "defendable" phenomenon. Needless to say, Murray stole this idea from me. True, he published this way before I even thought of it (I was 13 years old in 1954), but still, this is yet another example of the theft that Murray has perpetrated upon me. On a more serious note, there would not be any Defending series were it not for Murray, I would not have a career as an Austro-libertarian but for him, so I dedicate this book to him with great love and respect. He was for many years my mentor, my guru, my friend, I am honored to be able to say.

# Contents

# Part I
# Politics

# Chapter 1
# The Federalist

A federalist is someone who takes the side of the federal government vis a vis state governments. When the two are in conflict, such a person sides with the former. The anti-federalist of course takes the opposite position. By extension, when it comes to a dispute between state and local levels of government, such as counties or cities the centralist (federalist proxy) supports the former, and the decentralist (anti-federalist proxy), the latter.

This is a crucially important question, particularly in this era of the Covid 19 pandemic. Why? This is due to the fact that often, the federal and the state governments are at odds with one another as to which is the best way to deal with the coronavirus. That issue is beyond the scope of our present considerations. The bottom line, here, is that we should take neither a federalist nor an anti-federalist position. Rather, we should support whichever policy it is, centralist or decentralist, which has the best chance of dealing with this disease, or, indeed, any other challenge.

How do the various political factions fall out on this important question? It cannot be denied that there is some correlation; the left, or the Democrats, tend in the direction of centralization, while the right, or the Republicans, tend toward decentralization. However, there really is no right answer. It all depends upon whose ox is being gored. In past decades, the conservatives favored states' rights (mainly in support of the south), while the liberals opposed it. Nowadays, the tables have turned, and "progressives" are looking to states such as California, to over-ride federal immigration programs vis a vis what they see as unwarranted federal incursions. During the violent protests in Seattle and Portland in 2020, the local mayors adopted a hands-off policy while President Trump wanted a federal presence there. Here, the leftists were localists, the rightists, centralists. Similarly, when President Reagan threatened New York City with a cut off in funds unless it eliminated its prized rent control law, all of a sudden the shoe was on the other foot.

Similar goings-on occur at the state versus city level. In Parkland, after the deadly shooting that took place there, local citizens demanded stricter gun control laws.



W. E. Block, *Defending the Undefendable III*,
https://doi.org/10.1007/978-981-16-3957-9_1

However, a law passed in 2011 in Florida gave that state the right to over-ride such policies implemented at the more local level. These pre-emption laws hold city and county officials personally responsible for violating state firearms strictures.

So, which is the rational position for the various contending political advocates to take? Federalism or anti-federalism, that is the question? The correct view is neither. If you favor rent control, then you should be an anti-federalist, at least in that one instance when Reagan wanted to quash it. If you are an open-borders opponent, then at least under the Trump administration, you should veer in the direction of federalism.

Presumably, if there is a tie, or if nothing much is at stake, anti-federalism should win out. After all, it is a lot easier to pull up stakes in a city, and move elsewhere (job, home, school for the children) in the state; than it is to transfer from one state to another. And, it is very much more convenient to leave Georgia for Wyoming or vice versa than to immigrate to another country. But with regard to all other issues, the rational position is to jettison the federalism—anti-Federalism controversy and stick to one's principles.

There is one caveat to the above, however. If one or the other side of the centralism—anti-centralism is heavily supported, it may well have aggregative effects: it may well tip the balance in one direction or the other. What then? There is thus no clear answer to this conundrum, then. Most libertarians are anti-federalists; they tend to support the smallest jurisdiction in confrontations with larger ones. In so doing they veer from libertarian principle.

# Chapter 2
# The Anarchist

At first blush, the anarchist does not belong in this book; not within a million miles of it. For do not members of this ilk "throw bombs" in general, and, specifically, blow up innocent people? This cannot be denied. Of course it is true. History is replete with such despicable goings-on. Thus, this chapter does not concern such persons. However, not all anarchists do any such thing. Therefore there is still hope for supporters of this philosophy.

While we are discussing bomb throwing, let us look at the facts. In the last century, governments have killed some 200 million of their own citizens, and this is totally apart from those unfortunates who lost their lives in the wars incessantly fought by states. (Nor does this horrendous figure include motor vehicle deaths on government highways, another 35,000 per year in the U.S.) No, when it comes to bomb throwing, the government leaves the anarchist entirely in the shade.

Nor will I defend "left-wing" anarchists such as Noam Chomsky, Mikhail Bakunin, Peter Kropotkin and Murray Bookchin. For they would if they could prohibit private property, money, hierarchy, and other non-invasive institutions. I rise to the defense, instead, of libertarian (philosophical) anarchists such as Murray N. Rothbard, Gustave de Molinari and Lysander Spooner. Only the perspective of the latter variety is fully compatible with the non-aggression principle of libertarianism. And not only compatible with it; logically implied by it.

What is free market or libertarian anarchism? Etymologically, the prefix "an" means "against." As for example in "anti" or "Anabaptist." What, then, does this perspective oppose? It rejects archism. And what in turn is that? Archy is the unjustified rule of one person over another. Slavery, rape, murder, etc. are all instances of archy. Free market anarchism is the only philosophy consistently and bitterly in opposition to all such rights violations.

Exhibit "A" in this contention is that governments, all of them without any exception whatsoever, presume to "tax" their subjects. Sometimes their spokesmen go so far off the rails as to claim that these compulsory payments are actually voluntary. But nothing could be further from the truth. Yes, true, if you do not pay the


W. E. Block, *Defending the Undefendable III*,
https://doi.org/10.1007/978-981-16-3957-9_2

government what it thinks you owe them, the initial response will not be very invasive. Rather, it will be along the lines of, "Hey, did you forget to send us a goodly portion of your hard-earned money? We can really use the money, and it is all for your benefit, the taxpayer." But this will be followed up by letters of escalating harshness, until one day, if you ignore them all, a man in blue, with a badge and gun will come and offer you a visit to the local hoosegow. If you resist, he will shoot you dead. It is amazing, and appalling, that anyone in his right mind could consider such a process a voluntary one.

But did we not agree to pay taxes? Are they not, instead of coercive, akin to club dues? After all, if you join the tennis or golf club, you are expected to pay your fees, which go for the upkeep of the premises. We can hardly have such organizations if its members refuse to contribute in this way. In like manner, all citizens of the country, and all those living there, too, must pay for the care and well-being of the country. If you do not wish to call what the state collects, "taxes," fine; but, pay up! Let us not have here a mere verbal dispute.

Not so fast. When a man joins a club, he does so voluntarily. He fills out a membership form and agrees to pay dues. Did anyone sign any such contract with the U.S. government? Hardly. (New immigrants may well have done so, but it is a circular argument to deduce from this any tax justification; for it assumes the very point in question. Namely, that the government has the right to extract taxes from newcomers in the first place.)

Another argument is that the U.S. Constitution was agreed upon by a majority. True, representatives of nine out of the thirteen colonies did indeed assent to that document. But it was not a *contract*. The latter is unanimous; the covenant amongst these colonies was not. Even in the nine that initially supported the Constitution there was far less than unanimity. Yet this is the criteria for all contracts; purchasing a car, borrowing from, lending money to someone, and, the proverbial joining of the golf or tennis club.

What about the common refrain: "If you don't like it here, leave." This, again, argues in the circle, assuming the very point of contention to lie in the direction of the state. It posits that the government has the right to collect taxes, the very point under dispute. But why posit this conclusion? Why not the very opposite? That is, that the statists, criminals since they mulct taxes from the unwilling, should be the ones to leave?

One argument for government is that without it, we would each be at each other's throats. Murder, rape, theft, would be the order of the day. (Sounds familiar, no?) We must therefore cede to the state the monopoly of licit violence so that we can all be safe (They do a great job of this, right?) This claim, too, fails. How, then, would law and order be attained without government? This will be difficult for many people to wrap their minds around. However, in the free (anarchist) society, there will be private police-court corporations. Will they be perfect? Will they attain heaven on earth? Of course not. They will be staffed with imperfect human beings. There will be temptations to rule in favor of the richer of the two legal adversaries, not the one with justice on his side. But it is a matter of comparison. An economist was asked, "How is your wife?" Came the answer: "compared to what?" Precisely. The private justice system need not be perfect, merely better than the government, a low bar indeed. A judge who ruled in favor of someone who bribed him would more quickly than under the present system lose all of his customers, even wealthy ones.

Posit five actors in our little drama: Al, Bob, Charles, David and Ed. The former and the latter get into a legal altercation. Al invites Ed to seek justice from judge Bob. Ed splutters, but Bob is your brother, cousin, father, son, friend; he will not be fair. Instead, let us patronize judge David. Whereupon Al mutters along the same lines: David is Ed's brother, cousin, father, son, friend; he will not be fair. So, each takes his case to the judge of his choosing: Al appeals to Bob, Ed, to David. Neither as much as shows up in the other's court.

There are four possible results. First, both Bob and David rule in Al's favor. That will pretty much be the end of the matter; Al wins. For Al and Ed both signed a contract with, respectively, Bob and David, obligating themselves to be bound by the decision of their respective judges. In any case, both judges are replete with a police subdivision, to enforce their findings on recalcitrant customers. A similar conclusion applies if both judges find in favor of Ed. The third option is that Bob supports Ed and that David rules on behalf of Al, violating friendship and familial obligations. Let us ignore this option and focus instead on the fourth possibility. Just as we all feared, consanguinity prevails; Bob favors his buddy Al and David takes the side of his main man, Ed. Ayn Rand would say at this point that libertarians "blank out" at this point, but that is not at all the case. Rather, let us probe more deeply.

We note that there are two types of courts; rational, civilized ones, that have anticipated just such an eventuality, and bandit courts, which either have not foreseen any such possibility, or, if they did, would insist on prevailing in any case. Call the former legitimate courts, and the latter bandit courts. What will Bob and David do if they fall into the former category? We have not so far mentioned Charlie. He now comes into the picture. Both Bob and David have previously agreed with each other that if they should ever find themselves on the opposite side of a ruling, they would use this worthy (or a group of honorable judges, one of whom will now be chosen by a random number selection process) as a court of appeal. This they proceed to do, and the case is settled as fairly as human beings are capable of doing.

However, if one or both of our judges belongs in the bandit category, there will have to be a resort to violence, at least theoretically. Why theoretically? Because banditry simply does not pay. Bandit courts will have to fight each other, as well as licit judiciaries. The latter will only have to engage in fisticuffs with the former. Violence is expensive. Bandit courts will tend to be driven into bankruptcy. They will not exist in the real libertarian anarchic world. Then, there is that little matter of legitimacy. The pen is mightier than the sword. At the outset, it would appear that the latter would win any battle with the former. But no. The pen determines in which direction the sword is pointed. If that is not winning, then nothing is. The point is, not only will the bandit courts of the day, should there be any at all, have to fight everyone, they will do so with 1.99 hands (I calculated this exactly to the nearest decimal point) behind their backs, given that they will have not a scintilla of legitimacy to rely upon.

The case against anarchism is also subject to a powerful reductio ad absurdum. If the U.S. is needed to keep Smith and Jones from creating mayhem against each other, then what about governments themselves? Must they not be kept apart from one another? At present, Albania and Argentina are in a state of *anarchy* with each other. That is, there is no World Government to act as a referee between them. The exact same situation applies to Bolivia and Burundi; to Canada and Chile, to Denmark and the Dominican Republic, to Egypt and Ecuador, to France and Finland, to Greece and Ghana, to Haiti and Hungary, to Ireland and Israel, to Japan and Jamaica, to Korea and Kenya, to Luxemburg and Liberia, to Mexico and Morocco, to Netherlands and New Zealand, to Oman and … wait, I need a country that begins with an "O" if I am to continue my alliterative march through the alphabet, and there is none. I'll press on in any case: a state of anarchy exists, also, between Pakistan and Panama, Qatar and (uh, oh, I've run out again), Romania and Rwanda, Singapore and Somalia, Tunisia and Turkey, Uruguay and Uganda, Venezuela and Viet Nam, Wallis and Futuna Islands and Western Sahara, Yemen and I don't know who, Zambia and Zimbabwe. Whew! Not only does a state of anarchy obtain between these pairs of countries, but it does so also between any one of them and all the rest. We live in an anarchic world!

Should we then address this lacuna? Should we fix it? Should we end this state of anarchy that now exists amongst nations? If we do, we must impose world government! That is the only solution to world-wide anarchy. But this institution comes with problems of its own. If it is at all democratic, the world government will tend to resemble China and India since they are amongst the most heavily populated nations on the planet. They each have over one billion people. Together, they comprise almost 40% of the world's population. Do we really want to be governed by people with philosophies of this sort? The next most highly populated states, apart from the U.S. are those in this order: Indonesia, Brazil, Pakistan, Nigeria, Bangladesh and Russia. Not very attractive. No, the western countries would be simply overwhelmed by the force of sheer numbers. Then, there is always the (outside?) chance that the leader of the world government would be someone akin to Mao, or Stalin, or Hitler, or Pol Pot, with devastating results for all civilized peoples. With over 200 nations, despised groups can sometimes, often, find a refuge. With the end of anarchy between countries, there would simply be nowhere for them to run.

Then there is the matter of secession. One of the main building blocks of libertarianism is free association. No one should be compelled to associate with anyone else against his will. All interaction between people should be purely voluntary. That lets out slavery, rape, and other such forced associations. The slave master, the rapist, want to "associate" with their victims; the latter wish to disassociate, have nothing to do with, the former. It is the same with secession. Those who wish to depart from the nation to which they belong to, wish to leave; to secede. Suppose that that South wishes to disaffiliate from the North. May they do so? Of course it may do so, at least on libertarian grounds, based on the philosophy of free association. (There are some who claim that this constitutes not so deeply hidden support for slavery; not so, not so. The North had slaves too. Further, the first state to wish to secede was the abolitionist Massachusetts in 1825; they could hardly be accused of pro-slavery sentiments.) But then suppose Louisiana wanted to separate from the Confederacy. Would this, too, be allowed. You bet your boots it would, on the basis of the same perspective. However, suppose New Orleans wanted to vacate from the state of Louisiana? Again, we offer the same response: indeedy do. But the Garden District no longer wishes to be associated with New Orleans. Must the latter allow the former to do so? Yes, once again. But now, horrors, one city block in this neighborhood wishes to strike out on its own. Permissible? Of course. Patience, gentle reader, we are soon coming to the end of this process. There is one individual who wishes to secede from all of the other political entities. Kosher? Yes, this too. The goal here is seven billion or so sovereign states, one to each person (then, you can no longer ask out a woman on a date; your foreign minister has to first deal with hers ☺). What would we have if we pushed the envelope this far? Why, anarchy, of course. Unlimited secession, then, is yet one more argument in favor of that institutional arrangement. Nowadays, it is not likely that the South would want to separate from the North. Far more likely would be both coasts splitting themselves as one or two countries from "flyover" territory and/or vice versa. But the same analysis applies.

How is it that a government starts up initially? The state has not always been with us. Which came first, the people or their government? This is not an insoluble chicken and egg problem. Obviously, there can be people without a state, but there can be no such thing as a government with absolutely no people belonging to it. So, there were people in existence, and then, only later, came the state. How did it come into being? Well, possibly, someone got up on his hind legs and said, hey, let's start a government. Did everyone else in a given geographical area immediately give their consent to this new apparatus of control? This hardly seems likely. People disagree so much, nowadays, and it is difficult to see how our forebears were very different from us in this regard. Five friends want to get together for a movie and then dinner. Chaos almost erupts over the various choices. Imagine them all agreeing to set up a government of any one type. All but impossible. No, wait, scratch that "all but" business. It is logically impossible for a state to arise in any such manner. If it did so, it could not be a government. Rather, it would be a (large?) voluntary association. We quite properly reserve the word, "state," for an organization that came into being in violation of the libertarian non-aggression principle.

Here is another hypothesis. Governments came into being by conquest. One gang was more powerful than the others, and took it upon itself to regularize its tribute. Instead of continuing as hit and run gangsters, they settled down in Murray N. Rothbard's "Hector's Valley" there to batten down upon the local innocents. The monarchist eventually gave way to the tyranny of the majority, that is, democracy. But it is difficult from this perspective to see the government as anything other than born in subjugation of some by others. This is not very attractive. Sad, really, that so many people would be taken in by so illicit an institution.

One last nail in the coffin of the state: economic efficiency. We all want to be rich; or, at the very least, to ward off poverty. All men of good will would wish this. How to attain this goal? Why, by reducing the government to the smallest size possible, and that would be zero. Why? This is due to the fact that the market is much more efficient than the bureaucratic state. Look at the Fortune 500 for the last few decades. Notice anything? Yes, corporations, even large ones, come and go. Where is Packard anymore? Where is Trans World Airlines? Bankrupt, that is where. In contrast, the U.S. Post Office continues on its merry way. When a private concern no longer pleases its customers, investors, suppliers, it automatically goes the way of the dodo bird (unless of course it is "too big to fail" and garners government bailouts). The same cannot be said for the Army Corp of Engineers, which killed some 1900 people in the aftermath of Hurricane Katrina, due to its failing levees.

To summarize. There are utilitarian and deontological reasons to oppose the state and its power. These all point in the direction of supporting statelessness, or, anarchism.

# Chapter 3
# The Election Purchaser

Language is important. Apart from smoke signals, hand gestures, facial expressions, it is the only known way we have of communicating with each other. Thus it is important to be ever vigilant in protecting this vital resource of ours.

When he was a candidate for the Democratic presidential nomination in 2020, Former New York City Mayor Mike Bloomberg was widely accused of buying votes. Later he pulled out of this race in support of Joe Biden, and could no longer be accused of "buying" anything of the sort. For himself that is. But when he donated big bucks to Biden, he was again accused of buying up the Democratic electorate, this time for the presidential nomination for this former Vice President.

These accusations must stop. Such charges constitute an undermining, a vitiation, of our major means of sharing information, accurate language.

What's wrong with all of these claims? Isn't it true that Mayor Mike was indeed trying to buy the Democratic presidential nomination for Biden, and, since he succeeded in this "purchase" of his, he continued down this path in November against Trump? He might well have been trying, but this cannot be done. Mr. Bloomberg might as well have tried to draw a square circle.

If we are to respect language, we must reject all of these charges against the former Big Apple mayor, whether on his own behalf, before, or, later on, so as to support Joe Biden. It cannot be denied that Bloomberg had spent over $400 million of his gigantic fortune in the presidential race. Contrary to these widespread allegations, however, Mr. Bloomberg hasn't "bought" anything of the sort, nor did he do so for Mr. Biden.

What is it to "buy" something? It is to pay someone for services rendered, or goods shipped from vendor to purchaser. Did Mike Bloomberg ever pay a single solitary penny directly to any voter so as to obtain a vote? Of course not. That would be illegal. Even his most bitter critics, see above, do not allege that he has done that.

Instead, what the former mayor of the Big Apple bought advertising time in newspapers, radio, television, etc. So, yes, he purchased something of value, but not votes, not elections, not a nomination for the top spot on the Democratic Party's list.


W. E. Block, *Defending the Undefendable III*,
https://doi.org/10.1007/978-981-16-3957-9_3

He was only "guilty" of buying advertising space. He did no more for Joe Biden in the general election.

Has Donald done this? What about Bernie, Joe, Elizabeth, Mayor Pete, and all the others? Yes, they too are guilty of committing this self-same "crime." Their only mitigation is that they have done so to a lesser degree. But if Mike has done something wrong, they are all complicit.

Let us get literal for a moment. Suppose Big Apple Mike really wanted to buy votes. He offers the next person to enter the ballot box $100 to pull the lever for himself when he was still in the running, and later, when his own candidacy failed, for Joe. The former mayor could indeed engage in this illegal act, but could he ever be sure of obtaining what he wanted to "buy"? Of course not. The recipient could pocket the money and cast a ballot for anyone at all. We have a secret ballot in this country, or at least we did the last time I looked. Thus it would be nothing less than idiotic for the "buyer" of elections to spend his money thusly.

But what of the fact that Mr. Bloomberg has also doled out billions in grants to political and non-profit groups whose support comes in very handy? Did he buy them, literally? Well, no, but he has done far more than what any other politician in history has, when it comes to simply giving politically helpful groups and individuals rolls of cash—all perfectly legal, of course.

Does this undoubted fact undermine my thesis? No. Mr. Bloomberg still "buys" literally nothing. He is only "guilty" of edging down a slippery slope to a greater degree than anyone else, all of whom have done precisely the same thing. If the former mayor of the former greatest city on the planet has erred, it is one of degree, not kind, as alleged by his many detractors. It is thus unfair to single him out for special condemnation.

My purpose here is not at all to defend Mike Bloomberg or Joe Biden. It is rather to make a linguistic point. Let us strive to be more accurate verbally. Words are too precious to tolerate our abuse of them.

There was true bipartisanship in this unwarranted attack on Mike Bloomberg on this ground. Who says the two major parties can't agree on anything? But on this matter, both progressives and conservatives are wrong. There were flaws in Bloomberg's candidacy to be sure, but this was not one of them. Nor did Mike do any such thing for Joe no matter how much money he was willing to spend in this quixotic attempt to "buy" votes, or elections.

Why this fetish of mine about accuracy in language? We can either talk or write to each other or punch or shoot each other. Surely, the former is preferable. But, if we are to reach full communication, words are our only tool. We increase misunderstanding at our peril. ("Rent-seeking," too, must be confined to the dustbin of history. People who engage in the act all too often depicted by this phrase are not seeking "rent"; they are seeking booty).

# Part II
# Free Speech

"...ARE YOU BUYING THAT TO SPRAY PAINT GRAFFITI, SIR? IF YOU ARE, IT'S EXEMPT FROM THE SALES TAX UNDER THE STATE 'FREEDOM OF EXPRESSION' LAW."

# Chapter 4
# The Flag Burner

According to Donald Trump, 45th President of the United States, "Nobody should be allowed to burn the American flag—if they do, there must be consequences—perhaps loss of citizenship or (a) year in jail!"

There are problems here, even from the point of view of the most patriotic American. For what is to be done with old flags, worn out from use of which even the Donald would approve: damage from wind, rain or hail, use over many years which wears out the cloth from which they are made? According to long-standing practice on the part of the government itself, these flags are to be—wait for it—burned! Does our former resident really want to banish and or incarcerate thousands upon thousands of patriotic Americans who have burned, respectfully, tattered US flags? Hardly.

From a libertarian perspective, the outlawing of flag burning is on even shakier ground. Now, of course, it would be improper to burn someone else's flag, for it would have to be stolen from those people in the first place, and then the crime would be compounded by the destruction of other people's property.

But what about one's own flag? The essence of ownership is to be able to do with one's property exactly as one wishes, while of course continuing to respect the NAP. The owner should be able to refashion the flag into a shirt, use it as a wash-cloth, and or burn it, respectfully or, even, non-respectfully, as a matter of protest. If he is prohibited from doing all or any of these things, his ownership rights are to that extent attenuated. And, we have a pithy word for offending other peoples' private property rights; it is called stealing.

But what of the fact that other people are likely, more than probable, to take umbrage at the spectacle of someone burning his own flag without the reverence some think is due to this bit of cloth? Should not their feelings be taken into account? Yes, if we were to believe in stake-holder theory. There, every busy-body—suppliers, employees, neighbors, passersby—have a right, in addition to the owner, to determine the use of any given item.



W. E. Block, *Defending the Undefendable III*,
https://doi.org/10.1007/978-981-16-3957-9_4

Would it not be nice to refrain from flag burning, given that others' feelings will be hurt by such action? Well, yes, perhaps, maybe. But the matter is surely reciprocal. If patriots will be psychologically harmed by protestors burning our nation's emblem, or in any other way in their view of "mistreating" it, the very opposite prevails as well. That is, protestors will take it amiss that patriots refrain from this practice. Are not the subjective feelings of all people to be considered equal?

If so, perhaps, then, a majority vote should determine whether or not to prohibit or compel, flag burning. I answer that there is no warrant to make any such determination. As an Austrian economist, I deny there is any way to make such interpersonal comparisons of utility. Further, the lover of liberty never counts noses. It is a clear violation of the NAP to either prohibit or compel flag burning.

Here is the proper conclusion: let each person deal with his own property exactly as he sees fit and let the devil take the hindmost. We can applaud both those who burn their flags, as well as those who do not. The flag burner, and, also, the non-flag burner, are both heroic in that they engage in activities that should be legal, and are hated, detested, by others.

# Chapter 5
# The Demagogue (Written by Murray N. Rothbard)

For many years now, demagogues have been in great disfavor. They are not sober, they are not respectable, they are not "gentlemen." And yet there is a great and growing need for their services. What, exactly, have been the charges leveled against the demagogues? They are roughly three in number.

In the first place, they are disruptive forces in the body politic. They stir things up. Second, they supposedly fail to play the game in appealing to the base emotions, rather than to cool reason. From this stems the third charge: that they appeal to the unwashed masses with emotional, extreme, and, therefore, unsound views. Add to this the vice of ungentlemanly enthusiasm, and we have about catalogued the sins of the species demagogue.

The charge of emotionalism is surely an irrelevant one. The problem of an ideology is not whether it is put forth in an emotional, a matter-of-fact, or a dull manner. The question is whether or not the ideology is correct. Almost always, the demagogue is a man who finds that his ideas are held by only a small minority of people, a minority that is apt to be particularly small among the sober and respectable. Convinced of the truth and the importance of his ideas, he sees that the heavy weight of public opinion, and particularly of the respectable molders of this opinion, is either hostile or indifferent to this truth. Is it any wonder that such a situation will make a man emotional?

All demagogues are ideological nonconformists and therefore are bound to be emotional about the general and respectable rejection of what they consider to be vital truth. But not all ideological nonconformists become demagogues. The difference is that the demagogue possesses that quality of mass attraction that permits him to use emotion to stir up the masses. In going to the masses, he is going over the heads of the respectable intellectuals who ordinarily guide mass opinion. It is this electric, short-cut appeal direct to the masses that gives the demagogue his vital significance and that makes him such a menace to the dominant orthodoxy.

The demagogue is frequently accused by his enemies of being an insincere opportunist, a man who cynically uses certain ideas and emotions in order to gain



W. E. Block, *Defending the Undefendable III*,
https://doi.org/10.1007/978-981-16-3957-9_5

popularity and power. It is almost impossible, however, to judge a person's motives, particularly in political life, unless one is a close friend. We have seen that the sincere demagogue is very likely to be emotional himself, while stirring others to emotion. Finally, if a man is really an opportunist, the easiest way to acclaim and power is to play ball with the ruling orthodoxy, and not the opposite. The way of the demagogue is the riskiest and has the least chance of success.

It is the fashionable belief that an idea is wrong in proportion to its "extremism" and right in proportion as it is a chaotic muddle of contradictory doctrines. To the professional middle-of-the-roader, a species that is always found in abundance, the demagogue invariably comes as a nasty shock. For it is one of the most admirable qualities of the demagogue that he forces men to think, some for the first time in their lives. Out of the muddle of current ideas, both fashionable and unfashionable, he extracts some and pushes them to their logical conclusions, i.e. "to extremes." He thereby forces people either to reject their loosely held views as unsound, or to find them sound and to pursue them to their logical consequences. Far from being an irrational force, then, the silliest of demagogues is a great servant of Reason, even when he is mostly in the wrong.

A typical example is the inflationist demagogue: the "monetary crank." The vast majority of respectable economists have always scoffed at the crank without realizing that they are not really able to answer his arguments. For what the crank has done is to take the inflationism that lies at the core of fashionable economics and push it to its logical conclusion. He asks; "If it is good to have an inflation of money of 10 percent per year, why isn't it still better to double the money supply every year?" Only a few economists have realized that in order to answer the crank reasonably instead of by ridicule, it is necessary to purge fashionable economics of its inflationist foundations.

Demagogues probably first fell into disrepute in the nineteenth century, when most of them were socialists. But their conservative opposition, as is typical of conservatives in every age, never came to grips with the logic of the demagogues' position. Instead, they contented themselves with attacking the emotionalism and extremism of the upstarts. Their logic unassailed, the socialist demagogues triumphed, as argument always will conquer pure prejudice in the long run. For it seemed as if the socialists had reason on their side.

Now socialism is the fashionable and respectable ideology. The old passionate arguments of the soap box have become the tired cliches of the cocktail party and the classroom. Any demagogy, any disruption of the apple cart, would almost certainly come from the individualist opposition. Furthermore, the State is now in command, and whenever this conditions prevails, it is anxious to prevent disruption and ideological turmoil. In their wake, demagogues would bring "disunity," and people might be stirred to think for themselves instead of falling into a universal goose-step behind their anointed leaders. Furthermore, individualist demagogues would be more dangerous than ever, because they could now be equipped with rational arguments to refute the socialist cliches. The respectable statist Left, then, fears and hates the demagogue, and more than ever before, he is the object of attack.

It is true that, in the long run, we will never be free until the intellectuals--the natural molders of public opinions—have been converted to the side of freedom. In the short run, however, the only route to liberty is by an appeal to the masses over the heads of the State and its intellectual bodyguard. And this appeal can be made most effectively by the demagogue—the rough, unpolished man of the people, who can present the truth in simple, effective, yes emotional, language. The intellectuals see this clearly, and this is why they constantly attack every indication of libertarian demagoguery as part of a "rising tide of anti-intellectualism." Of course, it is not anti-intellectualism; it is the saving of mankind from those intellectuals who have betrayed the intellect itself.

# Chapter 6
# The Yellow Journalist

Competition amongst the British newspapers often really heats up. No longer content with lurid stories of political peccadillos, sex scandal, labor unrest, punk rock and teenage gang warfare, the various dailies are offering gigantic cash prizes for various and sundry game winners.

Publisher Robert Maxwell, for example, in an all-out struggle to pole-vault his *Daily Mirror* into the top circulation position, instituted a numbers game called "Who Dares Win." Cash prizes of £1 million are bruited about. Such flamboyant policies have catapulted his newspaper's readership.

Australian-born publisher Rupert Murdoch has responded in kind. His newspaper, *The Sun*, offered "the Biggest Bingo Prize in History." Says Murdoch to his readership, "Trust *The Sun*, folks, we're gonna make you super rich."

And the *Express* newspapers, publishers of the *Daily Express* and the *Daily Star*, have also jumped on the sweepstakes bandwagon. Not to be outdone, they have offered even bigger prizes in their own newspaper bingo games.

This is a highly competitive situation in the British newspaper industry. The denizens of Fleet Street, Britain's newspaper row, have been struggling to outdo each other regarding the size of cash prizes offered in an attempt to capture larger readerships. Rupert Murdoch of *The Sun*, Robert Maxwell of the *Daily Mirror*, and the *Express* chain have all been banner-headlining multi-million dollar cash prizes for their daily newspaper games.

Should we whine about the fact that local publishers have, at least so far, showed no signs of emulating our British cousins in this regard?

This orgy of prize giving has not gone unnoticed. According to newspaper purists, cash prizes simply have no place in a modern newspaper. And games, if they appear at all, should be confined to highbrow past-times such as bridge and chess, and buried deep within the bowels of the papers, not flashed on page one. The present huckstering after circulation increases, in this view, is highly regrettable. The fact that it is successful is even more to be regretted.


W. E. Block, *Defending the Undefendable III*,
https://doi.org/10.1007/978-981-16-3957-9_6

But not every Briton wants to read the staid, safe and unspectacular *London Times*. Some readers like the fluff and excitement of games with large cash prizes. In many cases, this is the only way to involve them in the print news medium at all.

"...AND LOCALLY, THE BIG STORY IS THE WINNING OF THE PULITZER PRIZE BY THE DAILY STAR TRIBUNE FOR THE BEST NEWSPAPER BINGO PROMOTION."

The innovative publishers are thus to be congratulated for their entrepreneurial efforts. Since the advent of television and the web, the newspaper industry has been a threatened species. If games and prizes and brou-ha-ha will swell the ranks of newspaper readers, this is all to the good.

That is what the competitive free enterprise system is all about—pleasing the customer. Even in the newspaper business, the customer is always right. Well almost always—apparently in local publishing the customer doesn't know what's good for him.

There is also an entirely different type of yellow journalism about. I refer here to the fact that virtually all the major newspapers occupy one side of the left-right political spectrum and nary an alternative exists. This would be fine and dandy if this referred, only, to the editorial sections of these dailies. Unhappily, this intellectual virus has seeped out into what is supposedly "all the news that is fit to print." For example, in the view of Jim Rutenberg (https://www.nytimes.com/2016/08/08/business/balance-fairness-and-a-proudly-provocative-presidential-candidate.html):

> If you're a working journalist and you believe that Donald J. Trump is a demagogue playing to the nation's worst racist and nationalistic tendencies, that he cozies up to anti-American dictators and that he would be dangerous with control of the United States nuclear codes, how the heck are you supposed to cover him?

> Because if you believe all of those things, you have to throw out the textbook American journalism has been using for the better part of the past half-century, if not longer, and approach it in a way you've never approached anything in your career. If you view a Trump presidency as something that's potentially dangerous, then your reporting is going to reflect that. You would move closer than you've ever been to being oppositional. That's uncomfortable and uncharted territory for every mainstream, nonopinion journalist I've ever known, and by normal standards, untenable.
>
> But the question that everyone is grappling with is: Do normal standards apply? And if they don't, what should take their place?

Well, we now know full well "what should take their place." Opinionated, biased reportage has substituted for the old-fashioned "Just the facts, ma 'am" practices previously in place. And this is not just one reporter, publicly confessing his sins. His essay appeared in the prestigious *New York Times*, and has been emulated, over and over, not only in the "newspaper of record," but, alas and alack, in virtually every other major American newspaper.

This is true "yellow journalism." The important issue for the present book is, can this variety, too, be defended on libertarian grounds?

The answer is, Yes and No. Yes, if the periodical is not part and parcel of the apparatus of the state: its owners do not contribute funds to the government; they are not protected by political office-holders; they are not crony capitalists, benefitting from special privileges denied their competitors. No, if any of these conditions hold true. That is, if and only if there is a complete arm's length separation between journalism and state would this biased news reportage be defended on the basis of libertarianism. In all too many cases, this simply does not apply.

# Chapter 7
# The Blasphemer

Junaid Hafeez has been held in a Pakistani jail for 6 years, from 2013 to 2019, for the crime of blasphemy. A former professor of English literature at Bahauddin Zakariya University run by the government of Pakistan, he has recently been sentenced to death by a court in that nation. He was formerly a Fulbright Scholar at Jackson State University in Mississippi.

Professor Hafeez was found guilty of anonymously posting messages on Facebook, accused by his own Islamic students.

Blasphemy is uttering or writing a critique of religion. Islam is far from the only religion to have violated free speech rights in this manner, nor is Pakistan the only country to have done so. Other laws abound in many other nations for rather different but not totally dis-similar reasons. For example, it is a crime in Canada and many western European countries to deny that the Holocaust took place, or to weaken claims against it in any way: it would be a criminal act to claim that fewer than six million Jews perished under its auspices. David Irving was found guilty of violating this law in Europe, which has similar restrictions on free speech.

Nor are blasphemy-like legislative enactments confined to religion or historical events. They also encompass environmental issues. Serious attempts were made to find Exxon guilty of similar thought crimes in opposition to the majority opinion on this matter.

Then there is that little matter of using the perfectly good English word "niggardly." It has nothing to do with the N-word, which I dare not mention even in this essay dealing with free speech incursions. Rather, it depicts a person who is stingy, non-generous, miserly, parsimonious. A great controversy arose over its use; certain people, not well-versed in the English language objected, strenuously, to its correct employment.

Nor can I leave unmentioned political correctness. "Mankind," "man," "he," are all verboten in certain circles. Even words such as "human" and "person" are seen by some as objectionable. You don't see why? You are a sexist pig! (Hint: take a peek at the last syllables of these words.)



W. E. Block, *Defending the Undefendable III*,
https://doi.org/10.1007/978-981-16-3957-9_7

It is bad enough that few conservative and libertarian speakers are invited to campus. It is far worse that those rare scholars who are offered a podium, are all too often disinvited, or not allowed to speak by protesting fascist students. Even worse is that the professoriate almost totally excludes scholars with these viewpoints. (An outside speaker is on campus once per year; some professors brainwash students every day).

What can be said about all these disparate attempts (religious, historical, environmental, racial, political correctness, academic) to quell free speech?

For one thing, they can all be interpreted as undermining their own presumed beliefs. For example, if God supports murdering those who deny His existence, or negatively question Him in any way, this bespeaks a weakness on His part. Surely, if He is as all powerful, wise, benevolent as His supporters maintain He is, He would not need such laws protecting Him.

Similarly, holocaust denial or disparagement laws can be interpreted as an attack on historians. If their views need buttressing by jail sentences, this undermines their evidence and the coherence of their interpretations thereof. The case they have been so far able to adduce in support of their contentions is to that extent weakened.

The same applies to left-wing environmentalists. If their logic and evidence were as impregnable as they believe it to be, there would be no need for them to characterize critics as "deniers" and to try to have even tenured professors fired from their academic posts for disagreeing with them, or to attempt to rein in the free speech rights of firms such as Exxon.

We cannot end without considering what John Stuart Mill had to say about such goings-on in his magnificent "On Liberty":

> He who knows only his own side of the case, knows little of that. His reasons may be good, and no one may have been able to refute them. But if he is equally unable to refute the reasons on the opposite side; if he does not so much as know what they are, he has no ground for preferring either opinion. The rational position for him would be suspension of judgment, and unless he contents himself with that, he is either led by authority, or adopts, like the generality of the world, the side to which he feels most inclination. Nor is it enough that he should hear the arguments of adversaries from his own teachers, presented as they state them, and accompanied by what they offer as refutations. That is not the way to do justice to the arguments, or bring them into real contact with his own mind. He must be able to hear them from persons who actually believe them; who defend them in earnest, and do their very utmost for them. He must know them in their most plausible and persuasive form; he must feel the whole force of the difficulty which the true view of the subject has to encounter and dispose of; else he will never really possess himself of the portion of truth which meets and removes that difficulty.

# Chapter 8
# The Hater

Hate is not a good thing. Hatefulness has all sorts of dire imprecations. Not least of which, it hurts the person doing the hating. Yes, he too is hurt by this emotion. Not for nothing is that famous aphorism often muttered: “Don’t get mad, get even!” Hatred hurts the hater. It raises his bile, and the ensuing acid eats away at his innards. It is a poison, an acid, directed inward.

All of this is as nothing compared to what happens to the target of detestation. Hitler, Stalin, Mao, Pol Pot, murdered millions of innocents. Were they filled with the milk of human kindness? No, the very opposite was the case. Their lives centered around abhorrence for others, whether because they were Jews, or blacks, or kulaks, or non-Aryans, or members of the bourgeoisie. Animosity was their middle name.

Hatred is the devil’s workshop. Were it banished entirely from the human breast, we would all be better off for it; at least that is the view of the overwhelming majority.

But the libertarian is not concerned with niceness; nor, even, with human welfare, at least not directly. Rather, this philosophical tradition is focused on the well-being of our species via the intermediation of the legal system: which acts ought to be licit, and which ones not? The bottom line is, does an act, or a thought in this case, constitute an uninvited border crossing; does it amount to a rights violation?

It is difficult to see how mere hatred can fit this bill. If hating someone were akin to a voodoo system that worked, where merely seeing another person through that lens could actually physically harm him, then, yes, hatred should be outlawed (I don’t see how that is possible; maybe some sort of Nozickian machine?). Back in the real world, this emotion does not at all work like that. Rather, hate, alone, is impotent to violate anyone’s rights. In order to attain that goal, the hater has to actually do something to his target, invade him in some way or other, an entirely different matter indeed.

What about hate crimes? Should they be outlawed? There is such a thing as mens rea, roughly translated into engaging in an act with a guilty conscience, or,


W. E. Block, *Defending the Undefendable III*,
https://doi.org/10.1007/978-981-16-3957-9_8

purposefully violating rights or full-well knowing that what you are doing is wrong. If you hit my car with yours by accident, you have no mens rea. You are not a criminal. You are a tort-feasor, and must pay damages to me for the repair of my automobile. But if you purposefully ram your vehicle into mine, presumably with hatred in your heart for me and my possessions, then you are a criminal, and must pay far more than my collision bill. To that extent, there is nothing incompatible with the "hate crime" doctrine and libertarian legal theory.

However, this is not at all what is mean by this position. Rather, it refers to one motivated by prejudices concerning race, or gender, or sexual preference or animus toward a certain nationality, or any other such "protected" group. There is even a question as to whether or not a hate crime can be perpetrated against a white, heterosexual male. And, of course, a "hate crime," at least according to this malevolent doctrine, can be punished more severely than a non-hate or ordinary crime, even, given, that the actual initiatory violence is otherwise exactly equal. This sort of thing, in contrast to the mens rea condition mentioned above, is entirely incompatible with justice, e.g., libertarianism. For it should not be relevant to the criminal law what is going on in the perpetrator's brain while he commits his dastardly act. It might be, indeed, hatred for the minority group of which the victim is a member. Or, possibly, it is "just business" on the part of the criminal as Mafioso hit men were wont to say, at least in the movies. Such a person only wants the money belonging to his prey and could not care less about that person's race, nationality, gender, sexual preference, etc. But the crime is identical. Why should the one be punished more severely than the other?

Let us try to employ a reductio ad absurdum. Suppose A beats up B in order to seize his money, but one, A does not hate B; two, A is indifferent to B; three, A loves B, and is only engaging in assault and battery against him out of this positive emotion (A is paternalistically robbing B so that the latter will not have sufficient funds to purchase harmful drugs, for example). We posit that in every other regard, these three crimes are identical, the ones based on hate, indifference and love. According to the "hate crimes" philosophy, the first should be punished heavily, the second less so, and the third? Here, the punishment should be very light, and perhaps not even exist at all. Perhaps we should pin a medal on the criminal.

For all we know, hate might have kept us alive when all we had were sticks and stones, and we were contending with the lions and tigers and bears and other creatures far stronger than relatively weak human beings.

One of Murray Rothbard's favorite aphorisms was "Hatred is my muse." What he meant by this is that he would read some horrid socialist tract, or peruse some "monstrous" (a favorite word of his) economic fallacy, and become determined to blast away at it. He would not rest until he intellectually obliterated the error in question. There is of course nothing wrong with that sentiment. Indeed, I am following my mentor in this right now as I write these words. (I always struggle not to turn the hatred inward). So, to conclude, not only should hatred be legal, there are indeed some positive things to be said on its behalf. So let us legalize hatred, and even appreciate it.

According to Thomas Sowell: "… it took centuries of struggle and people putting their lives on the line to get rid of the idea that a crime against 'A' should be treated differently than the same crime committed against 'B.'"

Why is the hater in this book? Why am I defending him? Why is he a hero? First, he does not violate the NAP, at least not necessarily so. Second, he enables us to probe even deeper into the real meaning of libertarianism. Third, most important, he is at present subject to criminal sanctions, and he should not be.

# Part III
# Discrimination

"...AND IN NEW DELHI TODAY, DR. RAVI MUKKERJEE, THE LEADER OF THE UNTOUCHABLES, ISSUED A STRONG CONDEMNATION OF THE RACIST SOUTH AFRICAN POLICY OF APARTHEID..."

# Chapter 9
# The Obese Disparager

Overeating is a compulsion. There is even a twelve-step program set up to deal with this malady: Overeaters Anonymous. It is akin to Alcoholics Anonymous and utilizes much the same literature. There is a low rung in hell ready for those who go out of their way to denigrate, make fun of, otherwise humiliate, the obese.

But should doing so be a crime? Should people be legally able to discriminate against the corpulent? From the libertarian point of view, one of the basic pillars of just law is free association: no one should be compelled to associate with anyone else for any reason. And this certainly includes disfavoring those who are overweight.

Many people will sharply discriminate between the job market on the one hand, and personal relations on the other. They will maintain that discrimination in the former should be strictly verboten unless it is relevant to the job, while in the latter case, apart from really radical commentators, it should be allowed.

Let us consider the former, first. Employment slots may be distinguished between those where weight is relevant, and where it is not. For example, even those bitterly opposed to discrimination against fat people might well make an exception for the trainers in the television series "Biggest Loser." In that show the professional actors were all thin, muscular, in good shape; they served as role models for those who were trying to lose poundage. If they themselves tipped the scales at 500 pounds, the image would be all wrong (although some might query such fat "objectification").

Similarly, such a person simply could not fit into the pilot's seat in airlines; thus, firms might well be excused from hiring them (although at great expense these accommodations could be supplied). Then there is the issue that firemen (not that perversion of language, "firefighters") need to carry people up and down ladders to help victims to safety, and those with this debility could scarcely move themselves in such a manner, let alone while carrying someone else (however, requirements have been diluted for women, who are also incapable of shifting people in such a manner). What about the NFL or the NBA? Would they automatically preclude a morbidly obese person from team membership? Probably not, if the candidate were satisfactory in all other ways. Of course there would indubitably be a "disparate


W. E. Block, *Defending the Undefendable III*,
https://doi.org/10.1007/978-981-16-3957-9_9

impact." While there are indeed some athletes of 300 pounds or so already functioning quite well in these leagues, probably, apart from Sumo wrestling, this would not apply to those exceeding 500.

Then, there are numerous occupations in which this consideration is entirely irrelevant: accountancy, law, teaching, editing, the list goes on and on. Here, social justice warriors would insist that no invidious evaluations be levelled at heavy people. However, from the libertarian point of view, employers have a right to choose those they associate with on any basis they wish. What about the normally weighted? Do they have a right to discriminate against corpulent employers? This is not that easy to answer from the woke perspective. In the opinion of those who exemplify this philosophy, employers control employees, not the other way around, so, maybe, possibly, a thin employee might get away with spurning a stout employer. However, libertarians make no such fine distinctions: anyone would be legally permitted to snub anyone else, for any reason, or none at all.

Now, let us consider personal relations. While some men favor the Big Beautiful Woman look, many others seek less amply endowed females. Are they to be compelled to befriend, date, marry, those who did not fit their ideal appearance? And ditto for women seeking men. Very few see a corpulent man as their model. Only the most fervent advocates of "fat rights" would insist on any such thing. Most would draw a sharp distinction between the personal and the professional, allowing rampant discrimination in the former, but certainly not the latter (with some few exceptions, as listed above, where the job required the svelte look).

But the radicals, not the moderates, are logically consistent. If the overweight have a right not to be discriminated against on the job market, why does it suddenly disappear in personal relations, whether sexual or not? That is not the way "rights" properly work. We have a right not to be murdered on the job, and, also, in the home. We have an equal right not to be raped while at work, and, also, in our personal accommodations. Similarly, we have the same identical right not to be stolen from on the job, and, also, in the home. Etc. That is to say, we may employ a reductio ad absurdum against the views of those who see a relevant legal divergence between public and private discrimination, the moderates, but not the social justice radicals who do not, and insist that this practice be eliminated from both spheres.

"...LADIES AND GENTLEMEN, THIS IS A 15 ROUND TITLE BOUT FOR THE OVERWEIGHT CHAMPIONSHIP OF THE WORLD...IN THIS CORNER, WEIGHING 278 POUNDS, FROM OAKLAND, CALIFORNIA........"

From a libertarian point of view, however, the moderates are in a better position. At least they properly allow discrimination in personal relationships, although they fail, dismally in the business sector. The radicals (see the Fat Studies initiatives newly burgeoning on college campuses) are wrong on both sides of this equation. Perhaps the moderates, in rejecting the extremists' position, if they are at all rational, will see that pure logic undermines their own viewpoint as well. That is, they may come to see that non-discrimination in personal relations will be crammed down their throats by syllogistic argumentation if they adhere to their position in the public sector, and thus embrace the libertarian position on this matter.

# Chapter 10
# The Pay Gapper

The feminist move for equal pay is dead from the neck up. To be sure, legislatures are continually enacting this idea into law. But as the evidence continues to pile up, its intellectual foundation is crumbling. The first nail in the coffin is that there is no wage gap between never-married males and females. That much ballyhooed statistic according to which women's pay is only a fraction of mens' stems to great degree from the asymmetrical effects of marital status. Marriage enhances the husband's income, and reduces that of the wife. Why? There is an enormous divergence between male and female contributions to the household: shopping, cooking, cleaning, child care, etc. When the incomes of people who have never been married are compared, and thus marriage asymmetry can play no role, the gap disappears. Often, depending upon the country, the year, the educational attainments, it reverses itself. Never-married women sometimes earn more than never-married men. As for the ever-marrieds (widowed, divorced, separated, presently married) the gap is far greater than that which prevails for all males and females.

But is it "fair" that marriage has these asymmetrical effects? This stems from the economic law of opportunity costs: whenever you do anything, you do it at the cost of not being able to do something else as well, or at all. Hussain Bolt was for a time the fastest sprinter in the world; how well did he play the cello? Not too well, if at all, since he was far too busy doing sit ups, lifting weights, sprinting, running long distance, etc. Yo Yo Ma occupied a similar role with regard to playing this instrument. But what was his time in the 100 meters? Not at all world-class, again, due at least in part to this doctrine of alternative costs. In any case, the unequal sharing of household and childcare responsibilities is a voluntary one.

The second nail emerges when we consider the logical implication of the employer discrimination explanation of the pay gap. If this analysis were true, one would expect to find a systematic and positive relationship between profit levels and the number of women in the firm or industry. That is, the discriminators would make a bundle by exploiting females. But the mythical "sexist pig" employer would soon go the way of the dodo bird, courtesy of market forces. If he were stupid enough to


W. E. Block, *Defending the Undefendable III*,
https://doi.org/10.1007/978-981-16-3957-9_10

hire a male when he could have employed an equally productive female for less money (because of the so-called pay "gap"), his gender-blind competitors would hire her, and price right him out of business. Given that free markets tend toward equal pay for equally productive workers, what, then, is the effect of mandating this situation by law? The answer, in a word, is chaos. Feminists are urging a wage-control system upon us that will reward points – and thus higher salaries – to skill, effort, responsibility, and working conditions. These are all supply-side considerations. But a crucial determinant of the value of labor, and one ignored by this system, is the demand for the product.

The skill, effort, responsibility and working conditions of the horse-breaker, saddle maker and the blacksmith changed not one whit when Henry Ford brought his "horseless carriage" to market. But because people demanded cars instead of horses, the salary of the horse trainer plummeted. According to feminist proposals, the blacksmith's compensation would have remained the same since his skill, effort, responsibility and working conditions remained the same. When programs incorporating these criteria have been implemented, the results have proved embarrassing. Different jurisdictions rate alternative jobs in widely disparate ways.

Government involvement in such issues as human rights, discrimination, affirmative action, equal pay for equal work, etc., is commonly seen as productive, efficient, and just – in a word, as on the side of the angels. On the other hand, businessmen, employers, the marketplace, the profit system, are often viewed as the "devil" in the scenario as far as racial, sexual and other prejudices are concerned. Evidence cited for these evaluations are black-white and male-female earnings differentials, the discriminatory behavior on the part of private employers, and the widely trumpeted good intentions exhibited by those charged with administering human rights programs. The government, in short, is seen as a large part of the solution to the predicament of minorities; the private sector is viewed as most of the problem.

Yet at least with regard to several well-known and highly acclaimed public sector initiatives, this conventional wisdom is rather suspect. To show this, consider the argument that affirmative action, equal pay for equal work, and various anti-discrimination measures are unjustified – at least insofar as they are based on the presumed existence of a male-female earnings "gap." A whole edifice of public policy has been built upon the premise that the earnings gap between males and females in this country is "too high," "rising," and at the very best "not falling fast enough." It is also very widely held that this gap is the product, not of voluntary choice on the part of female employees, but due to "sexism," "prejudice," "discrimination," "occupational segregation," "capitalism," etc. Programs which owe their justification, and in many cases their very existence, to a belief in these two propositions include "affirmative action" programs, "equal pay for equal work" legislation, "human rights" enactments, and various "anti-discrimination" measures.

It therefore becomes extremely important to measure the true earnings gap between male and female income earners. Let us start by considering the spate of laws now being enacted and implemented and known under the generic term "equal pay for equal work." Although such interferences with the market economy are usually intended to benefit women, their analysis can be applied to blacks, native peoples, or, for that matter, the left-handed or redheads.

An essential point which must be brought forth is that downtrodden groups always have one ace-in-the-hole: the ability to work for a lower wage than everyone else. Although perhaps the object of scorn, derision and hatred, minority member are able to claw their way back into economic respectability because they are so eminently employable; willingness to work for less makes them an economic attraction even for those who are the most prejudiced and opposed. Take this one advantage away, and they are at the mercy of those whose greatest pleasure consists of discrimination.

But this is precisely the effect of "equal pay for equal work" (EPFEW) legislation. Although conceived with perhaps the best intentions in the world, such laws banish, at one fell swoop, the ability of a group, females, to counteract the economic discrimination they may suffer in modern society. The harm this will bring to the cause of women is immense. For EPFEW does not require that women be hired. It only mandates that if a woman is employed, she be paid the same as men of equal productivity. But what good is a law that can push female unemployment rates up through the roof while ensuring "equal pay" for jobs they don't have and will not be able to attain? No. EPFEW legislation is a field day for those who wish to drive women "back into the kitchen." Feminists support this only at the risk of whatever economic gains women have made in recent years.

Perhaps the starkest example of the operation of this particular economic law occurred in apartheid South Africa. In that racist society, job reservation laws were on the books, which, as the name implies, specifically reserved certain occupations for certain races. That is, the law compels that there be "white jobs," "black jobs," etc., and you can imagine who got the short end of the stick in that context.

But white racist labour union leaders, the beneficiaries of such legislation, are actually on record expressing a willingness to have job reservation laws abolished – provided EPFEW laws are substituted in their place. That would boost the wages of blacks so high they would be difficult to employ.

Another problem is that "equal opportunity" is a subjective, not an objective phenomenon. Women do not come equipped with a little lapel tag which indicates their productivity, once and for all, in a manner from which no dissent is possible. (Nor, of course, do men.) Productivity, rather, is a continually changing phenomena that varies with education, intelligence, age, experience, presence or absence of complementary factors of production, etc., which can only be partially quantified, as well as with motivation, determination, etc., which are completely incapable of exact measurement.

Productivity must be estimated (or guessed at) by entrepreneurs who do so every day and lose money for each mistake they make. They are far more able to make such determinations accurately than are judges and juries who have little experience in this endeavor, and risk no personal funds if they commit errors. Since they assume that productivity measurements are easily ascertainable, EPFEW laws are at variance with the facts. They are thus incapable of fair and non-arbitrary implementation.

The difficulty is that there are several alternative hypotheses which can explain why women's wages, incomes, and salaries lag so far behind those of men. When these are acknowledged, it is no longer necessary to resort to discrimination on the part of the employer, business prejudice, or "capitalism," as explanations for the male-female earnings gap.

Men and women differ in a wide range of economic, educational, and sociological characteristics, each of which exerts an independent effect, raising expected male incomes and reducing expected female incomes. For example, working men tend to be older than women, more highly concentrated in the higher-paying professions, more heavily unionized in the highly skilled and legislatively protected blue-collar industries, and tend to work, to a greater degree, on a full-time, full-year basis. Not unexpectedly, when female-male income comparisons have been corrected for these factors, the ratio tends to rise.

As important as these variables are, the strongest determinant of the so-called male-female earnings "gap" is none of these things. Rather, it is marital status and the asymmetric effects of marriage on male and female earnings. That is, marriage increases male earnings and reduces female earnings.

This occurs for a myriad of reasons. Wives, to a greater degree than husbands, do a higher and disproportionate share of the housework and homemaker tasks; of childcare; are more likely to quit their jobs if their partner receives a better job elsewhere; to interrupt their careers for domestic reasons; to place their homes and families ahead of their jobs or professions; and even to purposefully attempt to keep their earnings below that of their spouses lest they undermine their marriages. It is impossible to quantify the effects of such phenomena in driving a wedge between married male and female incomes, but there is little doubt that they are important.

The private employers will not, generally speaking, be able to occupationally segregate equally well-trained people on the basis of sex (or any other criteria). For were the employer to try to do so, he would set up profit opportunities, which when exploited, would forestall any such attempt at occupational segregation.

There are more plausible explanations for occupational segregation by sex than employer discrimination. These include differential ambitions, talents, tastes, attachments to the labour force, etc. And, preeminently, the voluntary decisions made by wives and husbands in terms of sharing household and child care responsibilities.

# Chapter 11
# The Beard Belittler

Is it discrimination for a grocer to prohibit employees from growing beards? To fire them from their jobs if they disobey this order? Yes, would say most men of goodwill; they would undoubtedly urge the government to order the supermarket to reinstate all bearded employees who have been dismissed from their jobs.

However, from the libertarian perspective, all business establishments are within their rights to contractually compel all male employees who face the public (so to speak) to be clean-shaven.

According to some, this requirement is not meant to be discriminatory; but if a person is not prepared to abide by the appearance code, they are not considered for employment. That sounds like a logical contradiction.

What is going on here?

Is the anti-beard policy discriminatory or not? The answer is definitely "yes" and "no."


W. E. Block, *Defending the Undefendable III*,
https://doi.org/10.1007/978-981-16-3957-9_11

"No," in the sense that the employer is not reflecting a particular bias against beards. They could care less. Their only concern is with the customers and, in their best estimation, the customer prefers the neat-and-clean look to the beard—even if it is well-trimmed. So there's no question, that in that sense, the policy of "no beards" IS discriminatory because it does single out a specific behavior on the part of employees and penalizes it. While it is done by the employer, the emporium is only acting as an agent, as it were, for the customer. If it were the case that customers really did want bearded clerks, then the employer would presumably adopt a beards-only policy – at least for male employees!

Does the general public have the right to discriminate against those with beards and by their patronage to cause groceries to do likewise? Obviously, yes. Every shopper has the right to decide with whom he shall do business. If customers prefer to deal with clean-shaven clerks, then those employers who wish to attract their business must employ people of that ilk. Those business firms which correctly gauge the public mood on this as well as on other questions, stand to earn greater profits. The old adage: "The customer is always right" is the general rule in the marketplace and, of course, is the explanation why consumers are pampered and catered to. Rather than regarding such businesses as heinous employers attempting to dictate how its employees should dress, we ought to regard the employee who disobeys this requirement as attempting to force himself and his beard on unwilling customers.

That is the easy case. But suppose an employer becomes dictatorial and insists upon behavior not on the job, not on his work premises, but during the employee's private time; or which has nothing to do with pleasing buyers. For example, posit that the business firm insists that all workers be married (unmarried), be religious (or non-religious), engage in bowling at least once per week (or never do so), etc. Does a company have a right to engage in such authoritarian policies? Presumably not, according to extent law. But there is nothing in the libertarian legal code that would proscribe such rather outlandish behavior. This is part and parcel of what the third foundation of this philosophy mandates: free association. No one may be compelled to associate with another person except on a voluntary basis. If the company insists that all workers eschew modern transit and travel to work crawling on their knees wearing a propeller beanie, that is entirely within its rights. It may have difficulty attracting much of a labor force, even at astronomical wage levels, but that is an irrelevant consideration.

# Chapter 12
# The Diversity Demeanor

According to our friends on the woke left, black people comprise some 13% of the overall population. Therefore, we should strive for a situation in which that percentage of all physicists, doctors, economists, lawyers, chemists, politicians, researchers, computer nerds, musicians, artists, actors, singers, engineers, jewelers, bankers, judges, presidents of large corporations, should also prevail. That is, African Americans should fulfill roughly that percentage of all those jobs. To the extent they do not, this is due to toxic straight white male privilege. The cis-gendered white males are hogging up all these good employment slots for themselves, preventing people of color (I think we're no longer able to say "colored people": tell that to the National Association for the Advancement of Colored People, that racist organization) from obtaining them. They want these professions to "look like America" and at present, they do not. If we want to achieve "diversity," and we most certainly should in the view of the "progressives," then percentage representation, or at the very least a close approximation thereof, should be the goal.

If there is any one scholar who has done more to undermine this case for equal representation of all races in all occupations, it is Thomas Sowell. He just celebrated his 90th birthday and is still going strong in terms of debunking this desiderata of the "progressives." As for the dreaded white male responsibility for the present disproportionate situation in terms of numbers, his research stretches to every continent on the planet, and for decades, centuries, into the past. It is no accident, he demonstrates, over and over again, that Italians choose to be overrepresented in leather goods industries, Scots in distilleries, French in wine-making, Jews in academia, blacks in professional sports. These phenomena stem from the freely made decisions of the people in question and has nothing whatsoever to do with anyone restricting entry to anything, at least, certainly, not in the modern era. Anyone who has not read even a few of his books on this topic risks being an ignoramus. I highly recommend his *Race and Economics*, *Ethnic America*, *The Economics and Politics of Race: An International Perspective*, and *Race and Culture: A World View*.



W. E. Block, *Defending the Undefendable III*,
https://doi.org/10.1007/978-981-16-3957-9_12

Let me see if I've got this straight. Blacks take up roughly 85% of the positions in the NBA and some 75% of the NFL. So, what we are going to do, if "social justice" is to prevail, is to kick numerous players off these teams, and place them in operating rooms, behind the podium, in the courtroom, in the laboratories of the nation, etc. But suppose these splendid athletes don't want to do that. They want to stay put, right where they are, thank you very much. Shall we then castigate them as "Uncle Toms," or Oreo Cookies, since they would then be revealed as not "authentically black": dark skin on the outside, to be sure, but with an inner core of whiteness, since they would not be going along with this liberal program?

A similar problem arises on the other side of this equation. It is the rare physicist who can dribble the basketball. It is the rare economist who can do the 40 in under 5 seconds. It is the rare engineer who can make a foul shot, let alone a three-pointer. It is the rare lawyer who can throw a touchdown pass, or tackle anyone (well, at least not physically). Not only would our sports teams be less exciting, but specialization and division of labor would no longer apply to the extent it now does, in any of these other professions either. Suppose that members of these other professions simply do not want to play basketball or football for a living, and/or realize they would be inept at these callings. Are they to be forced to do so anyway, in the name of "progress?"

This is a recipe for ineffectiveness all throughout the labor market. Mediocrity in all realms here we come.

Do we want to cure Covid or not? Do we want a vaccine to prevent it or not? How about the next pandemic that comes down the pike? If so, and I mightily hope we do, and I fervently hope this vastly outweighs all such egalitarian considerations, then we want the best researchers on the job. If blacks are 13% of them, well and good. But if they hold fewer than that percentage of biological and epidemiological research jobs, or more, it does the human race no good at all to compel proportionality. If we give in to this egalitarian nonsense, it logically implies pulling some of our best researchers out of the labs of the nation, and plunking them down, of all places, onto a basketball court or football field.

This is not to say that everyone should not be encouraged to enter whatever field he wishes to engage in. But leftists say that if proportionality is not thereby attained, it is due to chicanery. This is highly problematic, to say the least.

The rejection of "diversity," and proportional representation of all races in all fields should of course not be interpreted as a call for discrimination against any group of people. The one simply has nothing to do with the other.

There is one arena, however, in which the diversity-ites do not at all welcome diversity: in terms of ideology. They rest content that virtually all university posts, editorial jobs, Hollywood actors, men behind the pulpits of the nation, subscribe to one side of the political-economic perspective. Where is the call on the part of the politically correct, for some egalitarianism in this context? That the next professor hired be a conservative? That the next editor be a libertarian? That the next priest or minister or rabbi represent a right-wing view? Nowhere, that's where.

# Part IV
# Labor

# Chapter 13
# The Wage Stagnationist

Wage stagnation, it would appear, is the latest stick with which to beat up on capitalism. Hence, the stagnationist enters this volume as yet another heroic character. What is wage stagnation? As its name implies, it is a description of the situation where wages neither rise nor fall, but remain the same, over time. They stagnate, got it? And who, pray tell, are the stagnationists, against whom we are instructed to protest? Actually, there are two, the employer and the employee. Guess who is the bad guy of the piece? If you guessed the former, go to the head of the class. The employer stagnationist dastardly refuses to increase the salary of his employee. He will not lower it (for which of course, we give him no credit), but he will not raise it, either. The greatly put upon worker stagnates at the same wage, neither having it lowered or raised. Boo hoo hoo?

Before we get out our crying towels, let us consider the economics of the issue. In order to know whether stable wage rates is a good or a bad thing, we must ask what is the source of job compensation in the first place. The uninitiated (Bernie Sanders, pay attention here) seem to think that the genesis of remuneration is employer generosity. Doctors, movie actors, professional athletes and computer techs earn high pay because they are fortunate to work for bountiful bosses; the take-home pay of dishwashers, floor sweepers and those who ask if you "want fries with that?" is far lower, since they face niggardly proprietors.

But this is just plain silly. Employers, like everyone else, want to pay as little for what they buy as they can and earn as much as they can from what they sell. If Jim Parsons of the Big Bang Theory television show and one of the highest-paid actors went incognito and worked in a car wash, he would earn a small fraction of his present salary, and this has nothing to do with how nice his firm was.

The main determinant of wages is productivity. LeBron James receives a huge salary since he can put lots of rear ends in seats at basketball games. Your local shoe shiner takes in far less, since he does not produce a service treasured, and to the same degree, by many people. Suppose John Smith's hourly productivity is $20. What this means is that for every hour Smith is on the shop floor, or behind the cash



W. E. Block, *Defending the Undefendable III*,
https://doi.org/10.1007/978-981-16-3957-9_13

register, his employer is richer by that self-same amount. What would the firm that hires Smith LIKE to pay him? If we disregard zero, and negative numbers (the employer pays the employee for working for him), then the answer is $.01 per hour. At that rate, the firm will profit from the blood, sweat and tears of the laborer to the tune of $19.99 per hour. But this cannot be the answer to the question since at that rate, this worker's labor will be a very desirable commodity. Someone, surely, will offer him $.02 per hour, "expropriating" from him $19.98 hourly. And, then, someone else will bid $.03, for a profit of $19.97. Where will this bidding process end (it is only hypothetical; I mention it only to introduce the process of wage determination)? Why, theoretically at $20.00 per hour, for only at that level no further profits can be made. We must also rule out any wage higher than this level, for if, for example, Smith is paid $21.00 per hour, his employer will tend to go broke, if we generalize this and hold other things equal, and thus not be able to pay him anything at all.

Thus wage stagnation implies that productivity has not changed. There is simply nothing wrong with that. It may take place because everyone stays in place. More likely, as people approach their peak productivity, their wages rise; as they move away from that point, they fall. If the two forces exactly balance out one another, we achieve "stagnation." It sounds awful when characterized in that manner, but there is nothing intrinsically wrong with such a situation.

This would be akin to a runner continually achieving his "personal best" time in races, neither worsening or improving his record. Or a chess player stuck at a rating of 1900, neither increasing nor decreasing it. Or a golfer scoring par time after time, neither more nor less. Or a worker suffering wage stagnation. All of these people would be in a rut. But the critics of economic freedom will lay the blame only regarding the last of these examples.

# Chapter 14
# The Gigster

What, pray tell, is the gigster? The gigster is a person who engages in a gig. And what, in turn, is a gig? A gig is a job, usually but not always constituting a temporary and/or part-time arrangement, but you are not an employee; rather, you are a single independent contractor. Why would anyone in his right mind prefer a gig to a permanent job slot with an employer? After all, in the latter case, you can enjoy a pension after you retire, health care, unemployment insurance, and a whole host of other benefits. True, with a gig you are "footloose and fancy-free" but the same can be said for more traditional employment. In that capacity, you can quit whenever you want. It is at-will employment, at least from the side of the worker. Sometimes, however, you are required to sign a non-compete clause when you leave the firm. This is far more rare with a gig; conceivably, this could also occur there.

Gigs started out in the music business. A band, or even a single musician, would get a contract to play at a bar for a Friday and Saturday night, or, at a wedding or birthday-party or some other such function, and that would be that. End of connection.

Why has the gig economy spread like wildfire? Why are there now so many opponents of this type of labor force participation that there are those who want to pass legislation actually outlawing it, or at least severely truncating its applicability?

A partial answer may be found in one phrase: labor unions. Organized labor finds it difficult, in the extreme, to enroll independent contractors. Our laws are such that to even try to do so would run afoul of anti-trust legislation. Another part of the explanation is that employers are trying to escape excessive governmental rule-making. The relationship between a firm and its workers is highly regulated, and companies greatly desire to free themselves of these stultifications. Regulations include compulsory unemployment insurance, overtime pay, minimum wages, worker's compensation, paid pregnancy leave, days off for sickness, the list goes on and on, depending upon jurisdiction. The business is not hemmed in, in this manner, with regard to independent contractors. Reclassifying Uber drivers from gig


W. E. Block, *Defending the Undefendable III*,
https://doi.org/10.1007/978-981-16-3957-9_14

workers to employees will cost this firm millions of dollars. In effect, this move from gigster to the regular payroll will price out of the market thousands of individuals whose productivity does not warrant the increased costs.

Let us extrapolate from this situation. If a company like Uber can be compelled to cease its temporary gig relationship with its drivers and place them on a regular payroll, what of the relationship between Walmart and a farmer who supplies it with, say, tomatoes? If Uber is exploiting its drivers, as organized labor contends, then for the same reason Walmart can be said to be doing the exact same thing with regard to farmers. And, also, to pretty much all of its other suppliers, who are not companies themselves. But this would mean that the farmer would be compelled to sell his product to Walmart and Walmart alone: equivalent to a government compelled monopsony.

But why stop at that point? If gigging is per se exploitative, why should we not include suppliers who are themselves companies? Coca Cola sells its wares at Walmart. Based on the logic of the anti-gig philosophy, the latter should make the former its wholly-owned subsidiary. Vertical integration here we come, and of the entire economy.

No, the attack on gigs is vulnerable to numerous reductios ad absurdum. But logic is not the only defense that can be made. Organized labor does not raise productivity, hence, it cannot, at least not in equilibrium boost wages. Getting rid of the gigster is a way of promoting unionization. That is, it is a way of reducing economic welfare. Yay, gigster!

# Chapter 15
# The (Voluntary!) Slave Owner

Coercive slavery is an abomination. It is despicable. It constitutes theft of labor. It is kidnapping on a vast scale; that is, for life (unless there is manumission on the part of the slave owner). Perhaps second to mass murder, it is just about the worst thing that human beings can do to one another. It ought to be banned forever, and salt sowed where once it stood.

But what about the voluntary variety of this "peculiar institution"? Would it, too, be illicit under libertarian law? Can there even be any such thing? Most people would say No: if it is voluntary, it cannot be slavery they would assert. And if it is slavery, it cannot be voluntary, they would aver. How wrong they are.

Consider the following case. One of my children, God forbid, has a dreaded disease. I am a poor man, and it would cost $25 million to cure that child of mine. You, gentle reader, had always wanted me to be your slave: to pick cotton for you, give you economics lessons, to use me as a punching bag, whatever; and, you may beat me to your heart's content if I displease you in any manner, shape or form. You are very rich. We agree upon the following deal. You give me that $25 million, which I turn over to my offspring's doctors, thus saving his life. Then I head off to your plantation to do your bidding and be punished for not fully pleasing you, for the rest of my days. I will call you Massa, try to be obedient to the best of my ability. You will treat me in much the same way as slaves were treated in the U.S. before 1865. The only difference between the two cases, and it is an absolutely crucial difference, is that I initially agreed to this transaction. I may even have initiated it with you, whereas those poor unfortunates, the actual (coerced) slaves, never approved of any such arrangement; certainly, they did not volunteer for it.

We both gain from this commercial arrangement in the ex-ante sense (this is true of ALL voluntary capitalist acts). I value my son's or daughter's life more than my freedom. I gain the difference to me between these two values. You also benefit, since you rate my servitude more highly than the money you expended in order to achieve ownership rights over me. Ex post, of course, I may well regret my decision. But,


W. E. Block, *Defending the Undefendable III*,
https://doi.org/10.1007/978-981-16-3957-9_15

maybe not. Even in the throes of a whipping, I can still contemplate the fact that my child is still alive, and would not otherwise be, and take great comfort from that fact.

"LOOK HERE, MOONEY, I'M SICK OF HEARING 'OL' MAN RIVER' OVER AND OVER, HALF THE NIGHT. YOU SIGNED THE 'VOLUNTARY-SLAVE' AGREEMENT, AND I GAVE YOUR FAMILY THE MILLION DOLLARS. AND <u>GET RIGHT OF THAT GODDAM HARMONIC</u>!"

The question is, Is this a legitimate contract? I respond with a big, loud, fat Yes, to this question. If I really truly initially own myself, then I have a right to sell myself into slavery. If the law prohibited me from so doing, beforehand, then I really did not fully own myself. Thus, my rights to myself should be alienable, not unalienable, as it states in the U.S. constitution. My pen is alienable. That means I can sell it, give it away, destroy it, etc. But suppose this right to my writing instrument was inalienable. Then, I would be prohibited from selling it to you or anyone else. The extent to which I may not legally engage in such an act is precisely the extent to which I do not really, fully, own my pen. Nor is there any real difference from this perspective between my ownership of myself and of my pen. Either I completely own these things, or I do not. If I do not, I am to that extent a slave, or a non-full owner of my writing implement. If I do, then I ought to be able, legally, to sell myself into this state of bondage.

But what about my will? Is my will alienable? No, it is not, I must acknowledge this objection to my thesis. Although I support the doctrine of free will (vis a vis determinism), I full well concede that at times, during my servitude, I hate my slave owner, I hate myself, I hate my predicament, I wish I could escape (although if I stole my master's property from him, that is, myself, what would happen to my child's life? Would it be forfeit? Maybe I had better stay on the plantation). So, alright, my will is not alienable. But, will, schmill. I am not selling my will. Rather, in very sharp contrast indeed, I am vending something far different. I am peddling, to wit, the right I would otherwise have to object to my master's overseer beating me. Consider the following scenario. I have just displeased my lawful owner, and he has instructed his overseer to beat me. (Or, I have not displeased him in any manner, shape or form; he merely has me whipped for the sheer pleasure it affords him). Along comes a policeman, representing law and order. I call out to him: "Help! I am being victimized by assault and battery. This whipping I am being inflicted with is a violation of my rights." The slave owner pulls out the voluntary slave contract he and I have signed, and shows that to the cop. What have I sold under this contract? My will? No. A thousand times no. Rather, what I have alienated is precisely the right to complain to the policeman that I am being beaten, and to call upon him to protect me, to free me. This has nothing whatsoever to do with any "will" of mine.

Voluntary slavery is an instance of a specific performance contract. (These are contracts, where consideration has been paid to ensure labor services; these are thus not mere promises, not actionable under libertarian law.) I am a tightrope walker. I perform 100 feet up into the air. I pay you in advance and hire you to hold a net under me, to catch me if I fall. You walk under me until I am in the middle of my act, and then start to walk off the job. I call to the proverbial policeman (who for some reason cannot take your place with the net, nor can anyone else) to compel you to fulfill your contract. May I do so? In my view, there is nothing, nothing at all in the entire corpus of libertarianism, that would prevent me from doing so. That is, specific performance contracts, always assuming no fraud, no compulsion, etc., are as valid as are any other voluntary agreements in the system of laissez-faire capitalism.

A note to all parents who love their children. Look me straight in the eye and tell me you would not give up your properly and highly-valued freedom to save the even more greatly-prized life of your son or daughter. I dare you to do so. No. I double dare you to look me in the eye and tell me that. If you do, I will reply that you don't really love your progeny all that much. If you cannot look me in the eye and say precisely this, then stop whining that I am incorrect, non-libertarian, in supporting the legality of voluntary slavery contracts. Note, I say not one single word about the morality of such an agreement. Libertarianism is a theory about just law, not all of ethics.

# Chapter 16
# The Labor Union Opponent

Do labor unions raise wages in the private sector? In order to answer this question, we must first ask what determines wage rates in the first place. Why is it that movie stars earn a ton of money, a college professor garners a middle-class salary and the person who pushes a broom around takes home a more modest remuneration.

The answer in technical terms is discounted marginal revenue product. In verbiage more suitable for a family newspaper, it is: productivity. Why does the employer want to have the employee on his payroll? Simple; because in that way his revenue will increase. Suppose a person, call him Joe, can add to the bottom line of the firm at the rate of $20 per hour.

The company might initially offer him an hourly wage of $12, but this cannot long endure. At that rate a profit of $8 will be earned on Joe's labor. Some other company will offer Joe $8.01, another $8.02, and a third $8.03. You see where we're going with this.

Eventually his wage will end up exactly equal to his productivity, if we abstract from the costs of finding him, interviewing him, testing him, and other such transactions costs. Nor need the impetus arise only from the perspective of the hirer. Joe himself can look for other jobs, and his pay scale can also rise from that direction. Nor can his wage long remain above his productivity level. At $30, if there are enough Joes, and they are kept on the shop floor for long enough, bankruptcy will eventually ensue.

So, the question of whether labor unions can boost pay packets comes down to one of, Do these organizations raise, lower or leave productivity levels unchanged? When put in this manner it is difficult to see how they can do anything other than lower productivity and thus equilibrium wages.

Even if they do not strike, their mere existence is costly. Organizing numbers of people so as to act together is not a free good. Then, when we add in all sorts of


W. E. Block, *Defending the Undefendable III*,
https://doi.org/10.1007/978-981-16-3957-9_16

labor union activities such as slow downs, job reservations, intra-union squabbles, sign-up activities, elections, law-suits, work to rule, collective bargaining, leaders' salaries, beating up scabs, establishing picket lines, publicity, secondary strikes, boycotts, lobbying congress, etc. These may all strengthen unions, but they lower member productivity, and hence, necessarily, wages (at least in the profit-making private sector; we economists do not have as airtight a theory of wages paid by governments).

The point we are making is not that unions cannot raise the wages of all workers. It is, rather, that they cannot even boost their own pay, at least not in the long run. Yes, to be sure, it cannot be denied, that in the short run, based upon violence and the threat thereof, the pay scales of the rank and file can indeed rise.

But, if they exceed marginal revenue productivity, which has been decreasing thanks to their activities, their employers will be rendered bankrupt. It is no accident that Detroit is an economic basket case; these types of organizations were very powerful in the automobile industry. Nor should it occasion any surprise that the entire "rust belt" came into being as a result of unions catapulting compensation above productivity levels.

Unions comprised some 33% of the labor force in 1955, and were down to single digits in the private sector by the 21st century. Wages rose markedly during that period. If organized labor were really responsible for this increase in worker well-being, it is more than passing curious it occurred during the time this institution was on the decline.

Why are labor unions falling on such hard times (except in government employment)?

Several hypotheses have been put forth to explain this radical reduction.

We are now much wealthier than we were in the 1950s. Unions are needed only for the poor, to help lift them up out of poverty. That is why Microsoft, Apple, IBM and their ilk have not been organized; they don't need this institution, since they already have high pay. But players in major league baseball, the NBA, the NFL, earn more than these high tech nerds, and they are unionized. There might be some explanatory power here, but maybe not all that much.

Here is another. Organized labor has been afflicted by corruption, mobster infiltration. The award-winning movie, The Irishman, encapsulates this charge in dramatic fashion. But this has always been roughly true, all throughout labor union history. It is difficult, then, to see this as an accurate account for the rise and then fall of this institution.

"...THEN IT'S AGREED, LADIES, IF THE MILFORD LEAGUE OF WOMEN VOTERS REFUSE TO CO-SPONSOR CANDIDATES NIGHT, WE'LL SLASH THEIR TIRES AND THROW ROCKS AND EGGS AT THEM."

Union leaders are invariably supporters of the Democratic party. Once upon a time that was also true of the vast majority of the membership. But it no longer holds. The rank and file in the age of Trump have to a significant degree embraced the Republican party. This might account, at least somewhat, for lessened support of the organized labor movement. (But it looks as if under the Biden Administration, this institution will get a shot in the arm).

Here is another hypothesis: The government has to a significant degree taken over the role played by unions in the past: promoting healthcare, pensions, etc. To the extent this is true, it might well at least partially explain the lessened interest in unionism.

Then there is the fact that labor has in the last little while been allocated away from customary union strengths: manufacturing, construction. It has flowed in the direction of restaurants, hotels, computers, healthcare, which traditionally, and also at present, were and are not now heavily unionized. This is a not unreasonable explanation, albeit a partial one at best. For it leaves open the question as to why these other zones of the economy have been so resistant to the blandishments of unionism.

Here is yet another entry into this sweepstakes. Before the Supreme Court's Janus decision, non-union members were required to pay so-called "agency fees" to organized labor. Why? It was thought that their wage increases were due to union activity, and that they were thus "free riders" on the efforts of that organization.

But the Janus finding put paid to all of that. It cited the first amendment, claiming that the free speech rights of the so-called beneficiaries were being violated by compelling them to pay their hard-earned money against their will to this group of people. Indeed, the entire pre-Janus justification was fallacious. First of all, wages are ultimately determined by productivity, not union threats. Second, even if A benefits from the acts of B does not justify B compelling A to pay him for them. I smile, take a shower once in a while, wear nice clothes, all of which (I claim), inure to your benefit. Yet if I sued you for these costs, I would properly be laughed out of court.

Several of these elucidations are at least partially correct, but none of them, even all together, can paint a complete picture. Here is another consideration to add to the mix. Wages are determined, ultimately, by labor productivity, and unions, with their strikes, work stoppages, internecine battles, downing tools in "sympathy" with their brethren, lower productivity compared to the level that would otherwise have obtained.

Unions are thus akin to a tapeworm, sucking the life out of an otherwise viable company. Detroit, anyone? Once upon a time this was a reasonably viable city. But the unions kept escalating their salary package demands, which choked off the profits of the automobile firms. Several of them headed south, and many of the others are now a shadow of their former selves.

The reason Lebron James earns a stupendous salary has nothing to do with unionism; ditto for your present author taking home more modest remuneration, nor for the guy who washes dishes at a still lower level. No, compensation is determined by how much each of us adds to the bottom line.

Wages are set by productivity levels, and unions lower, not raise them. This might be difficult to see, since many members of organized labor are paid generously. But that is despite union activity, not because of it. Without the "help" of this organization, their productivity would be higher, and so would their pay.

# Chapter 17
# The Precarious Labor Employer

Who are these rascals who are guilty of offering precarious jobs to their employees? Before we can answer this question, we must clarify what precarious employment is in the first place. This term refers to any and all jobs other than those that call for the standard fare of Monday to Friday, 9:00 a.m. to 5:00 p.m. (or any other fixed 8 hour day), with 2, 3, or 4 weeks vacation per year, depending upon seniority. What falls into this large category? Part-time work certainly does. And why, in turn, are there so many jobs featuring 39 or fewer hours per week? One reason is due to the fact that when this barrier is reached, all sorts of additional requirements (health-care, retirement, etc.) befall the employer. Another reason is seasonality. The skiing industry does more business in the winter than in the summer. The very opposite occurs in places like Cape Cod, and Seattle, where numerous people spend their summer vacations. Fishing season, too, must be served. Then there are those rainy days when the car wash industry is idled, along with the employer. There is also contract work, for jobs of limited duration. Once completed, all subcontractors are released. There is also temporary work, on a day to day basis, when the employer finds it difficult to predict the pattern of demand. Nor can we avoid cases where the impetus for this sort of thing stems from the employee not the employer side of the ledger. For example, a teenager may be saving up to purchase a motorcycle. When he has sufficient funds for this purpose, he downs tools without any by-your-leave from anyone. It is no accident that fast food purveyors such as McDonald's, Burger King, Wendy's, have over 100% employee turnover every year.

Do all of these eminently reasonable explanations for precarious employment have any effect on their critics. No, no, no. Labor unions and government bureaucrats, are seething with indignation that such a state of affairs persists. The former demand action to quell this institution, and the latter are only too happy to comply. Organized labor agonizes over precarious employment since, in their view, it is pernicious. Most workers presumably prefer traditional arrangement and if labor organizations had their way, all would be shoved into this Procrustean bed, whether they preferred it or not.



W. E. Block, *Defending the Undefendable III*,
https://doi.org/10.1007/978-981-16-3957-9_17

Thus, the employer who resists their threats and blandishments takes on the role of hero, for protecting a minority that wishes to avail itself of this option. If employer and employee wish to "do business" with each other, then, no matter what the level of precariousness, we can deduce that both gain thereby, at least in the ex-ante sense. That is, at the moment of agreement each sees benefits out weighing costs, otherwise they would scarcely consent to the deal with each other. And this goes for the worker as well as the boss.

But by far the greatest source of precariousness in the labor field is not employment but rather entrepreneurship. If we as a society really oppose precariousness, we must ban self-employment. For when people set up shop on their own, the failure role is substantial. But wait; large scale business is not either any safe haven. A perusal of the Fortune 500 over the last few decades will bear ample evidence of the fact that this is no safe refuge either. Where are Radio Shack, Kodak, Rand typewriters, Herald Tribune, Pan American, TWA, United Shoe Machinery, Nash, Studebaker nowadays? Gone, that is where.

Can the government, then, serve as insurance against economic variability? To ask this is to answer it: of course not. Countries for the most part survive, but their economic viability is subject to great oscillations. The fortunes of Cuba, Venezuela, and North Korea have plummeted while those of South Korea, Japan, Singapore, Hong Kong, and Taiwan have gone in the opposite direction. Precariousness is the human condition.

# Chapter 18
# The Housewife Non-payer

You may add the Vatican to that long list of distinguished and not-so-distinguished institutions, organizations and individuals that have advocated pay for housewives. A 12-article charter, which passed muster with the Pope, claims that families have a right "to social and economic order" and that therefore, wives should be paid a wage for working at home.

Now this would appear all well and good. Certainly, the salary will come in handy for millions of families the world over and, in any case, who could oppose a measure that would put more bread on the table?

A moment's reflection, however, will convince us that this particular apple comes fully equipped with worms at its core. To begin with, where is all the new-found money to come from?

The Rev. Jan Schotte, secretary of the Vatican-based Commission on Justice & Peace, stated that those bonuses should be paid compliments of the government. But this only places a veil on the financial proceedings, as the government has no money apart from what it first seizes from the private sector. So the real income transfer is from those who work for wages in the marketplace to those who can afford the luxury of maintaining an individual at home, there to provide all sorts of non-taxed services to herself and to the other family members.

Apart from the unjustified income transfers involved, this scheme also has serious allocational deficiencies. For the decision to work directly for oneself, in the household sector, or indirectly, in paid employment, is fraught with implications for the economic well-being of society.

Imagine the situation that would ensue were everyone to labor at home, in the direct production of consumer goods and services. We would have to do without the vast benefits of specialization, the division of labor, the ability to pool large amounts of capital, equipment and manpower. (On the other hand, a policy which artificially subsidizes co-operation through commercial enterprise would also reduce human welfare. Instead of brushing our own teeth, preparing our own meals at home,


W. E. Block, *Defending the Undefendable III*,
https://doi.org/10.1007/978-981-16-3957-9_18

dressing ourselves, shaving, combing our hair, we would find ourselves hiring other people to do these tasks for us, with a consequent loss in privacy.)

THE GOVERNMENT INSPECTOR FINDS DIRTY DISHES IN MRS. NORA DEVLIN'S SINK AT 11:10 A.M.– AN HOUR PAST THE OFFICIAL DEADLINE. THIS MEANS $7.00 WILL BE DEDUCTED FROM NORA'S HOUSEWIFE CHECK FOR THE NEXT 3 MONTHS.

Right now, presumably, we are all at equilibrium with regard to market and non-market work. That is, the allocation of time spent in and out of the home at least roughly conforms to our desires. However, let this latest Vatican plan be enacted, and it will artificially encourage people to remain home more than they would otherwise choose to do, with a consequent loss in economic welfare. This is so because pay for work at home would encourage those on the margin between market and non-market activity to devote more time to the latter. But with more than the optimal effort devoted to home-work, society would suffer the loss of commercial transactions, which have been judged by the participants themselves to have been more valuable than their other options.

However, it does seem unfair that woman A works at home and receives no pay, while woman B works as a maid dash housekeeper, dash shopper, dash babysitter, and is paid a salary for her efforts. That is to say, both A and B, let us assume, do identical work (we posit they are equally productive in these tasks), and are treated very, very differently.

But are they really? Not when we look at this matter a bit more carefully. For A, is really getting paid. Not in the form of money, to be sure, but in the coin of services which she performs for her husband and children. Had she not been doing such, and her family were to be at least roughly equally cared for, she would have had to hire someone else, such as B, to perform these services. A and B are in exactly the same position, assuming all other things equal. A performs these tasks, directly, for her family. B goes out into the market and does these jobs for another family. But what about B's own family? Who takes care of them? (Remember, we are assuming that A and B are equally productive, and start out in the same situation). Why, B has to hire someone else, presumably C. Thus, A and B at the end of the day are in the same exact position. Each family has the same efforts undertaken in its behalf. Again, this is done by A directly, and by B indirectly (via C). Why pay any more to A? She already garnering exactly the same recompense as B, who is being paid in the form of a money wage, which she turns over to someone else, C.

# Chapter 19
# The Minimum Wage Challenger

We live in an era of economic illiteracy. Consider the effects of minimum wage laws.

Most economists well know that such laws exacerbate unemployment for teenagers. A survey by the prestigious *American Economic Review* showed that members of the profession agreed, by an 87.7 per cent to 12.3 per cent margin, with the proposition that "a minimum wage increases unemployment among young and unskilled workers." (We have recalls for automobiles; we ought to do the same for that 12.3 per cent! Either they received their Ph.D. degrees in a package of Cracker Jacks, or they relish unemployment and poverty for the unskilled).

This finding has percolated very well into the economic mainstream—within the university, the business world, and the think-tank community. Even introductory textbooks, no matter what the political basis of their authors, typically include a diagram showing that when wages are set by law at a level above equilibrium, unemployment for the less skilled will ensue. (Nobel Prize-winning economist Joseph Stiglitz is no exception to this general rule. However, he also signed a petition favoring this law. When asked to reconcile these two different positions he was not even slightly incoherent. He was actually totally unintelligible.)

But the knowledge of the deleterious effects of mandated minimum-wages has not yet seeped into the consciousness of the public. Ministers, high school teachers, journalists, social workers, editorialists, and other well-meaning folk have been appalled at the fact that the minimum wage level is so low. The federal level in the US is $7.25. The reaction of many people is: "How can anyone live on such trifling pay?"

If we probe a bit more deeply, however, the case against legislative enactment becomes easier to see. For minimum wage law does not compel an employer to hire a worker at any given wage rate. Rather, it only stipulates that an employee cannot be put on the payroll unless he is paid at least a certain specified hourly wage. The loophole is wide enough to drive the proverbial large truck through: if the law commands that a low-skilled person be paid, say, $4 per hour and his productivity level is only $3 per hour, all the firm need do is take on several highly skilled employees


W. E. Block, *Defending the Undefendable III*,
https://doi.org/10.1007/978-981-16-3957-9_19

(and some sophisticated machinery) instead, and avoid like the plague the unskilled worker it would otherwise have hired.

If the minimum wage level is doubled from $4 an hour to $8 an hour, this will have very little effect indeed on a person earning $22 an hour. Why should it? But think of what it will do to a relatively unskilled laborer who can produce at the rate of only $5 an hour. If the firm is forced to pay $8 an hour, it will lose $3 for every hour the worker is on the payroll.

This is therefore the equivalent of a sort of black death for the employment prospects of very young and otherwise unskilled people. It also negatively impacts those who are the target of discriminatory practices. Suppose a white and black person have identical productivity levels of $10 per hour. If, due to discrimination the white earns that $10 (wages tend to reflect productivity), and the black only $7, then the latter in effect has a little sign on his lapel saying: "Hire me and earn an extra $3 per hour from my labor." But with a minimum wage of $10, this advantage of the black person disappears into the thin air.

The deer is a very weak animal. How does it survive? It's compensating differential is its great speed. The porcupine is a very weak animal. How does it survive? It's compensating differential is its quills. (How do porcupines make love? Very carefully/). The skunk is a very weak animal. How does it survive? It's compensating differential is its odor. The young black uneducated unskilled person is a very weak economic actor. How does he survive? His compensating differential is the ability to work for a low wage (a low wage is better than no wage at all.) But the minimum wage takes that away from him. Doing so to him is the equivalent of depriving the deer of its speed, the porcupine of its quills, the skunk of its smell. We do no favor to the unskilled by doing this to them.

But wait. There is such a thing as welfare. If the minimum wage creates unemployment for the unskilled, they can always rely on the dole. In order to see the fallacy of this rejoinder, consider the following case. Assume a 40 hour work week, a minimum wage of $7, productivity of $5 per hour, and welfare of 300 per week.

| | Minimum wage exists | There is no minimum wage |
|---|---|---|
| Welfare | A | B |
| | Job: 0 | Job: 200 |
| | Welfare: 300 | Welfare: 300 |
| | Total: 300 | Total: 500 |
| No welfare | C | D |
| | Job: 0 | Job: 200 |
| | Welfare: 0 | Welfare: 0 |
| | Total: 0 | Total: 200 |

Let me explain the four quadrants.

In A, the job pays zero since the person in question cannot be employed. He needs to be paid $7 per hour, his productivity is only $5 per hour; any company employing him will lose $2 per hour. That cannot endure in equilibrium. But there is welfare, so this person comes away with a total of $300.

In B, the job pays $200 (40 hours x $5 per hour) since the person in question can be employed. There is welfare, so this person comes away with a total of $500; $200 from work, $300 from the dole.

In C, the job pays zero since the person in question cannot be employed. He needs to be paid $7 per hour, his productivity is only $5 per hour; any company employing him will lose $2 per hour. That cannot endure in equilibrium. But there is no welfare, so this person comes away with a total of zero.

In D, the job pays $200 (40 hours x $5 per hour) since the person in question can be employed. There is no welfare, so this person comes away with a total of $200 from work, nothing from the dole.

Note, that when there is welfare, our subject is better off without a minimum wage law since B is preferable to A. Also, when there is no welfare, our subject is still better off without a minimum wage law since D is preferable to C.

But the law stipulates that the person who is working is not eligible for welfare, also. Thus B is a null set. A similar fate awaits D, since if a person is totally unemployed, he will qualify for welfare payments. To this I say, I don't give a rat's rear end about what the law is. The law, for this purpose, be damned. My focus is solely and only on comparing the presence or absence of the minimum wage, holding all else constant. I do so in two ways. One, in the absence of welfare, and find that the $200 of D is preferable to the zero of C. Secondly, I do so in the presence of this other governmental policy, and reach a similar conclusion: the B of no minimum wage ($500) is greater than the A with this law in operation ($300). Ceteris paribus conditions must be maintained if we are to make any sense of the situation when welfare payments are incorporated into the analysis.

Consider, now, this objection. Suppose that at free market wage 100 workers earn $5 per hour for a total of $500. Now we introduce a minimum wage of $7 per hour. As a result, 90 workers are still employed at this higher rate of compensation but 10 are unemployed. It is difficult to make any definitive conclusion about the well-being of the workers, since 90 are better off and 10 worse off. However, the workers decide to share both labor and pay. That is, a different 90 work every week and an alternative 10 become temporarily unemployed; but they are paid by the actual workers for those seven days. At the end of 10 weeks, everyone will have taken on both roles. How much will they then be paid, whether they work or not? Well, 90 employees at $7 per hour implies a wage bill of $630. If this was directed at the workers alone each would of course obtain $7 per hour. However, based on our assumptions the sum of $630 will be divided among not only 90 workers, but all 100, whether working during that particular week or not. Thus, each will receive $630/100 = $6.30. This is not as much as the $7 to which they would otherwise have been entitled were they on the job, but it clearly beats the $5 prevailing before the advent of the minimum wage law. Thus, we seemingly have a demonstration as to how this wage legislation can improve the situation of its supposedly intended beneficiaries.

Not so fast. The difficulty is that this section of the demand curve is inelastic (3/19, equal to about 16%). But the longer the length of run, the more elastic demand curves become. Give the employers a bit more time, and only 80 people will be employed. Then 70. Where will this process end? Assuming that worker productivity remains at $5 per hour, every last one of them will eventually join the unemployment lines, and stay there! This is why baseball pitchers hurl the ball at batters at speeds in excess of 80 miles per hour; they don't want to give their opponents time to adjust. The slower the ball approaches the batter, the longer the time he has to respond to it, the more likely he will hit it.

Lookit, when the minimum wage was raised from $0.40 to $0.75 in January 1950 (the largest percentage increase so far on record), how many manually operated elevator operators were fired the very next day? Not a single solitary one of them. That shows a zero elasticity. But, after a few weeks, months, all of these vertical conveyances were switched over to automatic status, and their previous operators lost their jobs. If the Card and Krueger of that day could not find evidence of this phenomenon, we would just tell them to look a bit harder. Their modern-day equivalents probably would not be able to find the earth after being ejected from an airplane with a parachute.

Are the intended beneficiaries of this legislation really the poor and the unskilled? Not hardly. Qui bono? We have seen that the fate of these workers is to become unemployed. Remember, this law is not a rising floor, raising wages; rather, it is a hurdle or high-jump bar over which workers have to exceed in order to obtain a job in the first place, and the higher it is placed, the more difficult it is for them to jump over it, into employment. Who then gains? It is organized labor. Skilled workers are always and ever in completion with those at the other end of the spectrum. When a union demands a wage increase from $30 to $40 per hour the first thought to enter the mind of the business owner is how to replace one of these high-paid workers with several of the unskilled. The last thing the unionists want is to be thereby supplanted.

They characterize these replacement workers as "scabs" and try to beat them up. One problem is that these youngsters can fight back. Another is that they are all too often of a darker complexion than the striking union workers, and this doesn't "look good" to the supposed "progressive" forces. Far better to get a law passed which obviates the entire threat: the minimum wage law, pegged at a high enough level to cancel competition from the unskilled.

I write at a time when President Biden is just about to take office. I have no doubt he will install a Bernie Sanders special: a boost of the minimum wage to $15.00 per hour if not even higher. This will have devastating effects upon the unskilled. They will be rendered unemployable. If they continue to look for jobs the unemployment rate will skyrocket. My prediction is that the Democrats will then install a federal jobs-for-all program.

"WAGSTAFF, I THINK YOU'VE GOT THE RIGHT STUFF—HAVE YOU CONSIDERED APPLYING FOR A SUPERVISORY POSITION?"

# Chapter 20
# The Academic Tenure Denier

Any attempt to end tenure in our universities always brings in its wake howls of outrage from virtually the entire academic community. Faculty associations, university departments, and even groups of professors from abroad typically protest vociferously along with the nations' editorialists, at what they consider this affront to all that is decent and right. But this should occasion little surprise since the professors are hardly a disinterested group in this matter. Rather, they have a compelling and vested interest in the perpetuation of tenure for themselves.

In contrast, the average Joe lunch bucket is highly bemused at all the fuss. If anything, he has witnessed this comeuppance delivered to the high and mighty professors with a certain degree of indifference, and even equanimity. And this is no surprise, either. For it is the average citizen and taxpayer who is called upon to pay for the trough at which the professors have been so avidly feeding these many years.

What arguments do the professors make in their own behalf?

1. Tenure saves money for the university. According to faculty members at one university, "(Without tenure) salaries would have to be raised to continue to attract highly qualified people. Tenure can thus be regarded as a way of making universities a more attractive place to work at no additional cost to the treasury."

This, as a matter of fact, is true, at least insofar far as it goes. Since most people, professors included, have an aversion to risk, you can usually hire people for less, other things equal, if you guarantee them life-long employment. So what else is new?

But the argument is too clever by half. For according to this logic, everyone should be given tenure. We could get away with paying lower wages for all employees in this manner.


W. E. Block, *Defending the Undefendable III*,
https://doi.org/10.1007/978-981-16-3957-9_20

Also, we gain out of pocket wage savings only at the cost of added inflexibility. For under this system, a university is liable to gather unneeded tenured professors in disciplines no longer desired by the students. Nowadays, this would include areas such as philosophy, ancient languages, literature, the classics, black "studies," queer "studies," feminist "studies," etc. In order to meet the increased demand for courses in commerce, computers and the physical sciences, the universities will have to hire additional professors in these "hard disciplines." Thus we can see that even with somewhat lower salaries, total costs may well be higher with tenure.

These professors have focused only on out-of-pocket expenses. But the relevant concept here is "alternative costs," which poses the more meaningful question of whether by saving a few pennies in monetary outlays now, colleges are undertaking pounds of costs further down the road.

2. Tenure promotes independent thought. Without tenure, it is contended, it would be more difficult for academics to challenge the powers that be.

This again is true—so far as it goes. But academics are not the only ones who from time to time point out that the "emperor has no clothes." Other boat-shakers and watch-dogs include editorialists, novelists, playwrights, essayists, rock and roll and folk, song lyricists, clergymen, journalists, critics, businessmen, movie producers, t.v. writers, cartoonists, and whistle blowers from many other walks of life. Shall all of these callings be given tenure—the better to upset the established order?

Then there is the question of independence from whom. The professors and their apologists, as could be expected, are concerned with undue or political influence from outside of academia. But that is where the paying customer—the taxpayer—resides, outside the groves of academe. Under our system of public higher education it is the politician who is the only representative of the voter and taxpayer. This demand for freedom from outside interference is thus a demand to do as one will with the hard-earned money of other people.

But what about undue influence on scholarly independence from within the university community? Anyone even vaguely familiar with the politics of tenure grantsmanship knows how strong and undue an influence the tenured professors can bring to bear on the untenured junior faculty. Let us consider an example we have already touched upon. Can anyone imagine that there were no implicit pressures brought to bear to go along with the statement on behalf of tenure, signed by the senior professors cited above? We may fear, and rightly so, that the young junior professors would be severely weeded-out by such a process, at the hands of the more senior faculty.

3. Tenure insures a high-quality, competent professoriate. According to this theory, tenure is granted after an arduous, exhaustive and intensive procedure, only to those who have demonstrated excellence in research and teaching. Actually, however, the process is marred by politicking, favoritism, and an "old boy"

network. There are dangers even when this process works well. For a young scholar who has shown great promise during a five or six-year period, will not necessarily live up to his potential. Then, the universities become cluttered with ancient incompetents, and useless time servers in their dotage waiting for retirement.

Perhaps a better plan might be to set a ten, fifteen, or even twenty year time period before tenure is granted. Under such a plan, there would be far fewer dead wood embarrassments. Professors would have more time to demonstrate that they were not just flashes in the pan. As well, such an alteration would have favorable effects on continued academic industriousness. No longer could people rest to the same degree on their earlier laurels.

But such a change would really undermine the whole logic of tenure. For if it is granted later in life, fewer are the benefits derived. If postponed until almost retirement, the tenure system would be virtually destroyed.

There we have it. On the plus side, tenure has the following benefits: it can save out of pocket expenses, it promotes independence from outside forces, it increases quality. As against that, this system increases costly inflexibility, it cuts the tie to the paying customer, it increases dependence on inside forces (the tenured professors), and it runs the risk of entrenching people who later turn out to be intellectual deadwood.

So is tenure a good or a bad system?

The answer is, we cannot say. There is nothing in the discipline of economics that would allow for an unambiguous answer one way or the other. For this is akin to a question of managerial technique, such as "What is the optimum allocation of labour and capital in a given plant or industry?" The answer, in both cases, is, it depends. On what? On the market!

Fortunately, however, economics can supply a methodology for answering all such questions. And the general answer is "Let the free enterprise system work." Allow freedom of choice. Operate a system where different entrepreneurs can try different proportions of labour and capital, and the competitive system will determine which are the best management techniques. But this experiment must be held in the private sector, so that the financial situation of the entrepreneurs is solely dependent on their allocational decision making.

"DOBBINS, I'VE HAD MY EYE ON YOU FOR SOME TIME. I LIKE THE WAY YOU HANDLE YOURSELF UNDER SEVERE EXCREMENTITIOUS CIRCUMSTANCES, I'M RECOMMENDING YOU FOR TENURE—CONGRATULATIONS!"

It is easy to apply this to the tenure system: privatize all colleges, and universities, make them directly dependent upon the choices of the paying customers (instead of indirectly dependent, via the tax system). Some universities would presumably maintain tenure. Others would not. Still others might institute variations on and permutations of this system. Then, from the competition between academies using different schemes, we would be in a position to judge. Perhaps, that is, tenure would work well in some sorts of institutions, and badly in others. But only on the basis of the free marketplace can such a determination be made.

Some people will be aghast at this "modest proposal." They will cry out that the poor will suffer. In this, however, they are wrong. Research on the public universities shows unequivocally that the children of the rich are the main beneficiaries of publicly financed higher education. True, all segments of society pay the taxes for these lavish centers of learning. But the rich are so overwhelmingly overrepresented, that on net balance, the poor end up subsidizing the education of the rich, who use this educational subsidy to widen the income gap further. This insight applies also to museums, libraries, symphony orchestras, planetariums, art galleries, and other subsidies peripheral to culture and higher education.

So let us move with all deliberate speed to the privatization of higher education. Such a step can right the wrong of forcing the poor to subsidize the education of the rich and will shed light on the tenure controversy as well.

There are some advocates of the market system, benighted souls, who will be unsatisfied with the foregoing. In their view, tenure in public universities is an abomination, to be fought tooth and nail. They regard the analysis above as just so much subterfuge and evasiveness. "Is public sector tenure a good idea or not?" they ask, and insist upon an answer. They regard the suggestion of privatizing public universities, and allowing the marketplace determine whether tenure survives or not. as no answer at all. Their dissatisfaction with this line of reasoning stems from the fear that it is, and will be seen to be, irrelevant to the question of tenure in the public university.

In this, the critics are correct. A call for privatization is, strictly speaking, irrelevant to the question of whether or not public sector colleges should maintain tenure.

Nevertheless, I still maintain the propriety of ignoring the question of tenure in public universities, and answering instead, as we have done above. For it is not the business of the free market advocate to become embroiled in questions of this sort. Indeed, it is counter-productive. It is a snare and delusion, and profoundly at variance with the philosophy of free enterprise.

At bottom, this question of public sector tenure is merely one of how can public enterprise best be administered? Should it be with a tenure system, or without one? But the implicit premise, here, is that public education is itself viable. Now, in the case of police, armies, courts—at least as far as the classical liberal position is concerned—this may indeed be so (this is of course not true for the anarcho-capitalist position I espouse, but that is another story—see chapter two above). But as far as education is concerned, especially higher education (any "spillovers" can usually be captured), there is no assumption whatsoever that this is true, even for moderate limited-government libertarians. On the contrary, the presumption is exactly the other way around. Unless and until the case is made, there is no room, in the classical liberal philosophy, for government educational enterprise.

To become involved in the public tenure controversy, then, is to accept the basic legitimacy of public education in the first place. And this is completely illegitimate, given that no case has been made against strictly private higher education.

Thus there is no option other than to do as we have done above. To list the pros and cons, perhaps, but then to insist, and steadfastly maintain, that the tenure question is a red herring. Our main concern is to see a system of private enterprise education, and then to let the tenure problem sink or swim on its own in a free environment.

# Chapter 21
# The Work Sharer

Work-sharing seems to be the "in" thing nowadays. According to this line of reasoning, unemployment is caused by people working too many hours; if they would just reduce their work-week to, say, 32 hours, there would be plenty of jobs to go around for everyone. According to some estimates, the 32-hour work-week could create more than a million additional jobs. If not halting unemployment entirely dead in its tracks, at least this would radically reduce it.

Superficially attractive as is this idea, it is deeply flawed. First of all, it flies in the face of the historical facts. Modern rates of unemployment were virtually unknown during the industrial revolution, and yet the work-week commonly lasted for 60, 80, and even 100 or more hours in that era. Surely if the long work-week created unemployment, our rate of joblessness would have been reduced as the length of the work-week fell; instead, the unemployment rate has risen as the work-week decreased to 40 hours per week, and even less in some cases.

The second major drawback to the work-sharing hypothesis is that it commits the lump-of-labour-fallacy. In this view, there is only so much work to be done in society. There is a definite upper bound to employment opportunities. If some people do more than their fair share of work, why, then, there will be less left for everyone else. Hard work, responsibility, great efforts, are thus not virtues, as tradition would have it. Rather, these qualities are evidence of greed. Ambitious and untiring workers are hogging up the available jobs.

But these are dubious propositions. There is no particular upper limit to the amount of work. Over the long sweep of time, the scope for employment is continually rising. As long as people are unsatisfied with what they have, want more goods and services, and are willing to work for wages that reflect their productivity, there will be room for additional employment possibilities. At one time in our history, virtually all laborers were tied to the farm. They were needed merely to keep body and soul together. But nowadays, thanks to vast gains in productivity, only some 2% of the work force is in agricultural employment, and we not only can feed ourselves far better than before, we can also supply foodstuffs to people in the rest of the


W. E. Block, *Defending the Undefendable III*,
https://doi.org/10.1007/978-981-16-3957-9_21

world as well. Where did all of these additional non-agricultural jobs come from? If the amount of work to be done had a strict upper limit, virtually our entire labour force should be unemployed by now.

"HEY, YOU GUYS, WHEN I CALLED FOR AN 'INSPECTION SLOWDOWN' ON THESE JAPANESE CARS, I DIDN'T MEAN THAT SLOW!"

And the same analysis applies to the knitting mill, automatic elevators, the computer, and other labor-saving technology. At one time or another in our history, it was feared that employment would become virtually obsolete because of these innovations.

The real cause of unemployment is not that ambitious workers are pigging out on the limited job opportunities left to us by new industrial techniques. On the contrary, unemployment is created when employees price themselves out of the market, by demanding wages in excess of their productivity levels. And this is precisely what will result from work-sharing schemes—when proportionate wage decreases are resisted, as they almost always are. For fewer hours, at the same weekly pay, translates into higher hourly remuneration. Work-sharing plans of this sort will exacerbate unemployment, not cure it.

A variation of this proposal is not to directly share work with one's fellow employees, but to legislate for a shorter work week for all of us. The problem is that such enactments seldom drive down the actual number of labor hours. Instead, they only succeed in reducing some of these hours as "overtime," to be compensated at higher rates of pay.

But what about work-sharing of this type accompanied by proportional wage reductions, so that hourly pay remains the same? Can this help? Well, this would be far better than work-sharing with in effect artificially increased hourly wages. At least it will not directly raise our already high unemployment rates. But there are still other difficulties.

First of all, productivity levels will fall. This is because the unemployed are likely to be less efficient, on average, than those already working. As well, it is extremely unlikely that each industry will have the same proportion of unemployment as every other. If the work is to be shared all across the board, this will mean that at least some people will be taken on in the positions for which they have little talent, aptitude, even inclination. With decreasing productivity, wages will thus have to be reduced even more than in proportion to the falling work-week, if the employment rate is not to be elevated.

"GET OUTTA MY WAY, TOM, YOU BLOODY REACTIONARY FASCIST!"

Secondly, the shorter work-week, with pay reduced more than proportionately, is likely to be resented bitterly by those forced to do the sharing. Unwanted leisure (see covid house arrests) is a burden, not a benefit. This alone would tend to make the scheme unstable. In addition, this contrived inactivity is just plain inefficient. In economic terminology, it creates a "dead weight loss." People who could be happily engaged in productive activity for 40, 45 or even 50 hours per week are forced to limit themselves to 32 hours, at reduced hourly pay.

And it is all so unnecessary! We can cure our unemployment rate without creating vast pockets of enforced idleness, bitterness and inefficiency. All we need to do is pursue public policies which do not encourage the boosting of wage rates beyond productivity levels.

# Chapter 22
# The Jury Refuser

A weird word comes to us from Joliet, Quebec, located in the country to the north of us. It is a small town lying some 40 miles northeast of Montreal. The local constabulary was on the loose, chasing down any adult citizens they could reach – in order to impress them for duty as jurors.

Say, what? It appears that only 11 members of a 12 member jury were selected for the trial of 10 Archambault Institute convicts charged with murdering three prison guards. The initial list of 225 candidates for the jury to try these men did not suffice. Each side could, and did, reject 20 potential juror without giving any reasons. The others were dismissed for cause.

When this unlikely event occurred, the Quebec Superior Court Judge ordered the local sheriff to go out onto the street and scare up a passel of new juror candidates. The honest burghers hid like desperados in the Joliette stores and homes, and many of them high-tailed it out of the community. Nevertheless, even though the word was out, the chief of police was able to lasso 44 more people into potential service.

The specter of an innocent citizenry hiding out from their duly constituted law officials must surely give us pause for thought. True, this jury round-up took place a century ago. At this rate, it is unlikely in the extreme, at least for most of us, that our lives will be interfered with in so cavalier a manner.

Nevertheless, even without these sorts of round-ups befitting cattle, our jury system is still a coercive institution. It is compulsory, and either totally unpaid (which reeks of you know what), or vastly underpaid, so much so that the compensation almost constitutes an insult. If "the laborer is worthy of his hire," surely in this year of our Lord 2021, it is time to end the medieval practice of drafting people for jury service.

But don't we need juries? If we didn't compel people to serve on them, that would mean the end of this system, and with it an important part of our legal culture, will be the defense of this modern bit of coercion of the innocents.



W. E. Block, *Defending the Undefendable III*,
https://doi.org/10.1007/978-981-16-3957-9_22

No, no, no, there is more than one way to skin the proverbial cat (trigger warning, animal rightsers; this has nothing to do with torturing any of our furry friends). Instead of drafting jury members, we could hire them! This may appear revolutionary, and unworkable to some, but this is the system utilized to attract service providers in every other nook and cranny of the modern economy. That it will appear strange to some that we apply this system to the functioning of courts is only based upon inbred habits of mind. Judges, court stenographers, uniformed guards, prosecutors, attorneys, the people who keep these buildings clean, are all paid, not compelled to contribute their services. Why should the juror be the only non-criminal at a trial who is compelled to be there? There need not be any more fear that a paid jury system will be co-opted by being "bought off by the highest bidder" than in any of these other instances.

Were such a plan adopted, henceforth, whenever there were not sufficient volunteers to form a twelve man jury, those who conduct trials will be forced to raise the wages offered until the supply of candidates increased to the extent needed. This is the system used to attract all other members of the judicial system. Why not this one too?

As at present, not every volunteer need be accepted. Plaintiff and defendant would still be able to reject a certain number of candidates. Judges could still rule out others, for cause. But people would likely have to be paid a fee merely for offering themselves, and a salary commensurate with alternative opportunities for protracted and intensive jury service.

There is also a utilitarian objection to be made to the present system. People compelled against their will to undertake any task are less likely to do it well. They might get angry, and take it out on the accused, which would be unjust. Equally problematic, they may attempt to get back at the source of their imprisonment, the authorities responsible for their plight, and lighten sentences or free criminals. It is an empirical matter as to in which direction the scales of justice will be misaligned. It is possible that these two effects may exactly cancel each other out, but we cannot rely on any such perfect balance. We want to approach as close as possible to justice in our courts (well, at least private ones, since governmental courts come with ethical difficulties of their own – they are financed based on compulsory levies). Drafting jurors is not likely to help improve matters in this regard.

Under a system of voluntary labor, the only one befitting a free society, the task of serving on a jury would take its place amongst all other honorable professions. And honest citizens would no longer have to fear arbitrary searches and seizures of their very persons.

# Part V
# Sex

# Chapter 23
# The Group Marriage Participant

It used to be, once upon a time, long, long ago, that marriage was between one man and one woman. More recently, we have learned that this is far too restrictive. The ties of holy matrimony may now be taken up by two males, or two females. Well, maybe not holy matrimony, the decision over which is made by institutions of religion, but, at least a pair of men, or women, may now link up with one another and enjoy all the secular prerequisites of that institution. (Or, maybe non-secular ones too, since nowadays some religious organizations have given their imprimatur to such arrangements, despite clear biblical mandates to the contrary).

What is the libertarian to make of all of this? We resort to "anything peaceful," "anything voluntary." We do not support such marriages nor oppose them, any more than we do for those between heterosexuals, one of each gender; or homosexuals, two of the same persuasion. We only say that since no rights have been violated by these arrangements, no law should set asunder what willing pairs of people have agreed upon. This means that government should treat all three types of marriage identically, with regard to such implications as people dying intestate, child adoptions, divorce, next of kin situations, and every other aspect of marriage. What about private employers and other such individuals? Should they be required to treat all such arrangements in an identical manner? No, of course not. Since free association is one of the basic bedrocks of this philosophy, firms, friends, business associates should determine for themselves exactly how to treat gay marriages.

But why stop there? Given that our touchstones are "anything peaceful," "anything voluntary," this encompasses far more than homosexual and lesbian nuptials. For example, it should also incorporate polygamy (one man, several wives) and polyandry (one woman, several husbands). Mormons have for many years in their history partaken of the former. When it joined the union, the state of Utah was bullied out of legalizing these arrangements, but there does not appear to be much justification for prohibiting them, at least not on libertarian grounds. If gays and lesbians may marry within their respective communities there is no legitimate reason why this should not apply, also, to polygamists, or polyandrists (my computer



W. E. Block, *Defending the Undefendable III*,
https://doi.org/10.1007/978-981-16-3957-9_23

program objects to the spelling of the latter word; it insists that I substitute for it "polyamorists." But this latter concept has to do with engaging in sexual intercourse with many people, not necessarily marriage).

We have only begun to scratch the surface of this issue. In Robert Heinlein's magnificent novel, *The Moon is a Harsh Mistress*, a group marriage played a significant role in the plot. That is, marriages, with all the credits and debits of that institution, may be enjoyed by groups of people: perhaps four men and six women; or, maybe, five females and seven males. There would not appear to be any limit as to the size or make-up of such marriages. One with hundreds or thousands of members might be a bit unwieldy, but that is an issue to be decided by the members thereof, not by the government, God forbid, nor even by private busybodies. (The latter would be free to boycott any one for any reason, but not to prevent this form of organization).

Yes, this does sound somewhat outré. Presumably, "nice" people never enter any such agreements. But, not too long ago, the same was said about gay marriages. It would appear that there is no logical stopping point. Once a different type of conjugal association is allowed, it does not seem reasonable to prohibit this to other varieties. Extrapolation should be the order of the day.

It sounds as if I am making a reductio ad absurdum argument. Since most people, even "progressives" who support gay marriage will likely reject these other alternatives, and the same logic applies to all, perhaps we should go back to the status quo ante during which only heterosexuals, two of them, one of each persuasion, were allowed to be wed. Conservatives might well make just such an argument. But here, in sharp contrast, we are exploring libertarianism, not that right-wing philosophy. And in this viewpoint, there should be no legal barriers to any marital covenants desired by any types of people, any number of them at all. There is no reductio being employed here; none whatsoever.

# Chapter 24
# The Straight White Male

Why am I now apologizing for being a straight white male, in the midst of Covid 19? It is due to the fact that when the vaccine for this dread disease was discovered, there was, horrors!, a plethora of evil cis-gendered straight white males heavily involved in the laboratory. Hence, the timing of this apology.

That's it. I can no longer stand it. I am a straight white male and I've long been exploiting, demeaning, belittling, disparaging, depreciating, patronizing, deprecating, being mean to, sneering at, criticizing, sticking my tongue out at, saying neener neener to, ruining, undermining, disheartening, being unfair to, condemning, abusing—females, blacks, gays, the disabled, and all other categories dreamed up by the cultural Marxists. I apologize. Mea culpa. I'm sorry. I'll try not to do it anymore. But, I just can't help myself. It just comes so naturally to me to trade in on my straight white male privilege, to the detriment of everyone else on the planet.

Why just the other day I belted my friend the late Walter Williams in the chops (he's twice my size so if you believe this, I've got a bridge to sell you). Why did I do this? Simple, I'm a straight white male, and he's not. I had to put him in his place. Only last week I did the same thing to another friend of mine, Deirdre McCloskey (she's twice my size too, so if you believe that I actually punched her, I've got another bridge to sell you). Why did I do this? Simple, I'm a straight white male, and she's not. I just had to put her in her place. I tried not to do this. Honest Injun (so to speak; I apologize for saying this too). Speaking of Native Americans (see, I'm reforming) one of my many co-authors, Adam Crepelle, has that heritage. I was gonna sock him in the nose, but I thought twice about this, and chickened out. He's not twice my size, but he's younger than me by about 40 years, and lifts weights. See, I'm reforming. But, I was thinking about belting him one. Why, you ask? Not to be repetitive or anything, but, it is simple: I'm a straight white male, and he's not. I just had to demonstrate his inferior status in the proper white male manner.


W. E. Block, *Defending the Undefendable III*,
https://doi.org/10.1007/978-981-16-3957-9_24

But I'm really serious about giving up my straight white male privilege. I am now starting a new twelve-step program: Straight White Male Privilege Anonymous (SWMPA). We'll meet regularly. We'll study the Big Book. Only, instead of praying not to be overtaken by alcohol, we'll earnestly try to overcome, you guessed it, our straight white male privilege. Of course, SWMPA will be limited to straight white males. No, wait. Wouldn't that be discriminatory? Wouldn't that be an exercise of our straight white male privilege, instead of the absolute rejection of it that we shall be striving for? I honestly (to the extent that a straight white male can be honest, which is very limited indeed) don't know. I'll have to consult my local cultural Marxist on this matter.

To continue this litany of my faults: Yesterday I got another raise in salary (I wish!). This means that my income, along with other sick, disgusting, degenerate, evil, monstrous, revolting, repulsive, degenerate, decadent, debased, immoral, debauched, perverted, corrupt, wicked, malevolent, atrocious, gruesome, ghastly, monstrous, bizarre, sordid, malicious, horrific, straight white males, is even higher than it otherwise would have been. The pay gap between me and the noble members of the human race (e.g., those who are not straight white males), is even greater. Again, I apologize. I ask for forgiveness. I prostrate myself at everyone else's feet. I greatly regret earning more money, because it comes at the expense of everyone else who is not a dreaded, you guessed it, straight white male.

I am getting tired of listing my faults. I'm now going to get out there and do something about this (in addition to initiating SWMPA). The next time someone offers me a raise, or wants to publish a book or article of mine, or asks me to speak at their conference, or praises me in any manner, way, shape or form, I am going to decline. It is time, it is past time, that we straight white males started to ride in the back of the bus. No more inventions from the likes of us. No more creativity from the likes of us. No more medical breakthroughs from the likes of us; let people die from the coronavirus; there are more important things than saving lives; being politically correct chief amongst them. No more new computer programs from the likes of us. No more movies from the likes of us. (We are all Harvey Weinsteins). No more going to the Moon. No more listening to the music of Wolfgang Amadeus Mozart, Johann Sebastian Bach, Antonio Vivaldi, Gaetano Donizetti, Tomaso Albinoni, Georg Philipp Telemann, Jean-Philippe Rameau, George Frederic Handel, Wilhelm Hieronymus Pachelbel, Domenico Scarlatti, Francesco Geminiani, Giuseppe Tartini, Giovanni Battista Sammartini, Wilhelm Friedemann Bach, Carl Philipp Emanuel Bach, Johann Wenzel Anton Stamitz, Leopold Mozart, Armand-Louis Couperin, Johann Christoph Friedrich Bach, Joseph Haydn, Johann Christian Bach, Carl Friedrich Christian Fasch, Michael Haydn, Carl Ditters von Dittersdorf, Luigi Boccherini, Carl Stamitz, Antonio Salieri, Muzio Clementi, Ludwig van Beethoven, Johann Nepomuk Hummel, Niccolò Paganini, Louis Spohr and Franz Schubert (this is the merest tip of the iceberg of great music; believe me, as President Trump would say).

Sorry, I'm not going through the list of white males who have contributed to other aspects of our civilization. Enough is enough. Otherwise, one might be fooled into thinking that only white males have made such contributions. And this would be false. But, not by much. Oh, wait. I promised to reform. It is sooooo difficult, given the evidence. Oh, wait again. I'm not supposed to mention the "e" word. It is so straight white male (along with 2 + 2 = 4). A thousand pardons.

Straight white males all have certain anatomical features, and pigmentation, and desire for the company of members of the opposite sex, that make us the enemies of all and sundry. I have heard the word from the feminists, from the professors who offer courses in black and queer and other such whining studies at universities. I shall repent. Well, to the best of my straight white male ability. Which isn't saying much.

# Chapter 25
# Jessica Yaniv

Jessica Yaniv a transgendered Canadian male, was born Jonathan Yaniv, with all the plumbing features of a boy.

This transgender woman still has a penis (is this a typographical error? I'm not sure!) She had lost over a dozen cases argued in front of the so-called British Columbia Human Rights Tribunal in 2018 and 2019. He (she?) initially requested Brazilian bikini wax jobs from firms that supplied this service. The providers were mainly East Indian and Sikh women who refused to remove the hair from his (her?) male genitalia. The Tribunal dismissed his complaints as follows: "… human rights legislation does not require a service provider to wax a type of genitals they are not trained for and have not consented to wax."

Nothing daunted, the heroic (I'm serious about this; explanation below) Yaniv initiated two further complaints.

One was against the She Point Beauty Studio for refusing to wax Yaniv's legs. The Tribunal did not sympathize with this complaint, dismissing past such claims, since they found that this man has hostility for immigrant women who refused him service.

Secondly, our many-time plaintiff chose a gynecologist as his defendant. Stated Yaniv: "So a gynecologist office that I got referred to literally told me today that 'we don't serve transgender patients… And me, being me, I'm shocked… and confused… and hurt. Are they allowed to do that, legally? Isn't that against the college practices?"

He (?) may now file an action against this physician with the College of Physicians and Surgeons of British Columbia.

What has been the reaction to this spate of lawsuits? Jessica is the Rodney Dangerfield of law: "(s)he can't get no respect."

The Calgary-based Justice Centre for Constitutional Freedoms, a conservative pro-bono litigation concern, has taken a strong stance against Yaniv, defending his/her legal targets.


W. E. Block, *Defending the Undefendable III*,
https://doi.org/10.1007/978-981-16-3957-9_25

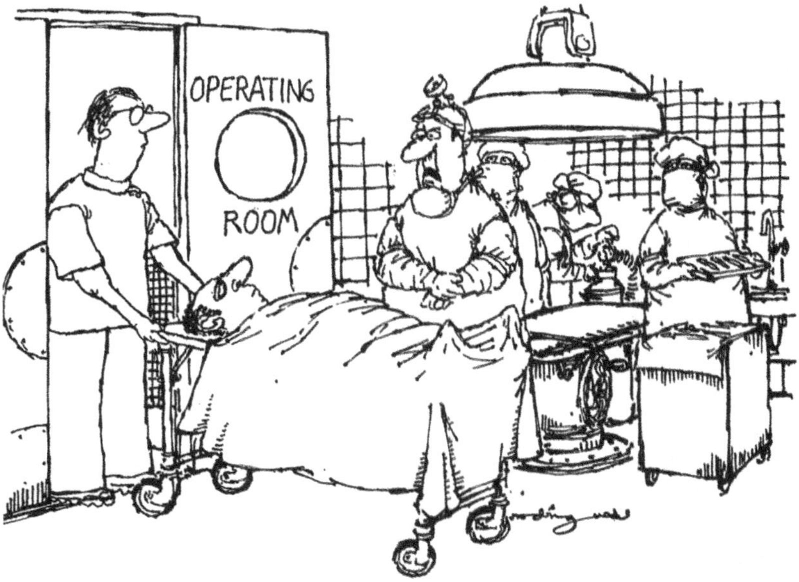


"WHAT? YOU'VE CHANGED YOUR MIND ABOUT BEING CHANGED TO A WOMAN, AND INSTEAD YOU WANT TO BE CHANGED INTO A HERMAPHRODITE?!! SO WOULD I, MR. FELDMAN, BUT I'M AFRAID THAT'S OUT OF THE QUESTION!"

Rod Dreher of the American Conservative was equally dismissive: "It is vitally important that we all understand that Jonathan Yaniv is a woman under Canadian law, because he says he is a woman. If we in the US adopt laws that require us to recognize people as of a particular sex solely because they say they are, there will be no stopping the Jonathan/Jessica Yanivs. The Equality Act, which was voted for by the entire House Democratic membership, would recognize Yaniv as a female solely on his say-so…As a philosophical matter, if you believe that maleness and femaleness is entirely a matter of individual will—and that's what gender ideology claims—then you had better be prepared to welcome Jonathan Yaniv into the changing room at the pool, where he will ask your middle-school daughters about tampons."

Let me now offer my support for Mr. Yaniv (I'm now installing myself as President of the Yaniv fan club. Anyone want to join?)

He is offering a blistering, magnificent reductio ad absurdum of the entire "human rights" philosophy. He is in effect if not by intention forcing us to look at the logical implications of every non-discrimination enactment. All such laws, without exception, compel people to engage in acts to which they "have not consented" in the words of the BCHRT. If this judiciary had the courage of its convictions, just an ounce of philosophical logical consistency, it would have ruled in favor of Jessica, and then, faced with the horror of any such decision, immediately disbanded.

The same applies to any other group: blacks, Jews, women, gays, natives, whoever. "Human rights" laws compel Christians to bake wedding cakes for gays, but would never in a million years require a black to bake a cake celebrating white supremacism. It all depends upon whose ox is being gored. How about a lesbian baker and a heterosexual or homosexual couple? Not bloody likely.

The impetus for these regulations is the fear that the discriminated against minority peoples will suffer grievous financial harm without then. But this is economic delusion. If blacks are paid less than they are worth due to a cartel agreement, there will be profits to be garnered by others to hire them. If Jews are not allowed in some hotels, other accommodations will spring up to house them, at a profit. No, mere boycotts are impotent to wound their target. Thomas Sowell and Walter E. Williams have done more good work to dispel this fallacy than any other two economists.

Jews and Asians have long been discriminated against, to no effect. Natives and blacks are poorer than others, but this is due to a lack of the development of their human capital, not to being targeted by discriminators. Blacks were not allowed in the front of the bus in the U.S. south for many years. Why did not some entrepreneur set up a competing transportation firm so as to rescue them? Did the free enterprise system fail? No. The same people responsible for this Jim Crow legislation in the first place were in charge of approving franchises for competing bus companies. They refused to allow alternatives to operate.

Hurrah for Jessica. She's my gal/guy.

# Chapter 26
# The Adulterer

Adultery is a breach of trust. People get married, pledging, among other things, faithfulness. Seeking sexual gratification outside of the bounds of marriage undermines that promise. There may be excuses for this sort of behavior. I do not say that they are valid, only that they exist. Possible examples include incapacity of one of the spouses, falling in love with someone else, physical or mental abuse. But, still, adultery is a violation of vows freely undertaken. Then, too, there are all sorts of practical objections to this practice. Hurt feelings, openings for blackmail, violence. All in all, it is not a particularly good idea to engage in this type of infidelity; actually, it is indecent. This type of behavior is roundly and widely condemned, and very properly so.

But should it be punished by law? Not, at least, under the libertarian conception of this institution. For in this philosophy, the use of violence (law is violence!) should be restricted to combatting previous utilizations of it, or the threat thereof, and adultery is a non-violent deed.

However, does it not constitute fraud? That act, plus counterfeiting, pick-pocketing, bad check writing, are not physically violent either, and yet, surely, they should all be proscribed by any legal system with even a vestige of justice embedded in it. Yes, for a certainty, these "peaceful" acts would be illegal in the libertarian code and should be. However, they all involve "violence" of an extended sort: they constitute unwarranted transfers of valuables from their proper owners to thieves.

But adultery is not fraudulent in this sense. There is no theft equivalent involved. In fraud, Albert sells Barbara a sack of potatoes for $10 which turns out to be rocks, instead. Albert has in effect stolen this amount of money from Barbara. But in the behavior now under examination, no such thing occurs. No one steals any item of value from anyone else. (Self-respect is not an economic good; in any case, when the adultery is not known, even this is not "taken." Yet it is equally vile whether discovered or not). Rather, this is a case of a broken promise, not out and out theft. According to libertarian principles, theft or fraud only occurs if a title to a piece of property is improperly transferred. This does not take place in the present case.



W. E. Block, *Defending the Undefendable III*,
https://doi.org/10.1007/978-981-16-3957-9_26

But do not broken promises cause the loss of real property to their victims? Yes. Charlie promises to marry Debbie and then reneges. Debbie has undertaken all sorts of expenses based upon this promise of Charlie to her: the purchase of a wedding dress, the rental of a hall, a band, flowers, etc. She undertook these commitments assuming that Charlie would carry through on his. Debbie suffers significant monetary (and of course non-monetary) costs. Yet, Charlie has not directly stolen any of Debbie's property, so the latter may not properly compel the former to marry her.

A similar analysis applies when Ellen promises to love Frank forever. Or when the grandfather promises the grandson that if he earns good marks in school he will give him $1000. The proper assumption of risk lies with the promisee, not the promisor. Why? Because failure to keep one's promise does not amount to a per se theft of any property of the promisee.

One last remark on this subject. There is an asymmetry between male and female adulterers. Trigger warning coming up. What I am now about to say will upset some feminists, and drive others of this ilk into an inconsolable rage. If a child results from the extramarital intercourse, the penalties suffered by the cuckolded male will likely be much more severe for the husband than the wife. If the affair is successfully hidden, he will spend years of his life helping to bring up another man's child. He will be expending the love, affection and treasure he had earmarked for his own progeny. In contrast, when the husband strays from the marital bed, the penalties suffered by the scorned wife will likely be less severe. She will not be parenting another woman's child for decades.

In saying this, I write not as an Austrian economist, who eschews interpersonal comparisons of utility. For there are no units of human happiness, no measurements, or utils. From that premise the above determination of asymmetry may not be made. Rather, I make this calculation based on prudential judgment. A straying wife hurts her husband more than the reverse.

# Chapter 27
# The Front Lawn Nudist

As the title of this chapter indicates, the front lawn nudist (FLN) is someone who appears sans clothes on his front lawn. He does not violate the non-aggression principle (NAP), nor private property rights. He engages in this act on his own land. Nevertheless, his actions provide a challenge to libertarians such as me who regard the NAP and private property rights as the be-all and end-all of this philosophy. We have a problem here. The FLN violates no rights the libertarian is required to respect, and yet, and yet, he makes his neighbors miserable. They just do not want to witness his rather depraved actions. Less so do they wish their impressionable young children to observe this behavior of his. Why is this a problem? It is because libertarianism aims not only at justice, but, also, at economic welfare, utilitarianism, broadly conceived. We libertarians maintain that not only is our system just, but, also, does not make vast numbers of people despondent, as would be true in the present case.

What then to do about this neighborhood maniac, while still adhering to libertarian principles? One possibility is to just plain tell him that "we do not do things like that around here; if you do this ever again, we will use violence against you." Such reactions might encompass public decency legislation, or zoning laws, or some such. The difficulty here is that it is rather more than just a bit difficult to reconcile such a reaction with libertarianism. Some advocates of this philosophy resort to culture or tradition to justify prohibiting this loose behavior. But it is unclear how this, either, can be squared with the NAP, or, indeed, with any other element of basic libertarian principles.

How then to deal with this neighborhood menace, and still stay within hailing distance of our precious philosophy? The answer lies in relying even more heavily upon private property rights, not jettisoning them at the first sign of difficulty with them as some right-wing thick libertarians counsel us to do.

How can we, then, best respond to this challenge? We have to go back a bit in time, before the neighborhood was first built. Imagine a residential housing development of one square mile, broken up into 640 parcels of one acre each. If the


W. E. Block, *Defending the Undefendable III*,
https://doi.org/10.1007/978-981-16-3957-9_27

developer sells these plots with no side conditions or stipulations, it is indeed possible that this FLN difficulty will arise. So, instead, he makes a deal with all 640 buyers: he sells his terrain to them in the form of a condominium association. Specifically, he requires them to eschew nudism on their front lawns. But here is something you learn in first year law school: it is impossible to anticipate all such possible annoyances, deviations, difficulties. If the codicil to the land specifies that this behavior on the front lawn is contractually prohibited, what about masturbation, sexual acts between adults, or other such practices which will also scare the horses and the children? What about engaging in such behavior on the back lawn, or the rooftop, which might also be in plain sight? Here is where the beauty of the condominium association comes in. With some supermajority, say 60% or 70%, they can make up any rules they wish. In that way, as these deviations crop up, they can also be mowed down. (Land developers will compete with one another as to which one can set up the best rules of the road, so to speak).

Will the FLN be banned from society, as some libertarians contend? Not a bit of it. There will arise in the free enterprise system all sorts of condominium associations. The pure libertine organizations will not only allow such practices to take place on front lawns, it will require them. Some, the real radical ones, will demand of all land purchasers that they engage in such behavior at least once per day, and twice on Sundays (weather permitting!). More moderate ones will require such acts once per month, or maybe weekly. Even more temperate libertine organizations will merely allow such behavior, not mandate it. Yes, the FLNs will be banned from traditional society, but the condominium associations of these nudists will turn around and give the back of their hands to those folk. It will be Even Steven for outdoor fornication and non-fornication. The straights, and the sexual libertines will be treated exactly equally by just law. There will be no fear nor favor for either of them under libertarianism.

In that way, people will sort themselves out on the basis of taste for conducting unusual sexual practices where the neighbors can see. And much more as well: taste for loud music, smells, wood fires, etc. (that can be confined to the one square mile of our example) fall under this rubric. There is absolutely no need to give up on libertarian theory merely to counteract this unusually creative FLN challenge.

Admittedly, it will be much more difficult to solve this problem in the present context, where people own land unconnected to each other via such restrictive covenants. But this is not a failure of libertarian theory; it is a difficulty because this type of law is not allowed to be applied. A similar situation holds true for questions such as Should the Nazis be allowed to march in Skokie, IL, a Jewish area, where this would be widely seen as offensive. There is no real answer emanating from libertarian theory, here, either, since the roads are publicly owned by the state. Thus, rights can indeed clash in such contexts. The answer is to privatize the roads, in the marching case, and to try to fashion, as best as possible, the kind of condominium associations that, contrary fact conditional coming up so beware: would have come into being had private property rights, not government meddling, always been the order of the day.

But what about culture? What role should this play in the free society? In some conceivable societies, if a woman wears a mini skirt, or has no face covering, this constitutes an invitation for sex. If men take her up on this invitation, it is not really rape, even if she protests or tries to escape. In others, such clothing, or lack thereof, is a per se invasive act, and forced sex is the proper punishment. In India, women are pushed, unwillingly onto the funeral pyres of their husbands. This is called suttee. In other cultures, slavery is acceptable, provided, only, that it applies to people with darker skin. In Germany, for a while, Jews, Romany, blacks, gays, were considered vermin, and were legally eliminated. How is the libertarian to react to such phenomena? The proper response is "culture schmultsure." These aforementioned cultures are evil. They are anti-libertarian. They are violating the NAP, the basic foundation of our beloved philosophy. All those who deny this are engaged in a sort of polylogism, from an ethical point of view. They are multi-culturalists, subjectivists; their views are incompatible with the freedom philosophy.

It cannot be denied that there are grey areas. Not all decisions can be deduced from NAP alone. It is not for nothing that all civilized societies need (hopefully private) courts to make determinations in such cases. But to jettison the NAP for this reason is to throw the baby out with the bath water.

Is culture, then, unimportant? Not a bit of it. This institution is of great significance. Those cultures that emphasize hard work, patience, science, learning, will do far better in every which way, other things equal, than those which place a high value on, even tolerate, drunkenness, laziness, inability to anticipate the future. But none of these latter characteristics are per se violations of the NAP.

Why is the FLN a hero of libertarianism? Why does he deserve an honorable place in the present volume? It is because he is widely reviled, even hated, and, yet, does not at all, in the slightest, violate the NAP. He serves as an insightful example of the power and of the importance of the libertarian emphasis on private property rights and the NAP.

# Chapter 28
# The Host Mother

U.S. Representative Trent Franks (R, Arizona) was compelled to resign from his House seat due to the fact that he had asked staff members if they would agree to bear a child for him and his infertile wife as a surrogate mother. For those not in the know about this relationship, the father, Mr. Franks in this case, becomes a sperm donor to the host mother who bears the child. In the case of traditional surrogacy, the baby is created through artificial insemination, and biologically, the baby bears the genes of the father and host mother. In gestational surrogacy, the father impregnates the wife, sometimes naturally, sometimes through in vitro fertilization, and then the fetus is transferred to the host mother. In this case, the baby is not genetically related to the latter. It is unclear which of these processes Congressman Franks was proposing to several female members of his staff; all that is apparent is that this request of his made them feel "uncomfortable." Suppose that the Congressman had asked an employee of his, for extra pay, to wash his car, or clean his house, or pick up his laundry, or get coffee for him—and that this had made her "uncomfortable." Would he have been drummed out of the lower house of Congress? Far less likely, would be the most probable answer.

This indicates that there is something widely seen as more nefarious about a substitute mother contract than others of these other institutional arrangements. It is widely seen as sexual harassment or sexual misconduct. But why should that be so? It is not as if the father is asking the host mother to engage in sexual intercourse with him. In our present Puritanical days, that would be totally unseemly. Rather, his request concerns what is in effect a purely medical procedure.

Let us leave off our discussion of the modern sexual mores now being imposed upon politicians, and return to our libertarian analysis. When host mother arrangements are made without pay, or, in the case that the substitute is given only room and board and defrayment of other maternity costs, there is little controversy about them. There are legal surrogacy agencies that operate openly, and even advertise their services. When sizeable amounts of cash, in addition, are transferred, many people will look askance at the practice, but from a libertarian point of view, mere


W. E. Block, *Defending the Undefendable III*,
https://doi.org/10.1007/978-981-16-3957-9_28

payment for an act that is otherwise legal does not undermine that status. Rather, in both cases, it is an example of a capitalist act between consenting adults, in the felicitous phrase of libertarian Robert Nozick.

There is only one relevant difference between this and other commercial interactions, even those that involve sex, such as prostitution: The host mother may not renege on the contract to which she has agreed. That is, she may not abort the fetus (nor engage in eviction; see on this below, Chap. 30). In gestational surrogacy, she has been paid to "house" for nine months a baby with whom she is not biologically related. If she rids herself of the pre-born infant, she kills a child "belonging" entirely, to other people. (The infant, of course, cannot be owned by its parents; but, they do have the right to be the baby's guardian). In traditional surrogacy, the host mother is in effect "caring for" the fetus which has half her genes and half of the client-father. Again, she is contractually bound to live up to the terms of the (presumably) nine-month contract.

In short, there is nothing amiss with a surrogacy contract. Apart from libertarian considerations, it is difficult to see why the offer of the same, even if it renders the recipient "uncomfortable," should be considered harassment or sexual misbehavior.

# Chapter 29
# The Rape Forgiver

On Wednesday, September 9, 2020, a particularly vicious gang rape took place in Pakistan: the woman's young children were forced to witness this act of brutality. The local police chief blamed the victim for driving at night on an empty road. Been there, heard that. Move along, nothing to see here.

But no. An interesting legal issue has (possibly) arisen here. According to the DNA analysis of one of the present accused perpetrators, he had previously raped a different woman 7 years previously, in 2013. But, that case had not been prosecuted because the victim had privately settled with the perpetrator. It is unclear at the present time as to whether this "settlement" involved a monetary payoff from the rapist to obviate the pressing of charges.

This leads to the question, Is a heinous crime such as this only perpetrated upon the victim, or also against society as a whole? If the latter, this woman in 2013 would have no right to accept fiduciary payment in return for the freedom of the rapist, or forgive him for any reason at all. She would be compelled by law to bear witness against him. The authorities would then have a right to jail this vicious and violent offender even if the victim is unwilling to cooperate; they could force her to do so.

How can we both have our cake and eat it too? We have here two desiderata. One, to not compel rape victims to testify against their victimizers against their will; they should be allowed to forgive them if they wish to do so, whether or not money changes hands. Two, to see to it that rapists are put out of commission once and for all, and not allowed to roam around perpetuating their evil deeds on other women, as may possibly have occurred in this case.

Wait for it: private property rights are the answer to this conundrum!

Where did the prior rape occur, the one in 2013? It must have taken place somewhere. Assume this abomination took place in the parking lot of a shopping center or in a hotel. The owner has a strong incentive to unleash the police on this rapist but he is unable to act, since (possibly) the victim was paid off and refuses to testify. That is seemingly the end of the matter. But not so fast. The owner does not want


W. E. Block, *Defending the Undefendable III*,
https://doi.org/10.1007/978-981-16-3957-9_29

this rapist to come back to his hotel or other property. He is going to widely broadcast what he did. The forgiven rapist will be persona non grata not only on his property, but on the terrain of pretty much anyone else who wants to maximize profits, by keeping such a scoundrel away.

I don't say no rapes (murders, thefts, etc.) would occur under such a system, but I expect they would be radically reduced. If so, in order to safeguard other women, we need not maintain that such crimes are perpetrated against "society." We can aver, rather, that they are against individual victims, only.

Let us now focus on that woman who in 2013 (possibly) allowed herself to be bought out from pressing charges against the rapist. Her name, too, would be bruited about. She would not escape attention. She is not a criminal, but, in refusing to press charges against the rapist, she was not very public-spirited. Indeed, the very opposite was true. She would have to pay a penalty in terms of loss of reputation, for in effect unleashing a rapist upon the community, who (possibly) struck again in 2020. Perhaps this would encourage females not to forgive, or be bought out by, rapists.

But suppose the former threatens the latter that he will kill her if she does not absolve him. The utterance of such a threat would also be a severe crime. To obviate this, property owners might well install a new rule: any rape victim who forgives her rapist, whether under threat or for financial compensation, is not welcome in his premises. If she goes there, she is therefore contractually bound not to fail to do her civic duty. Then, the rapist would know she is powerless to be bullied by him, and for this reason, in addition, there would be fewer such threats, and rapes.

# Part VI
# Medical

# Chapter 30
# The Evictionist

Let us consider a compromise between the pro-life and the pro-choice philosophies. Evictionism constitutes a principled compromise, not merely adding up the two positions and dividing by two. If Sally says 2 + 2 = 4, and Joe avers that 2 + 2 = 6, a non-principled compromise would be 2 + 2 = 5. Why is this unprincipled? It is because there are no premises from which this latter equation can be drawn, other than conciliation of the two positions.

"Abortion" really is a misnomer. It consists of two separate acts, not just one. First, evicting the fetus from the womb. Second, killing him (not "it"). The two are conceptually distinct, since even with present medical technology, it is entirely possible to evict the fetus without killing this very young person, in the third trimester. (This is similar to "labor strike;" it too consists of two separate acts: downing tools, on the one hand, and preventing "scabs" from taking over the jobs, temporarily abandoned).

When does human life begin? I posit, arguendo, it is with the fertilized egg. (In the Jewish tradition, it is when the fetus graduates from medical school!) Why? Two reasons. First, the baby one hour before birth, and one hour afterward, looks as much alike as all of us reading this chapter, two hours apart. Birth is merely a change of address. Second, so as to avoid a strawman argument. Evictionism calls for the killing of innocent human beings (e.g. fertilized eggs), and I want to make the case for this conclusion as difficult as possible for me.

So, what is evictionism? The pro-life side maintains that the pregnant woman may not evict the baby (of course until the nine-month period has elapsed) and certainly not kill it, while the pro-choicers take the position that she may both evict the young child at any moment of her choosing, and, she may also kill it, even if it is viable outside of the womb (partial-birth abortion in the third trimester). The evictionist compromise is that she may evict the pre-birth infant whenever she wishes, but may never kill it. That would be murder. Yes, the fetus will die if evicted in the first 6 months, but she will not be guilty of murder, only of expelling the baby from her body and allowing him to die, a completely distinct matter.



W. E. Block, *Defending the Undefendable III*,
https://doi.org/10.1007/978-981-16-3957-9_30

Consider, first, the case of rape. The woman now has, inside her body, a small human being. A very much unwanted one. This youngster is akin to an innocent stowaway on an airplane. If we adhere to strict private property rights, this rape victim has the right to evict, but not kill, the fetus. Now, it might well be nice, and moral, for the woman to keep this tiny trespasser in her body, and for the airplane owner to land the innocent stowaway, but the doctrine of strict private property rights, strictly interpreted, does not require it.

Now, take the case of voluntary sexual intercourse. One objection to evictionism is that the woman, in effect, agreed to carry the baby to term; she, in effect, signed a contract with the preborn infant. In the case of the host mother, she did indeed legally obligate herself to a nine-month stint; no eviction would be allowed in that scenario, let alone, abortion, which consists of ejection plus killing. Set aside the possibility of making binding contracts with under-aged persons. At the time of voluntary sexual intercourse, there was not even a fertilized egg with whom to make a contract of any sort. This is because it takes a period of time for the sperm to reach the egg. It does so only several long minutes after ejaculation. Even if we posit that "contracts" can be made with such an entity, voluntary sexual intercourse will still not qualify.

If present law is overturned, this will not constitute the death knell for the pro-choice position. Rather, one possibility is that each jurisdiction will have to decide this matter for itself. Presumably, those on either coast will tend in the direction of pro-choice, the ones in flyover country, pro-life. Some authorities might hit upon yet another compromise: abortions up to the 20-week mark, but not afterward. This time period roughly demarcates when the fetus is viable outside of the womb – at present. However, as medical technology improves, this dividing line will come earlier and earlier. Better to adopt evictionism, which is philosophically sound, than to choose a time demarcation which will have to change with every alteration in medical technology. The point is, that would not be a principled compromise. It is not based upon the ownership rights women have over their own bodies, as is evictionism.

This 20-week time period "compromise" cuts the cake somewhere near the middle, and, on a pragmatic basis, it might well satisfy both sides more than the present situation. But as a reconciliation based upon philosophical principle, it is a non-starter. Only evictionism passes muster in this regard. It is important to attain deontological clarity, since there are reasonable arguments on both sides of this debate. It is perhaps the most vexing and complicated issue our society now faces.

Why has this chapter been included in the present book? This is because, to the extent that either the pro-lifer or the pro-choicer has ever heard of evictionism, not too likely, each develops a visceral hatred for it. True, both see this solution to the problem as better than the one against which they have long been inveighing. But both are united in rejecting evictionism, often with great scorn.

# Chapter 31
# The Gay Conversion Therapist

At one time, in the United States, homosexuality was criminalized. (At present, in many countries, it is still illegal, and the death penalty is imposed on violators; that is, gays. There, they do not worry about whether or not they can get married to each other, or compel bakers to supply them wedding cakes; their very lives are always in danger from the government, and, indeed, from virtually the entire society). Then, we became more civilized, and this practice was legalized, but often subject to scorn, hatred and police brutality. Later on came their uprising in this country, when patrons of the Stonewall bath house physically and heroically fought the police who were raiding this establishment for no justified reason. After that, western society, in the main, adopted a more neutral stance with regard to gays. People were treated more equally in law; marriages between members of the same sex began to be allowed.


W. E. Block, *Defending the Undefendable III*,
https://doi.org/10.1007/978-981-16-3957-9_31

But then the pendulum moved in the other direction. A baker was forced to pay a fine of $130,000 for refusing to cater to a homosexual wedding. The same rights violation befell a florist and photographer who also declined to supply their services for gay nuptials.

What is the libertarian position on all of this? People, all people, whether hetero, homo, bisexual, or any other variation should have identical rights in law. No one should be considered as a criminal no matter what his sexual preferences, provided, only, that they expressed voluntarily.

With this background introduction, we are now ready to consider the topic of this chapter—conversion therapy.

For many years, the American Psychology Association listed homosexuality as a mental disease. Going with the tide of political correctness, this organization later reversed that assessment. Similarly, conversion therapy (converting homosexuals to heterosexuality) was allowed at one time, but, then, later, it, too, became prohibited.

In the free or libertarian society, would homosexuality be legal? Of course. All mutually agreed upon acts would be lawful. In the free or libertarian society, would conversion therapy be legal? Of course. So, if those who have prohibited this practice wish to align themselves with libertarian law, they will have to change their assessment yet once again.

As a purely empirical matter, is there any success associated with his therapy? That is a question outside the scope of libertarianism. Let us content ourselves by noting that heterosexual men, when imprisoned for lengthy durations, sometimes resort to this practice, and then when freed, resort back to heterosexuality. If people can in effect "convert" themselves in this manner, then there would appear to be no necessary barrier for others successfully helping them in this path.

# Chapter 32
# The Drug Price Raiser

Washington DC is continually nipping at the heels of big pharma over their high prices. An initiative along these lines comes to us courtesy of a 230–192 House vote (228 Democrats supported this) which would authorize the Federales to bargain down the price of drugs purchased by Medicare. But this is the merest tip of the iceberg in this vein.

Do we want a cure for cancer, heart attacks, the corona virus and other dreaded diseases or not? Thought so. From whence do we expect an antidote to emanate? From the drug companies or Congress? Thought so.

Given the undoubted unanimous goal of eradicating such ailments how can we best proceed to attain this end?

There are only two ways forward. One is obvious, the other highly paradoxical and controversial.

The first is to stop whining, threatening and bullying the drug companies over their pricing policies. Supply curves slope in an upward direction. The higher the price, the more quantity of any good or service will be forthcoming, other things equal. This applies to shoes, ships, sealing-wax, cabbages, kings and anything else you care to mention. Contrary to the denizens of swamp city Washington DC, pharmaceuticals are no exception to this general rule. The more money these people have to play with in their labs, the more likely it is that a remedy for whatever it is that ails us will be forthcoming from this industry.

Also, price ceilings, whether for drugs or residential apartment units (rent controls) lead to less supply, more demand, and hence to shortages. That's no way to run this particular railroad. So, lighten up, DC!

The second means toward this goal is to end patents for drugs (and anything else for that matter, but that's another story). Say what? Have I lost my marbles? Didn't we just get finished saying that big pharma needed all the incentive it can get to create new vaccines? And do not patents constitute an encouragement par excellance?

We answer yes and no to the latter question. On the one hand (where oh where is a two-handed economist when you need one?), when the patent system is first



W. E. Block, *Defending the Undefendable III*,
https://doi.org/10.1007/978-981-16-3957-9_32

inaugurated, it unambiguously promotes more innovation. No dispute there. However, after a while difficulties arise. Patent holders sue each other over infringement. Some people obtain these rights not so much to bring new technologies to market as to be able to launch lawsuits at others for intrusion. Scientists spend less time in the laboratories and more in the courts. Less and less innovation occurs. A turning point is eventually reached between the initial benefits and the later diminutions. It is an empirical matter, but my prudential judgment tells me that we have long passed this tipping point.

With proper public policy, we can now have our cake and eat it too. We can kill two boids (as they say in Brooklyn), with not one but two stones. First, eliminate drug patents. This will not reduce net productivity, but will decrease prices. Second, stop with the price controls. This will eliminate shortages and also call forth more medical innovations.

Prices are to the economy as are street signs to the urban geography. Not any old prices or street signs will do, however. In medieval times, the beleaguered city would turn around these markings, or eliminate them entirely. They did so to slow down the invading army. The locals still knew how to get around town as they had lived there for many years. We need not only prices to organize an economy, but accurate ones. The latter can only arise when price controls are eliminated.

This two-part program of removing both patents and ceiling prices will lead to more accurate prices, thus allowing us to approach closer to rational resource allocation.

Price is pulled up by patents and down by hassling this industry with controls. It is possible, it is conceivable, that the two balance each other perfectly, and, together, amount to what would ensue given a full free enterprise system; one, that is, where neither occurred. But this scenario is unlikely in the extreme. It would be much better, in terms of human welfare, to shelve both, and allow prices to more accurately reflect scarcity on the supply side and desire on the demand side.

However, given that contagious diseases might plausibly wreak havoc on the entire human population, should we not get rid of the price controls alright, but keep the patent system, and even add subsidies to the mix? No. Only markets, that is, all of us, can determine the proper allocation of resources. If we pour too many resources into fighting sicknesses, people may perish from cold, starvation or other debilities.

If there is one thing we learned from the dismal failure of central planning USSR style, it is that this system simply does not work. Far better to leave these challenging problems to the "magic of the market," that is, to Adam Smith's "invisible hand."

# Chapter 33
# The Non-licensed Doctor

According to critics more than 10,000 "doctors" are now practicing in the U.S. without benefit of proper medical licensing. These are not people with questionable credentials, or graduates from diploma mills, or physician's assistants or nurses practicing beyond their qualifications. We're talking about outright imposters, individuals who have no official qualifications at all. Apart from this, other critics contend that fully 10% of the 450,000 licensed physicians practicing are incompetent. The difficulties arise mainly with elderly doctors and family physicians, not specialists, it is contended.

How could this possibly be true? Are not this nation's doctors subjected to a complete and up-to-date medical school education, an exhaustive system of initial pre-diploma testing? This, at least, is the theory. But the system works not so much to ensure physician quality as to limit entry into the field, so as to increase the income, power, and prestige of those doctors already in practice.

What is the evidence attesting to these claims?



W. E. Block, *Defending the Undefendable III*,
https://doi.org/10.1007/978-981-16-3957-9_33

"SORRY, LOVELL, YOU KNEW THE RULES—YOU BEGAN ANSWERING A TEST QUESTION AND THE EXAMINER DID NOT SAY, '<u>SIMON SAYS</u>'. TRY AGAIN NEXT YEAR."

The medical establishment at one point or another in its history has banned price and other advertising for licensed doctors; has set minimum price schedules; acted so as to prevent "overcrowding" or an oversupply of physicians by setting up a whole host of irrelevant criteria for licensing; examples include a knowledge of grammar, mathematics, Latin, history, philosophy and other academic studies, language requirements, citizenship, etc. Doctors associations have outlawed the uncontrolled study of medicine, even for those who do not intend to practice; placed roadblocks against foreign doctors practicing domestically where they would compete with local physicians; imposed unreasonable entry examinations. If the certification of quality were the true goal of these exams, they would more likely be required of practicing physicians at least every decade or so. For there is little guarantee—certainly not on the basis of testing—that a 70-year-old doctor is still qualified, merely for having successfully passed an examination 40 years earlier. In addition, groups such as the American Medical Association has fought against prepayment contract practice, opposed doctors testifying for plaintiffs in malpractice suits, and discouraged charity work as undermining minimum fee schedules and professional prestige; they have raised medical student fees in order to increase the costs of entry into the profession; often succeeded in raising physicians' income levels beyond that of other, equally skilled, professionals.

Particularly egregious is the insistence of the American Medical Association that for a foreign doctor to be qualified domestically he must take the qualifying exam in English. This is why when Austrian and German Jews came to this country in the 1930s to escape Hitler, all sorts of professionals were able to continue their careers here: mathematicians, physicists, economists, chemists, biologists, statisticians, etc. There was one exception: doctors. A similar fate was experienced by Cubans who emigrated to this country to escape the Communists.

"PAPA, NOW THAT I HAVE MY DEGREE IN MEDICINE, I'M GOING TO DEVOTE MY LIFE TO HELPING OUR PEOPLE. THERE'S A PRETTY BIG COLONY IN MIAMI, SO I'M GOING UP THERE TO SET UP MY PRACTICE."

Superficially, proficiency in our common language would seem to be a reasonable requirement for licensing. After all, we don't want someone to visit a hospital complaining of pain in the knee and being operated on an elbow. However, there are unconscious patients; no need to understand the lingua franca would be necessary on such occasions. Secondly, non-English speaking doctors could certainly treat patients with whom they shared the same language. Viennese medical men could have treated speakers of German and Yiddish; similarly Cuban surgeons could have served Spanish-speaking patients. Then, too, there are translators. This would have added to costs, but hardly justifies prohibiting foreign medics from engaging in medicine on our shores. Further, there is always pantomine. Someone with knee pain could point to that part of his body, not to his elbow. No, this is evidence pointing in the direction of restricted entry to boost the wealth of physicians, not sound medical practice.

If the present licensing system has failed, what, then, can be done? The sensible public policy recommendation would be to install a system of competitive certification in place of the present system of monopoly licensing. Under licensing, if the applicant fails the test, he cannot practice (as with the motor vehicle license); under certification, a rejected applicant can still practice (a non-certified public accountant CPA may still legally help people fill out tax forms) but he may not pass himself off as certified. The problem with monopoly licensing (as with all other coercive monopolies) is that if the institution in charge does a poor job, consumers have no alternative. Under competition, there is an incentive system for all competitors to try to outdistance each other in terms of quality control, innovativeness, cost-cutting, etc. The weakest producers are forced to the sidelines, the strongest can expand the scope of their operations to the ultimate and ongoing improvement of the industry. Although the provision of knowledge to health care consumers about the skill, qualifications, experience, and general trustworthiness of doctors may not appear at first blush to be an "industry," the effects of competition would operate here as well as in any other sector of the economy.

"WHAT? ANOTHER TOPLESS BAR? WE HAVE TOO MANY TOPLESS BARS ALREADY! DON'T THEY REALIZE THE MORE TOPLESS BARS, THE MORE THE MORAL LEVEL OF THE COMMUNITY DECLINES?!!."

How might competition work in the medical profession? We should call a halt to the present monopoly system of licensing doctors. This would usher in a competitive certification system to begin at present, to coexist with licensing for the next decade, and to be launched out on its own at that point. What kind of firms might undertake such an endeavor? One likely scenario would have various certification agencies—the Harvard University Medical Faculty, major insurance companies, the ACME Certification Agency, for example—all competing with each other as to which might best be able to ensure the quality of physicians to the general public. Under such a system, the quality of medicine and the extent of monitoring medical practice would improve to the great benefit of the health care of the populace.

It would also reduce the felt need on the part of many for medical socialism. One of the impetuses of this initiative is that health care is so expensive. But doctor's salaries are an important contribution to this state of affairs, and would tend to be reduced under certification, regarding monopoly licensure.

# Chapter 34
# The Suicide Instigator

Suicide is a personal tragedy. A life that could have gone on for days, weeks, months, years, decades, is, instead, cut short. All human life is precious. Every second of all lives is also treasurable. (I make exceptions, of course, for murderers and others of that ilk who are serious violators of the NAP).

But, there is suicide, and then there is suicide. Suppose that the reason for this very radical act is that the person is suffering from terminal cancer, and the morphine no longer works. Life, now, is a living hell of constant, unrelenting excruciating pain. That is one not totally unreasonable justification for taking one's life.

A very different motive is that your spouse has left you (there are other potential spouses out there). Or you failed your exam (there are other exams). Or you were fired from your job (there are no other jobs available?) Or you didn't win the race or you lost the game (fill in the blank here). Or your firm went bankrupt (try, try again).


W. E. Block, *Defending the Undefendable III*,
https://doi.org/10.1007/978-981-16-3957-9_34

"... AND WHEN THE POLICEMAN TOLD ME THAT FRED COMMITTED SUICIDE BY DRINKING HEMLOCK, I THOUGHT, 'WHAT CLASS!'. THEN HE WENT ON TO SAY THAT HE DRANK IT FROM A STYROFOAM CUP."

From a personal point of view, I would aid and abet the first type of suicide, out of sheer humanity, and a hatred for pain and suffering. I would shrink with horror from helping the second type into the next world. However, the present book is dedicated not to my own likely behavior when facing such a challenge, but with a libertarian analysis thereof. So we ask the only relevant question from this perspective: should suicide (and/or helping someone else to commit this act) be legal? Or, should we use the violence of the law to prevent such acts?

In the bad old days attempted or failed suicides had the death penalty imposed upon them. The argument in favor of that unjust law was that God owned our bodies and that killing oneself was thus a theft; a crime against the Deity. In effect, the message from the king, the prime law-giver at the time, was that if at first you don't succeed, we will help you along. Nowadays, attempted suicide is not a crime, but helping someone to do so is.

"OH, ARTHUR, ARTHUR! WHAT IRRESPONSIBLE HARDWARE, HOME AND AUTO OR DISCOUNT STORE WAS NEGLIGENT AND SOLD YOU THAT PIECE OF ROPE THAT ENABLED YOU TO DESTROY YOURSELF?!!"

What is the libertarian take on all of this? Barring the horrific unending pain scenario, the forces of law and order should only be brought to bear on those who help children end their lives prematurely, but not for adults. Why? This is because youngsters are not yet fully in their right minds (this applies, too, to the senile, those with Alzheimer's disease, etc.). All law, and the libertarian version thereof, concurs in this distinction. But in contrast, those who aid and abet adults to engage in this practice, or urge others to do so, should not be seen as criminals, despite the otherwise despicable nature of their acts.

Michelle Carter, aged 20, urged her 18-year-old boyfriend, Conrad Roy, to kill himself; he did so. Both were adults according to the law; let us stipulate this, at least arguendo. She was found guilty of involuntary manslaughter and sentenced to two decades in prison. But under the libertarian legal code she would be found innocent. Was she despicable? Yes, of course, on the basis of ordinary morality. But she is not a criminal according to this philosophy, since it is set up to address one and only one question: When is force justified? and gives but one answer: only in defense or retaliation. Since Miss Carter did not violate libertarian law, it would not be justified to visit violence upon her. But from a personal point of view, "despicable" would surely be an accurate description of her behavior. Well, an understatement. No. A vast underestimation.

# Chapter 35
# The Prescription Drug Violator

Want some penicillin? How's about a shot of insulin for the likes of you? Can you go to the store and buy some? Well, yes. But first you have to get permission from one of your betters, a physician.

In this era of the Covid 19 virus, it is even more important than otherwise that economic freedom reign in the realm of medicine. People, now more than ever, should be able to make their own decisions regarding pharmaceuticals, and not rely upon Big Brother for permission.

Is the prescription system compatible with freedom, with individual initiative, liberty? Of course not. This arrangement is an aspect of the nanny state and should be ended. Salt should be sown where once it stood.

There is nothing wrong with paternalism. For children, that is. But adults, actual people of mature years, are treated in this infantile manner. A shonda.

Perhaps the most famous paternalist, nowadays, is former New York City Mayor Mike Bloomberg. He was adamant that no resident of his then domain, the Big Apple, be able to enjoy any large sugary drinks. We can all laugh at this unwarranted treatment of adults in need of such supervision.

But this is the precise system under which we all labor every day, insofar as prescription drugs are concerned. It is time, it is past time, to throw off this yoke of nanny statism.

Would it not be dangerous to use these drugs in the absence of expert advice? Of course it would be. But no such proposal emanates from the free enterprise side of the political-economic spectrum on this matter. Rather, the suggestion is that people would be free to seek all the advice they wanted, from doctors, pharmacists, whoever, before they made any such purchase. But it is demeaning to be treated like a child, told one *must* seek permission before deciding upon a course of action.

It is also undemocratic. That might not mean all too much to many people at present, but there are at least some who still revere this political system (albeit not libertarians). Consider, then, the following. If people are so stupid as to avail themselves of drugs in complete ignorance about their effects they do not deserve to be


W. E. Block, *Defending the Undefendable III*,
https://doi.org/10.1007/978-981-16-3957-9_35

allowed into the voting booth. But if they are allowed a ballot, this implies that they are not so intellectually feeble as to poison themselves with drugs which will harm them. It also bespeaks virtually a logical contradiction to posit that the average person is too befuddled to make good choices in the pharmacy, and, yet, wise enough to elect officials who will compel him to make rational choices via the prescription system.

Pharmaceuticals are not the only dangerous item for sale legally. Automobiles fit this bill as well. Some 40,000 people die on the nation's roadways every year. Yet, no one needs any permission from anyone else to purchase a car or truck. Imagine if we were to apply the prescription system to these purchases. The howls of outrage would be heard far and wide. That should hold in the present case too.

Why, then, do we tolerate these arrangements? Inertia might be part of the answer. Things are the way they are; best to let us leave them alone. But prescriptions do not date from cave man days. The first prescription drug monitoring program was introduced in New York State in 1918 (this was not Bloomberg's fault, although one can imagine he would have been an ardent supporter of this initiative). Before that time, people had the freedom to purchase medicinal drugs without any by-your—leave from anyone. Yes, health has improved since then, thanks to technology; this was in spite of compelling adults to seek permission for their purchases, not because of it. Free enterprise, not nanny statism enriches us, and wealthier is healthier, other things equal.

# Chapter 36
# The Socialized Medicine Debaser

It is particularly important to end this system while we are still under the (hopefully decreasing) threat of the corona virus. The fates willing we will soon have fully successful cures and vaccines for Covid 19 (it is too early to make any such determination at the time of this writing).

It is important, especially in this age of the coronavirus, to take on the sacred cow of socialized medicine.

Let us begin by rehearsing the basic economic element of this system. Instead of purchasing our own medical services, as we do for virtually all other goods and services (lima beans, bikes, cars, houses, haircuts), we are compelled to "chip in" to the central authority, government, for this benefit, and then, in return, we obtain it virtually for "free" from them.

One problem at the outset is that this is a compulsory system. If this is such a great idea, why mandate it? Why don't the authorities limit themselves to advertising its benefits and signing up all who agree to take part in this proposal? That, after all, is the way we handle pretty much everything else under the sun. If there were no compulsory socialized medicine in effect, we could "chip in" in an entirely voluntary manner, such as via private insurance, if we wished to do so.

Another difficulty is that at a zero or near-zero price for doctor or hospital visits, we tend to demand more of them than would be the case if we explicitly faced a price that accurately reflected the full costs of these services. This system constitutes a field day for hypochondriacs. Other people are lonely. They have no one with whom they can interact. The local general practitioner will at least talk to them as he pokes them with a stethoscope. Need a taxi service? Don't want to pay for it? Call upon a "free" ambulance. But this sort of thing afflicts even those of us who do not abuse the system in any such manner. I have a backache or a hangnail. If I had to pay, say, $100 to seek a remedy, I'd think twice before using scarce medical resources. But for "free," that's a no-brainer.


W. E. Block, *Defending the Undefendable III*,
https://doi.org/10.1007/978-981-16-3957-9_36

"WE'RE RUNNING A $2,800,000 DEFICIT THIS YEAR AND WE'VE GOT TO TRIM OUR BUDGET. JOEL, CAN YOU ELIMINATE SOME OF YOUR STAFF IN THE JOKE SHOP?"

Given this excessive and unwarranted demand, queues have to be set up. That is why there are long waiting lists not only for emergency services but also for pretty much everything else in this field of endeavor. There was the infamous case of the woman in Canada and her horse. They were both stricken with painful kidney stones. She took her pet to the veterinarian, and he was seen within 24 hours. Had she not done so, she would have been found guilty of cruelty to animals. As for her, she had to wait some 6 months for medical care. But this is only the tip of the iceberg of such unsatisfactory occurrences.

A possible defense of socialist medicine runs along the following lines. Health care is very expensive. Only government is in a position to underwrite its costs.

However, the state has no funds that we, the long-suffering taxpayers, do not first give it. Instead of funneling these moneys through that coercive institution, we can pool efforts through private initiatives, such as insurance. Government is hardly necessary for spreading out risks. If it were, we could hardly have insurance for cars, against fires, etc.

In any case, we must ask, why are medical services so expensive in the first place? That is because the all-loving government, through the American Medical Association, severely limits the number of places for entering students in medical schools and unduly restricts entry into the profession for foreign doctors who enter the country (see Chap. 33). End these roadblocks, and prices fall, drastically.

Other items, too, are pretty pricey. If socialism is such a great idea for medical care, why not apply it also to houses, food, cars? How would that work? Simple. We send lots of additional money to the capital. After the people running things there take their huge cut, they return these funds to us in the form of free houses, lima beans, bikes, etc. Anyone want to try that? Thought not.

Senator Bernie Sanders is now trying to impose the Canadian (Denmarkian?) system of socialized medicine on us. Wouldn't it be wonderful if, while he was attempting to socialize this industry there, Canadians moved away from this system that has impoverished the USSR, Cuba, East Germany, and North Korea and embraced laissez-faire capitalism?

The Vermont senator, and many others, maintain that modern health care is a right. Stuff and nonsense. If it were, who was guilty of rights violations in the twelfth century, when no such technology was available? In sharp contrast, we all have a right not to be murdered, raped, stolen from, and this applies all through history. Rights simply do not depend upon the level of expertise, level of technology, level of civilization.

What about the poor? Medicine would be cheaper without AMA-induced restrictions on entry. Doctors have a long history of pro bono work. There are private charities. The poverty-stricken also need to be fed. From that fact, it would be illicit to justify food socialism. In that direction lies starvation.

# Chapter 37
# The Ambulance Chaser

There is perhaps no lawyer more despised and disdained than the ambulance chaser. In contrast, even the member of the bar found guilty of accepting a bribe or engaging in fraud, does not have quite the same negative aura about him. The downright thief can at least claim a bit of class; not so—at least in the perception of a large proportion of the public—for the ambulance chaser.

On the face of it, the hatred is difficult to understand. For is not the ambulance chaser racing to the scene of the accident in order to bring aid and comfort to the victim? To be sure, this member of the legal fraternity does not come armed with bandages and life-saving equipment. But there are other non-medical professions whose members visit accident scenes in order to help—tow truck operators, for example—without earning almost universal scorn from the general public.

To be sure, the ambulance chaser intends his own good, not that of the victim. But as much can usually be said for other participants, such as the policeman, the fireman, the doctor, the ambulance driver, collision repairman, etc. Very few of these are Good Samaritans; virtually all are there only to earn a living, precisely the motivation of you-know-who. The ambulance chaser, like all other entrepreneurs, is simply going where the business is.

The ambulance-chasing solicitor is also charged with attempting to take advantage of the plight of the injured party. He approaches him at a time when he is unable to make a rational decision. But the same applies to all distraught people; are they to be prohibited from receiving commercial offers at such times?

Ambulance chasing, of course, is by no means limited to the legal fraternity. Although the connection between this activity and the stock market is not immediately apparent, there are strong similarities between the two.

A case in point arose with regard to two stock brokers who shifted through brokerage firm garbage cans in order to obtain lists of prospective customers. Then they telephone the residents obtained in this manner in order to promote stock, a violation of all sorts of bureaucratic regulations. As a result, they have had their trading rights revoked for a year and were fined big bucks.



W. E. Block, *Defending the Undefendable III*,
https://doi.org/10.1007/978-981-16-3957-9_37

Cold-calling in real estate, stock markets retail sales, analogous to ambulance chasing is also denigrated. But why should this be so? Cold-calling is merely a rather (sometimes) inefficient way of making a sale. It is hardly a violation of the rights of the recipient of the message. If such a person is not in the market to purchase stock or any other good or service, he need only decline; and if he is, a mutually beneficial business interaction will have been consummated.

We can define cold-calling (or, in general, ambulance-chasing) as a personal, but unsolicited invitation to engage in a commercial activity. Newspaper advertising is an unsolicited invitation, but since it is addressed to all and sundry, and not focused on a particular individual, it does not qualify. If you go to a real estate firm or an automobile showroom an agent or salesperson will invite you to make a purchase; but since this is not unsolicited, it, too, does not count as a cold call.

But this activity is far more widespread than appreciated. Purveyors of junk mail are in effect cold callers. You didn't ask for it, but there it is, right in your mailbox. Often we are telephoned at home by representatives of charities, who ask for a contribution. This, too, is a cold call. And the same applies to people who sell encyclopedias, magazine subscriptions, etc., on a door-to-door basis. And what are we to make of the purveyors of girl scout cookies? They, too, are cold callers, or "ambulance chasers."

If we as a society are to act consistently, we would have to prohibit them all. Happily, we do not. It is time then to recalculate our repudiation of the ambulance chaser.

# Chapter 38
# The Food and Drug Administration Challenger

The Food and Drug Administration must go. This organization is costly, is a gargantuan waste of time and causes needless deaths by slowing down innovation. The sooner it is disbanded, the better.

This seems a bit harsh. Ok, excessively severe. Does not the FDA stand between us and pharmaceutical firms that would exploit us—but for its heroic efforts? Does not the FDA ensure the quality of, wait for it, food and drugs? Does not the FDA serve as an excellent traffic cop in this field? No, no and no. Rather, this bureaucracy stands in the path of the very assurances with which they presumably provide us.

Their mandate is to ascertain that any products brought to market must pass a two-stage test. One, they must be safe, and two, they must be effective. Some commentators argue that while the first mandate may be a reasonable one, the second is unnecessary and only slows down the rate of progress. As long as a new offering is safe, it addresses the foundational medical requirement, "First, do no harm." Whether or not it is also effective should be up to the patients and their doctors. To insist upon the second as well as the first necessarily slows down new development.

This is all well and good, but we should also dig a bit deeper. The FDA is a monopoly. It, and it alone, makes all such determinations. But one of the most basic discoveries of the dismal science is that monopolies lead to extra costs, poor service and lack of accountability.

How else, then, can these functions of safety and effectiveness be attained. Milton Friedman hit the nail on the head in his book *Capitalism and Freedom*; he proposed, instead, a certification industry. The problem with the FDA is that it constitutes a licensing arrangement. Go ahead without its imprimatur, and you go to jail (and do not collect that proverbial $200). In contrast, without a certification, you may still bring your goods to the consumer, but without official approval. This system works in a myriad of other contexts. There are Certified Public Accountants; but any old book keeper can help you with your tax returns. For stocks and bonds there are Moodys, Standard and Poor and Fitch; but no one has to abide by their views. The Good Housekeeping Seal of Approval and Consumers' Reports serve similar



W. E. Block, *Defending the Undefendable III*,
https://doi.org/10.1007/978-981-16-3957-9_38

functions as do commercial testing laboratories; again, they can be ignored. Why not, also, have a group of private firms independently evaluating food and drugs? We rely on competition as the bulwark of our free economy. Why not here also?

Not only is the FDA a monopoly; even worse, it is also a governmental institution. That means no matter how many errors it makes, it can never, at least not automatically, go out of "business." Its employees are human beings, and we are the mistake-making animal. At least private monopolies are somewhat subject to market forces. Without bailouts, or the "too big to fail" philosophy, it is possible for them to no longer darken our doorsteps. Not so for the FDA (nor for the Post Office, the Motor Vehicle Bureau, the Departments of Agriculture, Education, etc.). Any private certification company approving of Thalidomide (great for morning sickness, but created birth defects) would quickly enough be bankrupted.

This brings us to Louis Falo and Andrea Gambotto. These gentlemen, both Professors at the University of Pittsburgh, were hot on the trail of a Covid 19 vaccine. The former, a dermatologist, the latter a surgeon, have concocted a medicine called PittCoVacc. It is to be administered to the skin via a patch exhibiting 400 tiny needles. One of its benefits is that it need not be continually refrigerated, a consideration very important especially in the underdeveloped world.

The bottom line was that the FDA took their own sweet time for determining approval for use with human subjects. Anyone see anything wrong with that? The FDA is now fiddling while Rome is burning.

Surely, there are some people, then at death's door, who would have given their eye teeth and more, to be the first human subjects for PittCoVacc. Safety and effectiveness be damned, in their view. They just wanted one last roll of the dice before meeting their mortal coil. Several of them have now passed beyond human care, thanks to the FDA slowdown. Is it totally unjust to think of Agency bureaucrats holding up the works as being guilty of manslaughter? Only if PittCoVacc really works, and we will not know that for quite a while yet.

With a private certification agency overseeing matters, human beings, on an informed consent voluntary basis might well have far more quickly determined whether or not PittCoVacc would be one of our answers.

Yes, this government bureaucracy has in its power the ability to in effect temporarily cancel its always unwarranted control. Right now, it has given the go-ahead to Remdesivir, a product of Gilead Sciences, under its Emergency Use Authorization policy. Thank goodness for this, as it may well save precious human lives, even though, I suspect, the motivation for this was more political than scientific. At present, some are calling for a packing of the Supreme Court. No one is mentioning setting up a governmental alternative to the FDA, hence in effect "packing" it. It is to head off any moves in this direction that might well explain its decision via Remdesivir.

But this humane decision undercuts the very case for its existence! One would think that now with the dire threat of a pandemic we would need the safety and efficiency provided by the FDA even the more. But it now lays down its "weapons" when they are presumably needed the most. What would we think of soldiers who disarmed in the face of the enemy? We would surmise they were not needed in the first place. "Emergencies" occur all the time. There are always a few patients, with no other options in sight, who would like to take a chance on a non-FDA approved remedy. If the FDA utilized its Emergency Use Authorization in all these cases, there would be in effect no FDA; it would be converted from a licensing agency into one properly limited to certification.

Says Michael Milken in this regard: "We send 19-year-olds into war zones knowing that no matter what we do, some number – greater than zero – will lose their lives or their limbs. But we tell a patient who is going to die not to try something because it could be dangerous."

Henry I. Miller, writing in the *Wall Street Journal* (April 23, 2020), has a very different suggestion in mind to meet this challenge: streamline the FDA process. To wit, he urges:

- animal studies to be allowed to take place at the same time as Phase I clinical trials
- lower wait times from 30 to 10 days from application to start of Phase I
- "publish a template 'master protocol' for streamlined Covid 19 vaccine development"
- unblind trial results earlier
- share data better
- allow approval for only parts of Biologics License Applications
- accelerate approvals for drugs tested on limited populations
- establish approval reciprocities with other countries.

None of these proposals are counterproductive. Mr. Miller is to be congratulated for making them. But none have so far been effected by that dinosaur, the FDA. Why is it that in reading this list, "rearranging deck chairs on the Titanic" comes to mind? The reason is that these suggestions leave in charge the very people responsible for not implementing them in the first place. What else can be expected from a governmental bureaucratic monopoly?

End, don't mend, the FDA.

# Chapter 39
# The Gene Editor

Doctor He Jiankui was sentenced to a three-year prison term, fined $430,000, and fired from his academic position as Associate Professor at the Southern University of Science and Technology in Shenzhen, China.

Did he engage in groping a patient? No. Poisoning a client? Again no. Plagiarism? Not a chance. According to the official Chinese Xinhua News Agency, Dr. He and two others, Zhang Renli and Qin Jinzhou, were convicted of gene editing fetuses.

His clients were a healthy mother and a father who was HIV positive. Dr. He engineered their twin girl babies so they would be resistant to HIV, the AIDS-related virus.

At the outset, this appears to be a voluntary agreement. The couple knew of the risks involved in this new medical technology. According to the defense, He Jiankui did not hide these from the mother and father. They agreed to the procedure since they weighed the dangers of AIDS for their daughters more heavily than the perils of the new, unproven, technique.

Why, then, were He and his two colleagues arrested and convicted? It is all too easy to surmise that this was done because it occurred in China, and that is a lawless country beyond the pale of civilization.

The fact of the matter is that if He had performed this Crispr-Cas9 gene-editing operation in the United States, a similar fate would have befallen him. This is because the Food and Drug Administration has not yet approved of this technique for human beings in terms of reproduction.

What are we to make of all of this? Let us adopt a set of private property rights economic freedom spectacles through which we can best perceive all such controversial acts.

We start by asking, who were the owners of the property in question? This, presumably, would be the parents. Did they receive informed consent from the supplier of the service? Not according to the local Shenzhen court. Let us, however, abstract from this finding. Instead, we adopt a Platonic perspective. This is because although we are indeed interested in this one case, we also want to derive a principle to deal


W. E. Block, *Defending the Undefendable III*,
https://doi.org/10.1007/978-981-16-3957-9_39

with all such violations of the law. So let us assume that there was no fraud involved here.

Should He and his colleagues have then been found guilty? Well, they did break an extant law. This leads to another question: is it a proper law that prohibits voluntary trades of this or any sort? The answer emanating from the free enterprise philosophy is a clear No. Rather, this would be a victimless crime, and all those even properly found guilty of violating it, should be set free.

Was there a victim here? Yes, possibly. If the dangers of this procedure were indeed of greater moment than these two children suffering from AIDS, then, yes, they might be considered victims. After all, one day that now manageable disease might be fully cured in the absence of this procedure. But this is clearly a judgment call upon which reasonable people can disagree. The parents would certainly not be guilty of child abuse even were this contrary to fact conditional to come into being. They were only guilty of doing what they thought best for their children, and in a reasonable manner.

What of the doctors involved? It is difficult to see them in any other way than as heroes. They put their careers, and their freedom in line, in order to help this mother and father be good guardians.

Yes, Dr. He jumped the legal gun, whether that of the FDA in the U.S., or the Chinese counterpart.

But the monopoly powers of these government bodies are incompatible with the free enterprise ethic through which we are viewing their behavior. These organizations, too, can err. But when they do (thalidomide, anyone?) they carry on merrily into the sunset. They cannot be bankrupted through erroneous decisions. That is no way to run a railroad.

# Part VII
# Real Estate

"WHAT'S THIS, BERGER? MR. JOSEPHS TELLS ME YOU REFUSED TO STAND UP WITH THE REST OF THE STAFF THIS MORNING AND RECITE 'THE REALTOR'S PROFIT PRAYER'....."

# Chapter 40
# The Redliner

It sounds innocuous. You get a map. No, one of those old fashioned ones, on paper, not the electronic version. It is possible to do this in that way, but let's stick to the tried and true. You get your red pen out and draw a line around a given neighborhood. So far, no problem. But, then, you refuse to lend any mortgage money, or make any loans whatsoever, to the owners of property inside this red-lined area.

Why in bloody blue blazes would you do anything like that? It is simple. You are a bank that seeks profits and wants to avoid bankruptcy. The point is, if borrowers do not repay their loans, with interest, insolvency is just around the corner.

But why discriminate against an entire neighborhood? Why not just refuse to lend to individuals not likely to meet their mortgage requirements, but not blackball everyone in the locale? Surely some of them are likely to make good on their financial obligations?

There are several answers to this puzzle. One is that it is costly to distinguish between the fiscally viable and the non-viable. Another is that a person in a red-lined district, be he ever so reliable, if his neighbors allow their properties to falter, the ensuing negative externalities will envelop him and the other few non-guilty parties. If everything around them is falling apart, this will most likely negatively impact the few stalwart proprietors.

Are other lenders free to enter the red-lined areas? Of course they are. It is still a free country. Well, sort of. In such a venue, no one is compelled to lend anything to anyone, nor prohibited from so doing. If the red-liners make a mistake and boycott people in an area on the rise, other lenders will have a field day there, with the lessened competition. That is to say, the red-liners do not have the last word on this matter. Rather, the market does.

The refuse-niks, possibly, can err in the opposite direction. They can fail to ignore regions on the decline. That is, they can fail to red-line when good business practice indicates they should. When they grant mortgages there, they can lose their shirts.


W. E. Block, *Defending the Undefendable III*,
https://doi.org/10.1007/978-981-16-3957-9_40

Investment bankers are akin to the white corpuscles in the blood stream. The successful ones direct savings to geographical locales where they will do the most good, and eschew places where the hard-earned savings of their depositors will be at too great a risk. Redlining is an integral part of this process. It should be protected from government interference. Instead, all too often, this practice is prohibited by law.

Why not, instead of refusing to make loans in these areas, just charge higher interest rates to the local property owners? There are usury laws on the books, that is why. They prohibit the charging of high enough interest rates that would defray the risk of lending in these areas. Were these to be repealed, as they should be, redlining in the sense of a boycott of all loans in an area would tend to disappear. This is but one more example of unwise government policies leading to difficulties, and subsequent attempts to remedy matters with still more regulations only further exacerbating the problem.

We have not so far brought into this discussion the topic of race. It is time to do so. Most red-line targets are in black areas. But this has nothing to do with the color of anyone's skin. There are very wealthy neighborhoods occupied by this demographic. Red-lining is unknown there, since with great collateral, mortgage delinquency is virtually unknown. Ditto for the negative externalities. No, the only color looked at by lenders is neither white nor black nor yellow, but rather green, as in the color of money. Red-lining is a result of usury laws, not racism.

# Chapter 41
# The Airbnber

When people leave their homes for a week or a month, they just sit there empty, not doing any good for anyone. Well, check that: their owners benefit from knowing that they can return at any time, and their domiciles will be available to them immediately. This is similar to the precautionary motive in macroeconomics: the motive for holding on to cash that pays no interest return. Why do people do any such thing? It is because there are unforeseen circumstances that might require payment all of a sudden. In similar manner, people retain ownership over their residences even when traveling or on vacation, out of a desire to ensure that when they return, their possessions will once again, instantaneously, be available to them.

But more recently the Airbnb company has been making an offer many find hard to refuse: turn your dwelling space over to us; we will find a temporary tenant, and more than make up to you any damages you may, but not likely will, suffer as a result of this occupancy. We will stuff cash down your throats to alleviate the distress you might feel at not having your property 100% under your control at all times.

How does this corporation make its business model work? By carefully monitoring both sides of this transaction (the homeowner's domicile has to be clean, safe; the temporary tenant must be reliable). As a result Airbnb has already made a large number of connections in this regard. They must be doing something right, otherwise they would not have satisfied customers on both sides of this deal, and garnered emulators as well. Another source of their success is that, per square footage, these rentals are often a small fraction of what a stay in a more traditional hotel would require.

But all is not well in Airbnb-land. You will never guess as to who could possibly object to these voluntary contracts! Yes, it is the mainstream hotel and motel industry. With help from the government, they have placed, or at least tried to do so, all sorts of restrictions on Airbnb. For example, they themselves are hemmed in by all sorts of government regulations; they favor visiting this sort of thing on their competitors. (The larger hotels, even the smaller ones, have a competitive advantage over private Airbnb renters in terms of filling out onerous paper work.) Also hotels


W. E. Block, *Defending the Undefendable III*,
https://doi.org/10.1007/978-981-16-3957-9_41

are prohibited from discriminating against minority clients; they have taken steps to ensure that this applies to Airbnb, even though the situation is somewhat different: one rents commercial space, the other personal homes. In the extreme, the industry under "attack" by Airbnb has called for their complete elimination. More moderately, attempts have been made through zoning legislation to reduce competition from Airbnbs.

Why the concern of the traditional hotels that Airbnb be tightly regulated? One hypothesis is that these mainstream hoteliers believe in the benefits of such regulations, and what to see them visited upon a wider and wider sector of the populace.

It is an old, old story, and not very complimentary to established business. When margarine first came on the market, it was naturally colored a not very enticing grey. Guess which state legislators passed laws prohibiting them from adding yellow coloring? Yes, those in the Midwest which produced a competing product, butter. Similarly, it is the barbering and hairdressing industry that is trying to prevent mostly black young female hair braiders from plying their trade without a license and years of schooling, none of which is even relevant to their occupation. The same sort of phenomena afflicted a religious order in Louisiana that wanted to construct wooden coffins, would you believe?

No, the alternative hypothesis offers a far better explanation of the untoward behavior of the opponents of Airbnb toward that company: they are competing for some of the same customers, and the more the latter attracts, the fewer will be left for the former.

If we are to attain (retain?) even a vestige of the free enterprise system that made this country great, Airbnb must be allowed to ply its trade free of impositions placed upon it by the all-loving state, at the behest of its competitors.

On the other hand, neighbors of Airbnb landlords complain of loud parties, continual changing tenants, an overall air of uncertainty. They want at least a modicum of stability in those who live next door to them. How would the free enterprise system handle this not at all unjustified objection? In the same manner as we dealt with, above, the nudist who likes to parade around on his front lawn: condominium developments.

# Chapter 42
# The Gentrifier

Gentrification has a bad press. It would appear that the gentrifier (he who engages in gentrification) is a malign exploiter, a bully, someone who takes advantage of the weak and the poor. And these are the nice things said about him.

What is the case against this practice? First and foremost, it pushes previous residents out of their homes. These people may have lived in their neighborhoods for years. They may be the third or fourth generation to occupy these premises. But when someone comes along, flashing big bucks, it is game over: the occupants have to vacate. What are the means through which the gentrifiers do their evil deeds? They simply try to purchase real estate in the target area, or attempt to rent accommodation there, thus bidding up rents and sale prices higher than would otherwise exist. The locals cannot compete with these hyped-up rates and are forced to retreat. Where do they go? Who knows? But wherever it is, they now occupy less preferred real estate. We know this since if they liked their new domiciles more than their previous ones, they would have already moved there, without any pressure being placed on the market by the new gentry. And it not only homes those forced to leave lose out on. These houses are part of neighborhoods, communities, associations. They have a history there. Their children are wrenched away from their friends.

Who are the main guilty parties in this sad story? College students who often have more money than the people they replace (or at least their parents do). When the Olympics come to town, people are moved en masse to make way for the new stadiums, swimming pools, ball fields, etc. Ditto for the World's Fairs. They, too, export inhabitants with a long history of occupancy, willy nilly. They, too, eradicate cultures and communities that were thriving before this economic rampage took place. Although this will not be politically correct, and we shudder to even mention it so beholden are we to the modern dictates and proprieties, but homosexual men are also offenders in this regard. This is the usual argument put forth by those who oppose gentrification.

There are grave problems with this account. Before we begin with our analysis, let us make one important distinction, that between owners and renters in the target


W. E. Block, *Defending the Undefendable III*,
https://doi.org/10.1007/978-981-16-3957-9_42

area. The former are in a far better position than the latter. Yes, when this process occurs, they, too, will leave the neighborhoods they have come to treasure over the years, but it will be "voluntary." That is, they will have so much money thrust into their pockets that they will prefer their new digs to their old ones. Otherwise, they will stay put, and not be "run out of town" by the newcomers. Community, togetherness, history, culture, neighborhood, are not the be-all and end-all of life, as opponents of gentrification would have us believe. At least some owners in target areas consider themselves lucky to be bought out at elevated prices.

The renters are in a far more precarious position. When their leases are up, the prices asked by the landlord will skyrocket out of their reach. They will be "forced" to depart, whether they like it or not. So, let us focus on those who lease real estate in the target area, not those who have taken up ownership positions there.

In order to put this into context, let us consider other arenas apart from real estate. For something very much like gentrification occurs all throughout the economy. Take automobiles for example. The rich get the pickings and the poor the leavings. The former walk away, or, rather, ride away, in cars such as the Mercedes, the Rolls Royce, the Cadillac; the latter have to content themselves with the vastly inferior Fords, Chevrolets, Hondas, Toyotas. The only difference between this case and the former is that the poor were never "pushed out" of luxurious vehicles, and into inferior ones. They never had the better cars in the first place. Otherwise, the story is the same: the rich eat high off the hog, the poor take the hind quarters. Ditto with food: it is lobster and steak for the wealthy, spaghetti and peanut butter for the impoverished.

But is this unfair? Certainly not. Assume that the rich came by their wealth in an honest way, not through government grants of special privileges, subsidies, bailouts, a la crony capitalism, but rather via laissez-faire capitalism. Thus they have contributed more to everyone else than have the poor. If anything would be unfair, it would be that the well-to-do would have to take the leavings and those without much honestly earned wherewithal get the lion's share. Or, that everything gets divided equally. We can see that opposition to gentrification is at least in part a disguised demand for equality. But this comes with particular ill-grace from those, for example, with two eyes. Were they to give up one of them to a blind man, they would lose mainly depth perception. This fades into nothingness compared to the benefits of imperfect sight to someone totally without. And, yet, these two-eyed egalitarians have the nerve to prate on about income inequality.

There is also more than just a little bit of economic misunderstanding involved in the case against gentrification. First of all, economic freedom, as Adam Smith so clearly saw in 1776, creates the Wealth of Nations. Those so concerned with the poor and with eradicating poverty, as we all should be, must realize that opposition to gentrification is an attack on the marketplace. To the degree that people are not free to buy and sell, to "barter and truck" is the extent to which the economy is more impoverished than it need be. The free economy is in a continual state of flux. People are being outbid every day for resources, up to and including housing they would otherwise prefer to keep to themselves. Outlaw gentrification, and if we are logically consistent, we must prohibit this entire process of bidding for goods and services, which implies, yes, the rich outbidding some people, disproportionately the poor.

Those ignorant of economics also fail to appreciate the distinction between residential housing ownership and tenancy. If real estate prices go down, and they sometimes do, it is the former, not the latter, who take the major hit. Owners are risk bearers, in a way that tenants are not. But there are also benefits to investing in this way: when gentrification occurs, they gain in a way unavailable to those who merely rent.

Forget housing for the moment. Consider the plight of a person who frequents a restaurant for many years. All of a sudden this establishment raises its prices because it can now attract a more affluent clientele. Our man can no longer afford to eat there. According to the anti-gentrifiers, this diner has rights that are now being abridged. But no. Engaging in a commercial interaction, even over the long haul, does not give either party any special dispensation to continue it on the same terms. One could with equal logic argue that if the diner shifts his custom to a competing restaurant, the eatery that had long served him would have a legal case against him. Stuff and nonsense. Both sides have for years benefitted from this long-standing arrangement, otherwise they would not have continued to partake in it. If one of them wishes to discontinue, either one, he has every right to do so.

It is the same with a person who rents an apartment. His long tenure there avails him nothing as a matter of justice if the landlord wants to raise the rent and substitute a richer tenant for him. And the opposite, too, holds true. If a long-standing tenant wishes to depart for greener pastures, the owner may not compel him, in law, to remain where he was.

It is sometimes said that the market benefits all participants. But what about the tenant, when due to gentrification he is booted out of the domicile he has occupied for many years, decades even. He has lost his friends, community, culture, etc. Surely, it is a cruel joke to say he is a beneficiary of any market which includes gentrification. Would this not constitute a counter-example to that general rule? No.

The correct state of affairs is that this tenant used to be a part of the market, but no longer is. For a long duration, he and the landlord reached an agreement as to rent and other aspects of tenancy, and he was a market participant in good standing. But now, due to gentrification, the landlord doubles or triples the rent; our man can no longer afford these higher rates, and moves out. He may well become a market participant in his new home, but he is no longer one in his old domicile; he can no longer afford to be one. It is the same with the blacksmith, before the advent of the horseless carriage. He, too, was once a market participant, but no longer was, at least not in terms of shoeing horses. He can become one again if he starts working for the automobile company, but that is entirely a different matter. So, yes, whether tenant or blacksmith, a man benefits as a market participant when he can make a commercial offer acceptable to at least one other person, but sometimes, changing conditions, gentrification, the invention of the car, this is not true anymore.

Gentrification is a very powerful market phenomenon. It sweeps all before it. It enables the rich to enjoy what they should be able to revel in. It shuts out the poor from luxuries. There is, however, one institution that stands in its way: government in general, and its public housing in particular. Consider those vast projects just west of the FDR Drive on the east side of Manhattan, and, indeed, littered all throughout that borough. New York City has some of the most expensive real estate on the planet (well, it did before covid and the mismanagement of the Big Apple mayor, DeBlasio). Have these poor people been gentrified to lesser valued real estate? To ask this is to answer it: they have not. Why is it important that they be banished to the hinterlands, which would surely occur, were gentrification to be given its head? This is because there is no earthly (economic) reason they should occupy such luxurious real estate, any more than that they should drive around in Rolls Royces. No. It should be the outer boroughs, New Jersey, Connecticut, for the likes of them. Why? Because, if we are ever to overcome poverty, we much make it easy for very productive people to locate in places where they can be even more so. E.g., Manhattan. The people in the projects are now located in places where doctors, lawyers, computer nerds, financiers, in a rational world, would have occupied.

The libertarian solution would be to privatize all of this public (socialist) housing. It should be sold to the highest bidders, and the money given over to the long-suffering taxpayer at whose expense these monstrosities were first built. Is this likely to happen? Not very likely. Objections would immediately arise to the effect that the poor are being turfed out of their private property. A practical solution is the following. Give the apartments to each of their present occupants, or, charge them a nominal fee ($100?) for them. Will the present tenants object? Of course not. Instead of having to pay rent, they will now own some quite valuable real estate. Then, sit back and watch the magic of the market do its work. Soon enough, the low productive people who occupy these premises (only such poor people qualify to rent them in the first place) will soon enough sell them for the vast sums they are really worth, and move a bit further away from Fifth Avenue and 42nd street. They will have longer commutes. But the high powered businessmen who take their places will have shorter and easier trips to work. Hence, productivity will increase, and poverty lessen.

Suppose you were a long-time regular patron at a small neighborhood restaurant. Then one day management decided to upgrade. New rugs, new lighting fixtures, new tables and chairs, a new kitchen—and a new top-grade chef with a new, improved cuisine. Naturally, with these changes to the premises, the prices were raised—way out of your reach. Or assume a similar occurrence took place at your local tailor, grocer, flower shop or another retail business. You would, of course, be disappointed with any of these scenarios. At the very least, you would have to find a replacement for the goods or service on which you had long relied.

But would you feel affronted and victimized? Would you feel so outraged that you would picket these business improvements, in an attempt to prevent them from taking place? And, moreover, would you feel morally righteous in doing so?

That is almost exactly what happened in a middle-class neighborhood in a northern city. According to a study commissioned by the city government, more than 250 tenants—half of them senior citizens—have been evicted from their long-term residences to make way for luxury condominium developments.

And they are fighting mad. Their demonstrations have been so successful that the city government came to their rescue. According to the recommendations of the author of this report, the city should: put a moratorium on rental housing demolitions; make public land available for co-operative and nonprofit housing; increase the notice period for evictions; enact rent review and rent control; rezone multiple-dwelling areas to protect affordable housing.

These suggestions are ludicrous. If similar restrictions were proposed for other businesses they would be summarily rejected.

Home and hearth, however, are considered to be different: with housing it is widely believed that rent-paying gives someone, in effect, ownership rights. Were rental housing compared to any other good or service, it would become clear that the only legitimate way to ensure continued supply is to become an owner, or at least to secure a long-term contract for this provision.

That the city government would even consider protecting these people is a moral disgrace. It amounts to no less than the usurpation of the value of these properties from their rightful owners. It is also economically inefficient. These recommendations are all designed to interfere with the free market process which continually transfers resources from those who value it less to those who value it more. Further, it is an attack on economic progress. At bottom, gentrification is only an improvement in material conditions. Also, it is undemocratic: the only people who "vote" for protection are the present renters. The political voice of the many more people who might otherwise occupy the luxury condos is not heard at all.

# Chapter 43
# The Holdout

A 94-year old man is derisively thumbing his nose at commercial progress. That at least is how many people interpret the travails of this senior citizen, owner of a tiny and decrepit turn-of-the-century house in a large city in North America. The family homestead is situated in the midst of two street-level parking lots, surrounded by high rise towers. As such, it is a prime development target in this land-hungry metropolis.

The builders have several options, none very savory from their point of view. They can build around his domicile; but this would put his rickety edifice smack dab in the middle of a spanking new multi-million dollar construction complex. They can try to wait out this nonagenarian; he is not exactly in the best of health. The problem, however, is that he plans to bequeath this property to his nephew, aged 70, and the latter is in relatively good health and is also unwilling to sell. They can try to buy him out. But he was offered a large sum and turned it down cold. Real estate experts estimate the current market value of this parcel of land at a lower value, but the holdout is adamant: he refuses to sell at any price. All of these options are consistent with the fact that this man is the undisputed legitimate owner of the property in question, and our constitution at least implicitly recognizes the rights of ownership of private property. There is one option open to the would-be builders, however, which is entirely in keeping with their short-run financial interests: get the government to expropriate the holding, and to turn it over to them.

At first glance, there are strong considerations which favor this course of action. New buildings would create construction jobs and after they are completed, thousands more city dwellers will be able to live, work and shop in them. Nor would the owner's needs be ignored; the government could figure out the "fair market value" of this real estate, and even tack on an additional amount for relocation costs. This would certainly enable him to obtain a vastly improved domicile, and have money left over.

However attractive, there are great dangers in this course of action. For one thing, it is by no means obvious this takeover would be economically advantageous. There



W. E. Block, *Defending the Undefendable III*,
https://doi.org/10.1007/978-981-16-3957-9_43

would be more jobs, but if that were our only goal, we could more easily achieve it by banning trucks, and employing people to carry cargo on their backs. The point is, we don't want jobs for their own sake. We want them only as a means of increasing utility. But it cannot be shown that stealing this man's land from him to turn it over to developers (that is precisely what eminent domain or expropriation amounts to, when the legalistic veneer is stripped away), would enhance economic satisfaction. Since there is no way to make interpersonal comparisons of utility, we cannot unambiguously conclude expropriation will promote the public good.

Moreover, this plan would undermine the system upon which our present level of well-being depends, as well as our future prospects. If government denigrates one man's private property rights, it does so for all.

So, let the hold out hold out. Permanently, if he wishes. He is a hero for demonstrating the rights of private property. Nor can it be shown that his action, or non-action, is economically inefficient.

# Chapter 44
# The Evicter

The Centers for Disease Control and Prevention, operating under the US Department of Health and Human Services, has effectively ended all evictions from residential rental units, during the Covid crisis. Until when? Until they get good and ready to end this taking.

It is interesting to note how very different the law treats food and clothing, on the one hand, and shelter, on the other. If someone breaks into a Walmart, grabs a cake and some shoes, and tries to leave without paying, the result is clear: that person is a shoplifter, and will be treated harshly not only by the forces of law and order, but will also lose out in the court of public opinion (I abstract here from when the person is a looter; then all bets are off, amazingly). But if a man occupies an apartment, and does not pay the rent, then, he is treated very differently. Yet, in both cases, there is theft. True, in one of them it is theft of services, in the other it is robbery of physical goods, but this can hardly explain the very different manner in which the two are treated. For, if someone obtains a massage, haircut, nail treatment, session with a psychologist, and declines to pay, this is also a theft of services but the perpetrator will not be gently treated by the police or the courts.

What is it that is so special about domiciles that failure to pay for them should be singled out for kid-glove treatment by all and sundry? Who knows? Perhaps the explanation lies deeply within us; maybe we are hard-wired from evolution when we lived in caves or trees to see home and hearth differently than all other items. All we can say for sure is that even under ordinary non-Covid circumstances, this bifurcation holds. For example, if you engage in shop lifting during the Christmas season, woe betide you. But if you are a few months behind in your rent payment, no court will grant the landlord an eviction notice until January arrives. However, both are theft. Who needs rent control when tenants can live fully free for the last few months of every year? Only a Bernie Sanders type of person can smile at this situation.

So much for the normative elements of freezing evictions. Now let us consider the positive ones. One bad effect of this slap in the face of landlords is that we will



W. E. Block, *Defending the Undefendable III*,
https://doi.org/10.1007/978-981-16-3957-9_44

have less shelter for people than otherwise. This policy reduces investment in this sector of the economy. Hence, the horrendous and multitudinous phenomenon of people living under bridges or on sidewalks. Eviction prohibition is not pulled on owners of commercial real estate or office buildings, hence we do not have the equivalent of homeless people in those arenas (apart from a very few trucks and hot dog stands).

What is going on vis a vis Covid, in this connection? We are now poorer than we would otherwise be, if the economy had not been to a great degree shut down. I abstract from the issue of whether this was wise or not. But the undeniable fact is that poorer people can afford less housing than otherwise. If evictions are allowed, where will the evictees go? Why, to smaller accommodations. Landlords don't relish empty apartments! If numerous people now occupy fewer rooms per person, there will be more space available. That is Adam Smith's "Invisible Hand" at work. How else can the homeless be rescued from their plight? We are not now building more rental units, for goodness sake. The mistake well-meaning people make in opposing Covid evictions is that they think the evictees will be consigned to living in the street. As Henry Hazlitt reminds us in his excellent book *Economics in One Lesson*, we should look not only at the visible immediate narrow effects of any public policy but also at the long run results for the entire economy. Evictions economize on space; they are a necessary condition for downsizing. Preventing them means more homelessness, not less.

Landlords are no more mean-spirited than other profit maximizers (that means pretty much all of us). If they cannot collect rents, their property will be foreclosed on them by banks. Will the CDC declare a moratorium on that sort of thing until the end of the year? Not at all likely.

# Chapter 45
# The Rent Control Adversary

The case for rent control seems rather simple and straightforward. Tenants are usually poorer than landlords. In a tight housing market without such "protection," rents will rocket and the unfortunate occupants of apartments will be forced into smaller and smaller dwelling spaces and greater and greater misery.

What better way of short-circuiting this vicious circle than by clamping a ceiling on rents? That would give tenants some measure of security against rampaging inflation and benefit a poor and helpless element of society. It is reasoning of that sort that is behind the well-intentioned movement to impose rent controls.

But alas, the truth about this policy is very different: Controlling rents reduces incentives to supply new rental housing. Even if newly constructed buildings are exempted, potential landlords still fear the re-imposition of controls.

Under such a system, moreover, landlords have little motivation to maintain their dwelling units in good repair, so dilapidation occurs more quickly than it need be. Nor are tenants led to economize on space, because prices are no longer free to signal just how valuable their units have become, so vacancy rates plummet. Labor mobility is curtailed because tenants are forced to reject more productive jobs since no apartments are available in the new areas.

Rent control is an unmitigated disaster for landlords, tenants, the work force, and property values.

Time and time again the lesson of rent control has been driven home. Landlords lose out but tenants suffer even more. It is not the landlord but the tenant who faces the possibility of sleeping under a bridge or in a tent on the sidewalk.

A low opinion of rent control is shared by all economists regardless of ideological bent. Strange as it may seem to the casual observer of the profession, economists appear to be unanimous in their opinion about the effects of rent control. That agreement ranges all the way from Nobel laureates Hayek and Friedman on the right to their fellow Nobel Prize winner Gunnar Myrdal on the left.

An important architect of the Swedish Labor Party's welfare state, Myrdal's opinion was that "rent control has in certain Western countries constituted maybe,



W. E. Block, *Defending the Undefendable III*,
https://doi.org/10.1007/978-981-16-3957-9_45

the worst example of poor planning by governments lacking courage and vision." Fellow Swede and fellow socialist economist Assar Lindbeck was responsible for this bit of immortal wisdom: "In many cases rent control appears to be the most efficient technique presently known to destroy a city—except for bombing."

The current housing shortage is a direct consequence of the boomeranging of various government policies designed to protect tenants. It is predictable now that unless rent controls are lifted the plight of tenants will worsen in the years to come.

If governments are serious about solving the housing crisis, they will make the removal of rent control one of their highest priorities. Since tenants outnumber landlords, and are usually convinced rent controls are in their best interests, it may prove "politically impossible" to act in such a statesmanlike manner. But do so they must, otherwise today's politicians will preside over the ruination of the rental housing market.

Like any law that freezes prices, or causes them to rise at lower rates than otherwise, rent control is a market signal. What it indicates to the entrepreneur is that none, or fewer rental housing units should be constructed. While it's true new rental units are specifically exempted from coverage by most rent enactments, investors are too cautious (perhaps too smart) to put their faith in rental housing—believing that they may well eventually be hit, despite the initial exemptions.

A question I often ask rent control advocates is: "Suppose you inherited $10 million or won it in a lottery; would you invest it in an apartment building, at a time when tenants are clamoring for more and stricter rent controls? Would you advise your elderly parents to place their hard-earned cash in this highly risky field?"

Some analysts have attempted to account for the shortage of residential rental construction and the near-zero vacancy rates in many parts of the country not in terms of rent control, but as a result of other factors. Alternative explanations include high interest rates, increased costs of construction (labor and materials), immigration and population growth. But there are grave difficulties in each attempt to defend this malicious system. Why characterize this law in such a manner? It constitutes an unwarranted "taking" from landlords. Imagine if this were applied to the owners of shoes, pencils, labor, or any other such product; then it would be far more obvious.

Other things equal, an increase in the interest rate leads to a decline in all long-term capital investments. But why then have high interest rates not punched as serious a hole in the construction of office buildings, factories, warehouses and commercial space? Pre-covid, vacancy rates for residential rentals were much lower than in office towers. A similar analysis can be applied to rampaging building costs: they decrease new building, but commercial, office tower, factory and other non-rent controlled construction seems, not so curiously, virtually exempt.

Nor do existing rental units fare very well under controls. Even with the best will in the world, the landlord cannot afford to pay his skyrocketing fuel, labor and materials bills, to say nothing of refinancing his mortgage out of reduced rent rises he may legally charge. And under rent control, he no longer has anything like the best will in the world; the incentive to supply tenant service he had under free-market conditions is vastly reduced.

His allowable rent rises, if they occur at all, are now arbitrarily set by outside political forces. They no longer depend, as they do in other fields of endeavor, on the standards he maintains, pleasing customers. The result is often improper maintenance, poor repairs, and painting, grudging provision of services and a gradual slide into housing deterioration. The sitting tenant is "protected" by rent control, but he receives no real bargain. The enjoyment he can derive out of his dwelling space tends to be reduced to a level commensurate with his controlled monthly payments.

Why is it so difficult to educate tenants and other members of the public about the economics of rent control? Economic illiteracy is one explanation. A free lunch at someone else's expense is another. The average voter either has not heard the economist on rent controls, or will not listen.

Although this can only be speculative, another reason may be because of the sheer durability and immovability of the large residential structure. No one in his right mind advocates a price control on carrots in order to ensure a lower-priced supply; everyone realizes that the farmer would switch production to other vegetables, leading to a shortage of this one. Likewise, when governments have attempted to place ceilings on the incomes of doctors, they have been faced with a brain drain to other, freer countries. While the farmer can easily change to a new product, and labor is mobile at a moderate cost, people quite correctly see it as exceedingly difficult, if not impossible, to move a big apartment dwelling into a non-controlled locale. The average man may think he can have the "benefits" of rent control without the attendant destruction.

But this is a mirage. When the market signals a lower need for apartments by holding down rents, entrepreneurs will take every step at their disposal to comply. They will attempt to convert rental units of condominiums, to build single detached units—which have never been controlled—for rental purposes. The will allow the slide of the rental housing stock into deterioration if it cannot otherwise be made into a paying proposition. These phenomena, however, are rarely seen by non-economists as the result of rent control. They occur years after enactment and are often interpreted as the result of other social forces.

Voters and politicians should not confuse appearances and reality. They must come to realize that however immobile residential buildings seem to be, economic law grinds on inexorably.

Recently, a new twist has been added to the argument in the defense of rent control legislation. According to this perspective, it is far too "simplistic" to assert, in a straightforward manner, that rent control leads inexorably to various types of housing disarray.

No, we are now told, the reality is far more "complex" than that: Different types of controls will lead not to the same conclusion, but to very different results, depending upon which specific types of controls are implemented.

The view does more than affront logic and common sense, it is a violation of numerous empirical studies of the effects of rent control.

Certainly, all instances of these legislative enactments have something more in common than a mere name. They all mandate that rents be legally forced below the level that would otherwise have been obtained in the absence of such an enactment. What common effects will all such laws have? They will all make investments in residential rental units a less attractive proposition than otherwise. This, in turn, will retard new building, promote housing deterioration, reduce vacancy rates, encourage racial and other discrimination and decrease labor mobility. True, the strength of these effects will vary with the strictness of the control in question, but from this fact it does not at all follow that rent controls – all instances of them – have nothing in common. There is little doubt that imposing rent control in a city is very much akin to reducing its stock of residential housing units. The only question that remains is one of determining how strong a blow has been struck in any given case.

New York city's early form of rent control, for example, was a real knockout punch. It did not provide for any rental increases whatsoever, nor even for vacancy decontrol. True, it has moderated in recent years, and rent "review" has come to take the place of rent "control" for many thousands of housing units, but the Big Apple's 80-year experiment with rent limitations (it started as a war time measure in 1941; quick question: which war?), by whatever name, has spelled the death knell for hundreds of thousands of people's homes.

Other jurisdictions, too, have unwisely passed rent control legislation. It is not as strict as New York's used to be, and some have only been in effect for a briefer period– too short a time to provoke a South Bronx-style response. But just wait!

This is all beside the main point. It deals only with the degree to which different regimes of rent control will attack the rental unit stock. On the fact that this will be so, there can be no question. Even eminent socialists, economists who have called for government intervention on numerous other occasions, have pulled back in the case of rent control as we have seen in the cases of Gunnar Myrdal and Assar Lindbeck. The proposition that "a ceiling on rents reduces the quantity and quality of housing available" was supported by an overwhelming 98.1% of economists polled in a survey reported by the prestigious *American Economic Review*.

Let's face facts. Rent control is an assault on the rental housing stock, and the sooner this elementary postulate of economics is recognized, the better the future housing conditions for tenants.

# Chapter 46
# The Pet Hating Landlord

Based on a recent pet-related tenant eviction, it would appear that the evil landlords are "at it again." They are exploiting tenants who wish to give a home to some of our furry or feathered friends. "Pet-hating landlords" is the way this phenomenon was described by a leading newspaper.

Nothing could be further from the truth, however. Actually, except for a minuscule number of cases, the landlord couldn't possibly care less about which pets inhabit dwelling units. Dogs, cats, parakeets or lions, elephants and alligators (on the assumption that no extra costs are thereby imposed on the landlord) it's all the same to him. The landlord, like all other businesspersons, is usually interested only in maximizing profits. And since the best way to increase profits is by satisfying renters, the "customer is always right" is the typical motto of the landlord.

Why is it, then, that virtually all leases prohibit pets if the landlord's self-interest lies in pleasing customers, and some of them not only like our brothers of field and stream, but revere them.

First of all, while all standard written tenant agreements prohibit pets, they also provide for landlord waivers. And rental accommodation owners commonly grant exceptions for goldfish, parakeets in cages, and other such four-legged and finned friends.

More importantly, we must reject the view that all landlords are pet-hating, misbegotten misanthropes. In actual point of fact, most do not care at all whether tenants maintain pets, as long as this practice (1) does not impose any additional (maintenance and repair) costs on them, and (2) does not annoy other tenants. The landlord typically brings no views of his own to this matter: he attempts to act as an agent for his tenants.

In a reasonably well-ordered world, renters who like pets would be segregated from those who dislike them, in much the same way that smokers and non-smokers are kept apart in restaurants and (previously) airplanes. For pets, just like tobacco smoke, are what economists call an "external diseconomy" or "negative neighborhood effect:" they impose costs on third parties without automatic compensation.


W. E. Block, *Defending the Undefendable III*,
https://doi.org/10.1007/978-981-16-3957-9_46

Encouraging people with such divergent tastes to live in close proximity with each other reduces welfare all around: non-pet owners object to pets, and pet owners are unhappy with this opposition.

The difficulty is that our institutional arrangements do not make it easy for the landlord to collect additional rent to defray the increased costs of tenants with domestic animals. This is why rental property owners are exceedingly reluctant to invite dogs and cats into their buildings, not because of any innate hatred of animals. But unless landlords can, without any red tape or legal burdens, be fairly compensated for these additional costs, they will have no incentive whatsoever to set up entire buildings devoted to pet-owning tenants. Under these conditions, the segregation of tenants by pet status will be an unreachable ideal.

Rent control is a particular problem in this regard. In the newer and luxury buildings to which controls do not apply, tenant wishes and desires can be met to some degree. But in units subject to rent control, there is not the slightest likelihood of the landlord collecting additional rent for allowing pets. Should it really be a surprise, then that the rental property owner would be completely unresponsive to tenant wishes?

There is one pressure vent open to the tenant in these circumstances: a condominium, or better yet, single-family ownership. In condominiums, strata title, or cooperative housing, the "neighborhood effects" problem still prevails. A majority of owners may vote to preclude pets. (And the high proportion of these groups which actually prohibit pets is further evidence that most people, tenants included, oppose this practice.) But, presumably, if there is enough demand for this accommodation, at least some condos will welcome owners with such tastes.

It is only by owning a home, with a backyard and a fence, that the pet owner need seek permission from no one. The problem, of course, is that many pet lovers cannot afford to buy a home of their own. All the more reason, then, to end rent controls, and to enact legislation which makes it easier for landlords to collect additional rents to defray the increased costs of renting to pet owners.

In this way we can separate tenants based on their desire for pets. We can thus help remove a minor but important irritant to living together in a congested, complex modern civilization.

# Chapter 47
# The Zoning Renouncer

Most people would not see much connection between zoning legislation, a rather prosaic government attempt to control land usage, and phone taps, conspiracy, bribery, and secret midnight police activity—things usually associated with treason, murder, kidnapping or drug-dealing. Yet bribery is spawned by this geographical central planning.

There is little doubt that zoning complexity and changeability have spawned graft and corruption. The reason for this is easy to discern: a less restrictive variance may be worth millions of dollars to the land developer. Be the bureaucrat ever so honest, he will be sorely tempted by a share in these gains. Paradoxically, this is not necessarily all to the bad. If a bribe can convert a land parcel to use more highly prized by consumers, wealth and the allocation of resources will have been much more nearly optimized. This is not the first case on record attesting to the benefits of black markets. A great loss, however, is the general disrespect for all law, including licit law, engendered by this practice.

In a free market without governmental zoning, there would have been no need for bribery.

Consider the allocation of land between industry and agriculture. Under laissez-faire capitalism, those wishing to erect factories would simply bid the land away from farmers and other such property owners. But some cities have agricultural land reserves at their periphery. There is strong evidence that land located near urban areas is far more valuable to the public in its industrial or residential or commercial use than as a farm. It is only by illegally converting such land into a use far more highly prized by consumers that their "sovereignty" can be attained.

Given these personal tragedies, economic inefficiencies, and the disrespect engendered for law and order, why do most cities have such zoning enactments?

In the view of many concerned professionals, this type of legislation is a necessary bulwark against chaos in urban land use. Without zoning it is contended external diseconomies will abound: pickle works will come to rest cheek by jowl with single-family homes; glue factories beside country clubs; and oil refineries in


W. E. Block, *Defending the Undefendable III*,
https://doi.org/10.1007/978-981-16-3957-9_47

proximity to family restaurants. Moreover, it is feared that rapacious land developers will erect, profit from and then abandon buildings, placing undue strain on the capacities of municipal services. Further, the un-zoned city will be one of haphazard construction, falling property values, instability, disregard for neighborhood "character," irrational allocation of property—and a haven for unscrupulous speculators.

The zoning idea has a certain appeal. What, after all, could be more simple and obvious? If land usage seems imperfect, all that is needed is the enactment of a set of laws compelling proper behavior.

There are, however, grave flaws here. Consider "Exhibit A," the City of Houston—which has rarely enacted zoning legislation. The very existence of a large North American city (an area in excess of five hundred square miles) which can function normally and continue to grow without zoning (at least for many years) is a major piece of evidence against the traditional view that zoning supposedly protects against chaos.

The reality appears to be either there are a few significant interdependencies and externalities in urban property markets or that "one man's meat is another man's poison." For instance, the presence of commerce in an otherwise residential neighborhood is interpreted in a positive way by some people and in a negatively by others.

We must not lose sight of the fact that market mechanisms exist naturally to eliminate such externalities that would arise from the proverbial glue factory on the corner of Fifth Avenue and 42nd Street in New York City.

Quite simply, land prices in the top neighborhoods are too expensive for the glue factory: they effectively prohibit any but the most valuable concentrated uses—such as large office buildings or high-rise residential dwellings. And, in the more marginal areas from which industrial uses cannot be precluded, the evidence is that the local inhabitants look upon them as a blessing, not a curse, because of the jobs they bring.

In Houston, the market has tended to create a reasonably well-ordered pattern. Because of private "marketplace zoning," we find no filling stations at the end of cul-de-sacs; ship-channel industries are, naturally, located along the ship channel; large supermarkets, bowling alleys, movies and department stores are placed at or near major intersections, not in quiet residential areas.

The days of the three-district zoning (residential, commercial, industrial) with two of the three pages of regulations have long since passed. Today's ordinances are continually growing to accommodate more detailed regulations of use, lot size, building height and bulk: more reasons for granting variances, bonuses, and special exceptions; and much more complicated procedures for appeals and reviews. Things have come to such a pass that no self-respecting set of zoning regulations dare appear in a tome of fewer than 500 pages.

The real issue here is between private and government zoning. What has been criticized above is government zoning, not the private variety.

"I'M SORRY, MR. MUKHERJEE, IT IS NOT PERMITTED, YOU MAY NOT ESTABLISH A CHUTNEY FACTORY ON LAND ZONED 'CLASS A-3 SQUALOR'."

What is private zoning? The most well-known example is Houston's system of deed restrictions. (Neighbors contractually tie each other to continued or similar land usage. These voluntary agreements thus preclude the arrival of a factory—unless all or a previously stipulated number of signatories desire it.) But private zoning also takes place every time a glue factory is priced out of a residential neighborhood, or whenever the gas station locates on a major thoroughfare, not in a side street.

The same process is at work in shopping centers. It is difficult to imagine two "incompatible" tenants adjacent to each other in a shopping mall. Any inclination toward such mal-zoning tends to be rigidly suppressed by the market. Go to any supermarket, and appreciate the private "zoning" that occurs there. In one aisle, all the soft drinks are gathered. Another houses all of the meats. A third is devoted to vegetables, and a fourth to fruits. Frozen foods are displayed here, cookies over there. Serious variants from this practice are limited to individual firms and lead to loss of revenues.

In contrast, when the bureaucrat makes a mistake he does so on a vast scale. He negatively affects millions of people virtually none of whom will be able to connect him with their suffering. He need not lose any of his personal funds, since he deals with other people's money. The public zoner can rest secure in his immunity from the "dollar vote" of the consumer, while his private counterpart, the land developer, the mall owner, the grocer, is dependent for this very existence on continually satisfying customers.

There are a few things feared more by the average urban property owner than declining residential values. That is understandable, for much of the real savings of many citizens is tied up in a single-family house. Perhaps that is the single most important explanation for the high regard in which many citizens hold zoning legislation: it is supposed to protect property values.

Of far greater reliability may be the system of dead restrictions, or restrictive covenants, whereby the property owner may contract with his neighbors concerning the uses to which land subsequently may be put. (This institution has a bad press since historically is was used for racial segregation; this no longer occurs in the modern economy.) Alternatively, land developers may require, as a condition of sale, that all buyers agree that specified land usage be continued, either for a stipulated period of time or until a majority vote of such buyers overturns the agreement. In contrast, government zoning is continually vulnerable to changing regulations.

Ultimately, of course, there can be no absolute guarantee against declining property values. A fall in the price of wood, a decrease in the market rate of interest, the sale of government lands, technological improvements in prefabrication methods, can all lower housing prices.

Value preservation is a will o' the wisp, because price is a manifestation of the worth placed on an item not by one person, but by two groups: potential sellers and potential buyers. Not only are we unable to speak with certainty of the value an owner will place on his home in the future, it is even less possible to assess the worth a future hypothetical buyer will give it.

Let us consider the "thin house" to be erected on lots that are only 15-feet wide. There has been no empirical research done concerning the likely effect of such construction on the value of neighboring houses. Surrounding property values might decline, as feared by some. On the other hand they might increase, if the new houses are well built and modern looking and replace unsightly vacant lots. Then a whole neighborhood might be upgraded.

But let us suppose, for argument's sake, that the negative externalities outweigh the positive, so that thin houses lower surrounding real estate prices or cause them to rise more slowly than they otherwise might. Is government action then indicated?

The difficulty with the externality argument is that it cuts both ways. If we assume that thin houses have negative external effects on fat ones, then we may with equal justification assume that the fatties impose externality costs on the skinnies. Surely if the fatties succeed in prohibiting house construction on the narrow lots, they will have reduced the value of the latter. And even in the absence of zoning prohibitions, common sense shows that if the obese houses were demolished, this would leave more room, air, and sunlight for the emaciated dwellings. Thus, neither

Fat Power nor Skinny Power can gain any ethical competitive edge from the concept of externalities.

Statist zoning has not worked well for another reason. In the absence of this institution, the economic surplus resulting from a change in land usage is usually captured by the private owner. But when there is zoning, it may be appropriated by the politicians and civil servants who are in a position to give or withhold permission. Since millions of dollars are often involved, it is little wonder that a zoning system can create massive graft and corruption of the sort so much in the headlines.

# Chapter 48
# The Housing Rights Repudiator

Housing is not a basic human right. If housing is a right we're in a moral swamp.

All rights involve equal and opposite obligations. If I have a right to property, you have an obligation to refrain from stealing it or trespassing upon it. If you have an inviolable right in your person, I, and everyone else, have an obligation to leave you unmolested.

Note that these are negative rights. They make it incumbent upon people to refrain, to cease and desist, to avoid certain aggressive behavior. But they impose no positive obligations whatsoever. Rights such as these, the rights to person and property, have been acknowledged since time immemorial. They are at the core of the Magna Carta, the constitutions and the actual practice of all Western democracies. They are the backbone of Western civilization.

Of late, however, some new types of rights have arisen. Widely trumpeted, these include a claim to everything from a "decent" level of clothing, food, housing, medical care, to rock music, sexual orgasms and meaningful relationships. If this were only an emphasis of everyone's right to seek happiness in whatever manner chosen, provided no one else's rights were infringed in the process, it would be unobjectionable. Indeed, this is the essence of the right to person and property.

But something quite different is meant by those who hold that "housing is a basic human right."

What is claimed is not the right to be left alone, free to build, buy or rent whatever shelter one can afford. Rather, it refers to a so-called right to housing which implies an obligation on the part of other people, to provide it. This claim involves the positive rights, not the negative rights of classical origin.

What is actually at stake here, however, has nothing to do with rights at all. On the contrary, it is a disguised and therefore quite insidious demand for other people's wealth. In the case of rights proper, all that is required of outsiders is non-interference. But in this fraudulent case, a myriad of material goods and services is demanded.


W. E. Block, *Defending the Undefendable III*,
https://doi.org/10.1007/978-981-16-3957-9_48

AFTER READING A N.Y. TIMES EDITORIAL DECLARING HOUSING 'A BASIC HUMAN RIGHT', LOWELL AND RHONDA, RESIDENTS OF THE PORT AUTHORITY BUS TERMINAL, PICK OUT THEIR WALLPAPER.

To see how radical a departure are the new "positive" rights, consider the following: Mankind could at one fell swoop, if it were so minded, completely banish all violations of negative rights. All that need be done is that each and every one of us resolves not to initiate physical violence or fraud, and then act on this basis. But all the agreement in the world would not be sufficient to provide the level of wealth necessary to fulfill our so-called positive rights to health, shelter, happiness, etc.; certainly not at the levels sought by the advocates of positive rights.

There are other grave problems with this contention. If housing is a basic right, imposing ethical imperatives upon strangers, each of us is immoral—not only if any of our countrymen are without "decent housing," but as long as anyone in the world is so lacking. For rights know no national boundaries. If it is morally incumbent on anyone to supply a good or service without his contractual agreement, then this applies to everyone without exception.

Another logical implication is even more insidious. For rights, by their very nature, are egalitarian. It is clear that all of us, right or poor, old or young, have equal (negative) rights. We are all equal in that, for example, murder committed on any innocent person is wrong, and to an identical degree. The mass murderer is guilty of the same immortality in each of the specific acts as he perpetrates.

If positive claims are also rights, then people must not only have a right to "decent" shelter, but an absolutely equal share of the world's housing, etc. Since there is no logical stopping place for positive rights, the claim of basic human needs as rights really amounts to a demand for absolute income/wealth equality.

And the situation is even worse. For there is nothing in the logic of the argument to prevent the demand for equal intelligence, equal beauty, equal athletic and sexual prowess, and even equal happiness. If these things could somehow be contrived. We must reject this claim, and with it the moral swamp in which it necessarily involves us.

# Part VIII
# Business

# Chapter 49
# The Metric Protester

Most countries in the world are on the metric system. There is even a movement afoot to convert the U.S. to these types of weights and measures. Inroads have already been made. Athletes race 5 k and 10 k distances, not 3 and 6 miles, respectively. Our swimming competitions take place in 25 and 50-meter pools, not yards, and our sprinters are timed for the 100 meters, not 100 yards.

Is metrification compatible with libertarianism? This cannot be doubted. Why then extol the virtues of the metric protester? This is because in all too many cases this system is imposed by coercive fiat; it is not implemented on a voluntary basis. We, then, applaud this protester to the extent he opposes the intimidation aspect, not metrification itself.



W. E. Block, *Defending the Undefendable III*,
https://doi.org/10.1007/978-981-16-3957-9_49

Take our neighbors to the north of us as a case in point. Based on the work of their Metric Commission, established in 1971, the Canadian Department of Weights & Measures (Ministry of Industry, Trade & Commerce) can order business to weigh, measure, and advertise in accordance with this system; it can impose fines of up to $5000, for violations and call upon an army of inspectors to keep a sharp eye out for transgressors. It also has the power to close down recalcitrant businesses, and even throw their disobedient owners in jail. Imagine, you can go to prison for selling a pound of cheese.

Forced metrication is an obvious violation of the rights of people to freely transact with one another on any commercial basis they choose. Although the Canadian Civil Liberties Association has been silent about this issue, metrication is a clear and present danger to our civil liberties, which encompass far more than rights to speech, drugs, sex, criminal procedures, and so on. Our civil liberties include, as well, the right to engage in "capitalist acts," whether measured in pounds or grains, inches or centimeters. People should have the right to sell by the handful if they can attract any customers that way. In the words of one metric protester, "Your freedom to measure is a measure of your freedom."

"NO, MADAM, WE NO LONGER USE A, B, C OR D FOR BRA CUP SIZES, WE'VE GONE METRIC. IT'S NOW CENTIBOOBS AND MILLIBOOBS."

Apart from this moral or philosophical problem, there are a host of economic fallacies in the Canadian metrication initiative.

- Despite arguments to the contrary urged by its proponents, metrication is not needed to promote international trade, nor will it have that effect. It is simply not true, as is claimed, that 90% or more of the world is either already on a metric standard, or soon to be converted. New Zealand, Australia and Britain are in varying stages of rethinking their initial enthusiasm with this system. In Japan, it is no longer illegal to use the ancient shuka ruler, nor the tatami and tsubo measurements for area. And in the U.S., PL96-86, enacted in 1979, specifically prohibits federal agencies from imposing, or even advocating metric conversion.

Metrication will also increase balance-of-payments deficits (for those who unwisely worry about such matters) in another way. Almost all metric scales used are produced elsewhere. The purchase of scales by local businesses will thus increase our import bill. Governments practically froth at the mouth every time an item is imported into their countries, and spend millions of advertising dollars telling citizens to "Buy Local." How can they then turn around and urge a program which will necessitate the importation of numerous expensive metric scales from abroad?

- The implicit premise underlying the international trade argument is that metrication will enhance standardization. But this is not true. A metric one-centimeter bolt on a Volkswagen need not interchange with one from a Toyota—even if they are of identical diameter—because of the number of threads per unit length. If different firms do not wish to make spare parts interchangeable, such standardization cannot come about merely through the introduction of metrication.

On the other hand, if standardization is desired, metric is not needed to accomplish it. Any item 10 inches long in Canada can be exactly duplicated as 25.4 centimeters in West Germany or 245 millimeters in Australia.

"WHY DOESN'T THE BUSINESS COMMUNITY FOLLOW THE GOOD EXAMPLE SET BY THE ILLICIT DRUG DEALERS AND USERS ?!! THEY ADOPTED THE METRIC SYSTEM WITH NO FUSS !"

- In a reasonable world, no responsible government would enact an expensive program—especially in these economically troubled times—without clear evidence that the benefits would more than offset the costs. Yet so far removed are we from rationality that numerous governments have carried on with this program without a shred of any such evidence.
- And the costs of metrication are very substantial! Replacement of a single supermarket produce scale will take several hundred dollars. The more complicated meat scale costs several thousand, secondhand, while the new model costs in the

low five figures, according to informed industrial sources. And since conversion costs more than replacement, the country's Imperial scales will have to be sold for scrap value, even though most are in perfectly good running order.

But this is only the tip of the iceberg. What is the total-cost estimate for conversion? Not too surprisingly, no such figure has been produced by our metric czars. But an authoritative U.S. study estimated costs for that country of between $40 and $100 billion.

"MR. POYANT, SOME NEWSPAPER'S ON THE PHONE. THEY WANT TO KNOW IF USING THE WORD, 'FORTNIGHT' IN A NEWS STORY IS A VIOLATION OF THE METRIC SYSTEM..."

These are only direct costs. We must also consider the lower national productivity during the 20-year replacement period it is likely to take to completely cram a different measuring system down our collective throats; the additional bankruptcies of marginal companies unable to adjust; the replacement costs for math, science and other school textbooks; the additional inventories of spare parts which must be carried; the necessity of junking perfectly good business, commercial and manufacturing implements, for which no spare parts are available.

- Given these costs, problems and difficulties, it is not surprising that many people, when given the choice, have overwhelmingly rejected coerced metrication.

Numerous retailers have attested that regular customers will drive to outside communities, where metric is not in effect, in order to do their shopping, if it is done on a state-wise basis. Customer outrage was so great in some cases, that local stores actually switched back to the Imperial system as soon as a year's delay in the forced march toward metric was announced.

- The moral, economic and cultural case against forced metrication is overwhelming. Why is it, then, that governments have set their feet firmly on this path, despite all evidence to the contrary? It does not appear that the answer lies in financial gain, nor even in political motivation. Indeed, it is more than likely that the government will lose votes over this issue.

Although this can only be speculative, the answer may be in what Friedrich Hayek has called the conceit of "rationalism" or "scientism": the idea that the human mind is capable of organizing an entire society from the top down, in complete disregard of institutions "which are the product of human purposes, but not human design." If this aesthetic or ethic of central planning is really what is behind the metrication movement, it will be very difficult to sway it by recourse to mere reason or evidence.

Which sounds better: "Give 'em an inch and they'll take a mile"? Or, "Give 'em (2.5) centimeters and they'll take (1.6) kilometers"? QED.

# Chapter 50
# The Cultural Appropriator

Did you ever wear a sombrero, and are not Mexican? Then you are a cultural appropriator, you heinous creature, you! Ditto for a sari, and are not Indian. Yalmica? Jewish. You are a monster. You are evil. You have appropriated the culture of downtrodden peoples, and thus exploited them. Opposition to cultural appropriation went so far at a politically correct university, that a free yoga class had to be cancelled. Not only did this constitute cultural appropriation, but, to add insult to injury, it was taught by, horrors!, a white woman. According to cancel culture, yoga was derived from cultures that have suffered oppression from toxic white males.

These people own their own culture. When you appropriate it, you steal it from them. You have misappropriated their property. You have stolen from them. Baaaad. Off to the pokey with the likes of you.

This at least that is the claim of woke cultural "progressive" (actually, regressive) Marxists who inveigh against cultural appropriation. I kid you not. There are actually people who believe in this bilge. Should we take them seriously? Yes, unfortunately. Jobs have been lost as a result of engaging in this "dastardly" practice, particularly on our social justice campuses.

The first thing to ask about this criticism, from the libertarian perspective, is does cultural appropriate amount to theft or trespass on private property rights? If a Chinese person wears a Viking hat, which he purchased from a willing seller (maybe even from a Frenchman), did the former rob anything owned by the latter? To ask this is to answer it. But I will supply the correct response in any case: of course not! The Swede does not own the hat; the Frenchman does, or, rather, did. He sold it to the Chinaman. From whom did the seller obtain this? He manufactured it himself; he did so from raw materials he dug up, or purchased from yet another vendor. Does the descendent of Vikings have a legitimate claim to all such head wear on the planet? It is difficult to answer this question in the affirmative. Thus, we conclude that the Chinese person engaged in cultural appropriation from the Scandinavians but was fully justified in so doing.


W. E. Block, *Defending the Undefendable III*,
https://doi.org/10.1007/978-981-16-3957-9_50

The point is, nothing that they properly own has been stolen from the "victim" of cultural appropriation. Thus, cultural appropriation is compatible with libertarianism. Since it is heartily and widely reviled, those who violate these tenets can be considered heroic.

So far we have only mentioned cases that irk the woke supporters of cultural appropriation. If dressing like a native American Indian by an Indian from the Asian subcontinent (or vice versa) is sufficient to commit this "crime," then so does the following:

All non-Austrians who listen to the music of Mozart.
All non-Jews who avail themselves of the Salk Vaccine, or benefit from the discovery that E = MC2, and other equations of that Jew, Einstein.
All non-black people who eat peanut butter.
All non-Arabs who utilize the concept of zero.

In a sense, the opposition to cultural appropriation is worse than the rejection of free trade. In the latter case, people can lose their jobs (they will tend to get other, better, ones), but that is a different matter. With cultural appropriation, no one becomes (temporarily) unemployed, and not even its harshest critics make any such accusation.

From whence, then, does this vitriolic opposition to cultural appropriation spring? From sheer bloody-mindedness. It arises out of a sense of pique, nothing more profound. What can we look forward to, if this movement increases, and is allowed to impose its will on innocents?

Here are some other arbitrary dislikes which may next come forward, with as much rhyme or reason:

Rejection of plain white clothing;
Plaid clothing; too multicultural.
Perhaps then, only white toxic males can be cultural appropriators?

"...I'LL BE HONEST WITH YOU, MR. LEGRAND,
THIS POEM OF YOURS,
'ROSES ARE RED
VIOLETS ARE BLUES
A LEAK IN MY WATERBED
HAS DAMPENED MY MUSE',
IS NOT WORTH \$2000;–\$750 IS THE BEST I CAN DO."

They still have their culture. You have emulated it, the highest form of flattery. But their culture remains with them. If you wear a sombrero you stole from a Mexican, then, yes, you are indeed guilty of a crime; theft. But this is not at all what the complaint amounts to. The social justice warriors will come down just as hard as the purchaser of this implement of clothing as someone who stole it (maybe even harder, who knows? After all, the robber, in their eyes, at least trashed the concept of private property rights, anathema to them, while the purchaser engaged in a "capitalist act between consenting adults.") They would still have plenty of sombreros and serapes and beans and rice with which to practice their culture.

Are not the Marxist cultural warriors hoist by their own petard? After all, Marx was a Jew from Germany. Therefore, according to the "logic" employed in this intellectual bedlam, only chosen people from this country should be allowed to utilize Marxism. All others are, wait for it, cultural appropriators.

The cultural appropriator (CA) has been reviled by all wokesters in good standing, by all those who oppose micro-aggressions, by all snowflakes, by all fine folk on the left side of the aisle.

Who is the CA? He (invariably it is a male, usually sporting white privilege, who engages, enjoys, partakes in, a practice created by a different cultural group. For example, if he wears a sombrero, a serape, or a poncho, or eats a burrito (even worse, cooks and sells one) he is CA from Mexicans. If he eats watermelon, or black-eyed peas, or shoots a 3 pointer in basketball, or sings rap "music," he is exploiting black culture. If he is not Jewish, but ingests or manufactures bagels, blintzes or gefilte fish, he is again guilty of this form of oppression.

Why is this bad? Our answer is that if you have to ask this question, you are a Neanderthal, a pervert, a weirdo, a racist, a white supremacist, a right-wing fascist, etc. Don't you realize that the *feelings* of blacks, Mexicans, Jews, other victims, will be hurt? And that hurt feelings are the be-all and end-all of the new politically correct dispensation, you unfeeling brute, you?

Now, yes, there is a question as to whether or not it is even possible to CA Germans for example. Is it alright for the rest of us to exult in the music of Bach, and Mozart, to eat Wienerschnitzel, to garnish this with sauerkraut, to engage in other activities that emanate from this country? After all, there are a lot of people who partake of white privilege, and it is unclear as to whether or not if a black or Mexican were to engage in these things it would constitute a rights violation. On the one hand, this is as clear and present a case of CA as can be imagined. On the other, while there is no doubt that when one type of ethnicity (whites, Europeans) engages in CA "against" some other ones (blacks, Hispanics) this is a case of micro-aggression. But when the shoe is on the other foot, when the member of the supposed downtrodden takes advantage of the products, life style, contribution of the exploiter, matters are far less clear. I leave this crucially important question of the ages to those more qualified to answer it. After all, I am a privileged white male, and thus any opinion I might have about this burning question (or indeed any other issue under the sun) must be counted as suspect. Who knows? I might be accused, horrors!, of "mansplaining."

But race and nationality are only the tip of the iceberg in so far as CA is concerned. There is also gender. In New Orleans, there are 5 K races in which everyone, without exception, wears a red dress. It is quite alright for women to utilize this product, but there are actual men, thousands of them, who adorn themselves in such garb. If this is not CA and hence disgusting, then nothing is. One must allow special dispensation for male homosexuals. If they wear red or any other color dresses, that is quite alright, if I correctly comprehend the ethics of CA. However, this does not apply to straight males. Thus, this 5 k race ought to be banned. On the other hand, if women dress as truck drivers, or stevedores, or construction workers, this, too, is CA; but it really does not count, since all men exploit all women and it is time it is long past time, that the fairer sex turn the tables on their gender counterparts. In like manner, if a male cooks, sews, darns, knits, takes up nursing, he is guilty of improperly appropriating female tasks. Have I got all of this straight? Probably not, given my genetic impairments; this isn't rocket science, but it is not altogether straightforward either.

A similar pattern applies to sexual preferences. If homosexual men dress up as drag queens, this is perfectly acceptable. Yes, it constitutes CA, but it violates no rights, for obvious reasons. But when evil heterosexual men engage in this practice it becomes per se despicable. No, wait, deplorable.

Since George Washington Carver, a black man invented the peanut (I exaggerate here, of course, but only somewhat), no white people should be allowed to eat any, nor spread peanut butter on their bread. No peanut butter and jelly sandwiches for the likes of them! On the other hand, if we follow this policy, non-whites would not be able to avail themselves of telescopes, the Salk Polio vaccine, dentistry, penicillin, computers, the music of Mozart and quite a few other things that make life worth living as well. Needless to say, we are precluded from even mentioning such considerations, lest the feelings of our friends on the left might be hurt.

If we decide that both men and women must refrain from CA from the other, females will get the short end of the stick. The fact is that men have invented and created many more items than women. Without CA, men will have to do without the far fewer following contributions of women: the car heater, the game "Monopoly," the fire escape, the life raft, residential solar heating, the medical syringe, the electric refrigerator, the ice-cream maker, the computer algorithm, ax, touch-tone telephone, solar cells, fiber optic cables, the dishwasher, wireless transmissions technology, CCTV, the paper bag, central heating, Kevlar, computer software, beer, circular saw, chocolate chip cookies (bless them for this!), liquid paper, the COBOL Computer Language, colored flare system, windshield wiper and nystatin. And what, pray tell, will women have to refrain from? Pretty much every other innovation under the sun.

At bottom the opposition to CA is really an attack on specialization and the division of labor. We *all* appropriate from each other, whether cultural (dress, music, dance, food) or not. When the rancher trades some beef to the farmer for corn, they each "appropriate" what the other has produced. When the pianist trades his craft to the artist in return for painting lessons, they are again "appropriating" the skill of the other. Norman Rockwell once painted a picture of the milkman and the pie man in front of their respective trucks, each chowing down on one of these products, and slurping on the other. In a bygone age, this illustrating comity, cooperation, the division of labor, the benefits of trade, friendship. But nowadays we know better. One, they were each exploiting the other, profiting from the other, and, two, you had better be sitting down when you read this, culturally appropriating each other.

Without such specialization and division of labor, some 99% of us would indubitably perish. Is this what the critics of CA wish? The death of most people on the planet? One fervently hopes that this is not the case. More reasonably, most of these people are simply economically illiterate. They do not realize that if we generalize from their opposition to people trading these contributions, cultural or not, with each other, the human race will be in dire straits.

# Chapter 51
# The Entrepreneur

Syndicalism is a system in which all the workers, together, own the factory, or the shop, or the farm. Given rampant political correctness, and hatred of capitalism by all and sundry, why do we not have more of that type of business organization in the free society? One would think that we would, given that there are so many people who are antagonistic to the ordinary authoritarian type firm, where the boss orders around his employees. There must be some reason why the syndicalist form of organization is rarely found when people are completely free to choose what type of business firm they will join.

As it happens, there are several reasons why traditional top-down hierarchical companies are more typical. But, before we discuss them, we ask, How does a firm get started in the first place? Suppose there was an economy consisting solely of independent producers; there was no hierarchy, no business firms, no corporations. No one bossed anyone else around (apart from the consumer wielding a thumbs up or thumbs down verdict on what all the one-man independents produced). How would someone be able to get up on his hind legs, and start the beginnings of the typical business we now see all around us?

Simple. All this entrepreneur needs to do is amass some cash. And how, pray tell, could he do that? All that is required is that he either earn more or spend less on consumer items; namely, pile up some savings, by depriving himself, at present, of desired goods and services he would otherwise have purchased. This more ambitious worker, perhaps no more skilled than any of his fellows, would then have the wherewithal with which to hire someone else. And, viola! The modern employer-employee firm was born. The point is that there is nothing particularly special about such a person. He certainly need not exploit anyone else in order to set up shop in this manner. All he need do is make a more attractive financial offer to one of this previous fellow self-employed workers, than the latter can earn on his own account. There would be no perpetrator, and no victim. Both parties would gain, at least in the ex-ante sense of anticipations, otherwise one or the other or both would refuse to enter into any such agreement.



W. E. Block, *Defending the Undefendable III*,
https://doi.org/10.1007/978-981-16-3957-9_51

What advantage would this two person firm now have? Specialization and the division of labor. The two of them working together, one bossing the other around, would be able to produce more than double of value that either could create solely on his own!

What, then, is the boss's contribution to the firm? Why are they better off with him, than without him and on their own? It is because he offers them three types of assistance.

First, there is timing. Let us suppose that from the point of time that the firm is set up, until the first product, say, furniture, rolls off the assembly line, is one year. During that period, the following must be accomplished: a plot of land must be found; a factory must be erected upon it; machinery must be purchased, as well as raw materials (wood, cloth, plastic, in this case); insurance must be sought. Without the entrepreneur, the workers, together, will have to put up the set up money, plus clothe and feed themselves for the duration. He, in effect gives them twelve months of time. Without him, they would have to dip into savings, which they may or may not have, and if the former, may not be willing to tap.

Second, there is risk-bearing. Suppose at the end of the year when the furniture is now available, no one wants to purchase it; or, it can only be sold at a price that does not at all defray the entire cost. Can the boss go back to his employees and say, "Sorry, I have bad news for you. Too few people wish to purchase our output. Remember that salary I paid you for the first year before any finished product was available? Well, please give back all or most of it, since the business has failed." No, the entrepreneur may not say anything of the sort to the workers. It is he, not they, who bears the risk of this type of failure.

And third, he is the one, usually, who initiates the entire process. He is the leader. He tries to choose the team that can work with maximum efficiency. He is the one who first eschewed his single producer status, and hired his competitor at a wage greater than the profits the latter could garner on his own.

Yet, he is reviled by all and sundry as a boss, as an exploiter, as a profiteer, etc. No, he is a hero.

# Chapter 52
# The Self-Dealer

Governments are typically concerned about mergers. Why? They subscribe to the notions that bigness is badness and are even more suspicious of such arrangements when they lead to industrial concentration. Both of these views are highly problematic. Large size is hardly per se problematic insofar as gigantic firms have made signal contributions to our economic well-being. Concentration, too, is a non-problem, given that the very concept is arbitrary and capricious. Do we look at paper clips only, or all office supplies? Is the industry to be defined as cars only, or all modes of transportation? Obviously, concentration will be far higher in the former than the latter cases, and, yet, there is no proper objective way to define an industry. No firm can ever tell, beforehand, with the best will in the world, whether or not it is ever guilty of "monopolizing." A similar problem arises geographically. There is only one restaurant in a small town. Is it "hogging up" the industry or not? How about if the next village is 10, 50 or 100 miles away? Again, there is no objective method to make any such determination. Legislation is not justified if, even in principle, guilt or innocence cannot clearly be determined when all the facts are in. Anti-trust law fails this test, miserably.

One of the pet peeves of the anti-trusters is self-dealing. This is sometimes defined as per se fraudulent. For example: "a trustee, attorney, corporate officer, or other fiduciary that consists of taking advantage of their position in a transaction and acting in their own interests rather than in the interests of the beneficiaries of the trust, corporate shareholders, or their clients." Or this: "when a fiduciary acts in their own best interest in a transaction, rather than in the best interest of their clients. It represents a conflict of interest and an illegal act." Well, yes, under definitions of this sort, this practice is a per se crime and ought to be prohibited by law.

But this is a stupendously unjustified way to look at the matter. Etymologically, nothing of the sort follows. All it should mean is that there is indeed a conflict of interest set up, wherein the fiduciary could commit fraud, or, even, is now in a better position to do so. Those who oppose such situations should be more linguistically honest and characterize what they (properly!) oppose as "unjustified self-dealing"


W. E. Block, *Defending the Undefendable III*,
https://doi.org/10.1007/978-981-16-3957-9_52

or "fraudulent self-dealing." It should be an empirical matter as to whether or not a trustee actually takes advantage of his position or not. As to being in a better position to commit financial shenanigans, this applies to earning a Ph.D. in finance, or a CPA degree or being a book keeper for 20 years. One would scarcely want to prohibit such attainments merely because they better enable people to engage in monetary swindles.

We are all in positions of interest conflicts. The employee has an interest in goofing off, using company time for personal tasks, as long as he can get away with it. Should we ban all employment contracts?

The implication is that financial and non-financial enterprises should not be allowed to coalesce. Should a bank, for example, and a retail establishment be allowed to merge? Or should this only be allowed to occur after the imposition of severe restrictions? The reason for such large-scale government intervention would appear to be fear of an alliance of a financial institution and a non-financial corporation, and the increased self-dealing thereby made possible.

Self-dealing has also been defined as a process in which a conglomerate uses its trust company to unfairly benefit related firms even though this unduly risks its depositors' money; or in which a parent company uses capital from its subsidiary to finance its own dealings, regardless of the best interests of the subsidiary's depositors. Based on the opposition to the merger vociferously made by many commentators, there would appear to be something particularly objectionable about a merger between a financial and a non-financial corporation. There are several difficulties with such a contention.

First, the concern is too general and overstated. Any merger may conceivably result in one party misusing the assets of another. There is thus no reason for the state to limit its misgivings to just those corporate purchases which combine financial and non-financial holdings. Of course, if two non-financial corporations form one larger one, no depositor's funds are put at risk; but there is as much of a public interest in protecting the property of shareholders as there is in protecting that of depositors.

Second, the concern is biased. Critics are troubled by the prospect of the conglomerate pillaging the depositors' property. But the reverse, which they ignore, is equally plausible. The history of economics is littered with sorrowful tales of bank failures. Who is to say that in order to ward off such an occurrence in the future no financial institution would engage in a raid on the non-financial membership of its conglomerate?

Third, the property of depositors may be ravaged not only by the takeover of a non-financial conglomerate, but by any one shareholder in the trust company or bank who attains a measure of control. To obviate such a scenario, the government has enacted legislation placing control over banks and has enmeshed trust companies in a welter of restrictions which limit the ability of owners to engage in fraudulent "sweetheart" deals. However, the government has also organized a scheme of mandatory deposit insurance. This sharply diminishes the creditor's incentive to insist upon the writing of efficient contracts to preclude such fraudulent behavior.

In the absence of deposit insurance and other government activities that retard marketplace incentives, if the investment community felt that a merger between financial and non-financial corporations would unacceptably increase the risk of improper self-dealing, the depositors would desert any such trust company or bank in droves. This would make it infeasible to engage in such a merger in the first place. Were markets allowed to work, there would be no need for any special government vigilance on behalf of the depositors against a merger with a non-financial business concern.

One solution is to recognize that legislation which at present protects the depositor from other would-be predators within the financial corporation will presumably serve as well against any threat from a non-financial source. More radically, public policy should contemplate the removal of the first unwise government regulation, subsidized deposit insurance, which deludes depositors into thinking they are safer than they actually are. Since we have seen there is nothing unique about a financial-non-financial corporate merger, the brouhaha about self-dealing may thus be interpreted as a general criticism of the propriety of mergers in the private sector. The visible hand of the government is far less able to protect the public against harmful and untoward mergers than is the invisible hand of the marketplace.

# Chapter 53
# The Religious Broadcaster

The Canadian Radio-television & Telecommunication Commission has been holding hearings to determine whether or not religious organizations should be allowed to broadcast on the Canadian air waves.

This is a crucially important decision. It has profound cultural, spiritual, religious and sociological effects on all Canadian citizens. It represents a major effort by the government to extend its power over the religious freedoms of Canadians. It brings into serious question the previously assumed separation of church and state. The implications of this decision will stretch well into the future.

All the more reason, then, not to allow a small group of people (five CRTC commissioners) to dictate such a choice to an entire nation.

The weakness in the present system of deciding such questions is easily seen. Suppose religious institutions were not allowed to publish newspapers, magazines and journals without government permission. Suppose, that is, that the top circulation Canadian religious publications had first to convince a Canadian Newspaper, Magazine and Journal Commission of the worthiness of their endeavors, of the public interest inherent in their periodicals, of the desires of millions of people that they be in existence—just to mention several of the arguments put before the CRTC. (Such a list would include the *L'Oratoire*, the *Anglican*, the *Canadian Churchmen*, the *Catholic Register*, the *Communicate*, the *Canadian Messenger*, the *Canadian Baptist*, the *Diocesan Times*, the *Living Message*, the *United Church Observer*, the *Canadian Jewish News*, the *Mennonite Mirror*, the *Presbyterian Record*, and the *Pentecostal Testimony*.) Imagine the hue and cry, the sense of moral indignation and outrage, that would ensue were the churches subjected to such a humiliation.

In actual point of fact, the religious periodical publication industry is in a far healthier state than indicated even by the above long and impressive listing. Ulrich's International Periodicals Directory lists no less than 60 tightly printed pages of religious periodical titles, equivalent to roughly 2700 separate entities. Many of course originate in other countries, but all are available to interested Canadians.



W. E. Block, *Defending the Undefendable III*,
https://doi.org/10.1007/978-981-16-3957-9_53

"But, but, splutter, splutter," say the opponents of a competitive enterprise in broadcast journalism, "a free market cannot function for the airwaves. People cannot be allowed the freedom to bid for broadcasting rights." And for the following reasons:

> The electromagnetic spectrum is not the sort of thing that can be privately owned, as can newspapers, magazines and journals. It is a public good, and must of necessity be administered by the public authorities.

"... ON THE CONTRARY, REV. THURBER, THE COMMISSION HAS BEEN MORE THAN LENIENT. WE GAVE YOU 90 DAYS TO FURNISH US WITH YOUR GOD'S ADDRESS AND PHONE NUMBER AND YOU COME HERE AND TELL ME YOU DON'T KNOW."

This argument is actually bolstered by early experience in radio. In the late 1920s, when radio was in its infancy, different stations would actually encroach on each other's frequencies, bringing disorganization and chaos to the entire enterprise.

But this was actually due to the failure to set proper boundaries on the spectrum between the frequencies of neighboring broadcasters, and to ensure broadcast property rights to those who had first "homesteaded" the airwaves. Without clearly defined and protected property rights, no industry can function properly. All that was needed in the 1920s, one century ago, was to bring lawfulness to this industry.

In the event, the government did finally set frequency boundaries, but also accorded to itself all broadcast rights—only doling these out on a temporary and periodic basis in the form of licenses.

Luckily for our relatively free society, the government did not seize similar power in the print industry. But the arguments are very similar. If the government can demand control over radio and T.V. on the ground that chaos will ensure without clearly defined and protected property rights, it can do so in the print (or any other) industry with equal logic. For surely newspapers and magazines could not be published if they were free to grab each other's scarce and valuable paper, ink, printing presses, and other factors of production.

> There aren't enough radio and T.V. frequencies to go around to satisfy everyone who wants one.

Welcome to the real world—one of economic scarcity. This is precisely the definition of any economic good or service: something which people want more of—at a zero price—than is available. The answer to this problem – when it arises in the case of limited ship and sealing wax, snails and puppy dogs, is to allow a price to be charged, so that the scarce supply can be rationed amongst the more numerous demanders.

It is a basic axiom of economics that there exists an equilibrium price, at which point the amount demanded will equal the amount supplied. This holds true for every other good or service, and would obtain as well in the market for broadcast rights as well. And if such a market were allowed into existence, no individual, group or firm which could afford a radio or T.V. station would have to do without.

The identical problem, moreover, has been solved in the print journalism field. There is not enough newsprint, paper, ink, typographical equipment—to say nothing of the highly skilled labour necessary to gather the news, work the machinery, and the talent necessary to co-ordinate the whole enterprise—to give a print periodical to everyone who wants one.

These scarce goods are rationed to the highest bidder, in the absence of a Newspaper Commission to oversee the whole process. There is no earthly reason this market system could not work for the electronic spectrum as well—without CRTC interference.

The above analysis holds true for AM and FM radio and for VHF television. But the situation is vastly different on the UHF television band. There, according to informal sources in the industry, only some 2% of all available bands are in actual use. This means that any religious broadcaster who wanted one could, at least theoretically, have a UHF band assigned to him—without displacing anyone else.

The "scarcity" argument is at least relevant to the VHF band (along with all other goods and services of an economic nature). But it does not even apply to the UHF spectrum at all.

> Allowing religious broadcasting would set a precedent for other special interest groups to seek similar treatment.

This argument has such power that even some champions of the rights of free speech of religious persons) are unsure about this. But surely the proper answer to this argument is to deny it any validity whatsoever. Of course other special interests will also seek broadcast outlets. And why ever should they not? Special interests—including groups representing virtually every stripe of opinion in politics, economics, philosophy, psychology and religion—have attained their own print outlets. There are newspapers, magazines, journals and other periodicals in glorious profusion which give vent to their views, with no obvious harm to our society. Why should it be any different for the electronic media?

> The needs of a modern pluralistic society can best be met under the guidance of the CRTC, which will ensure that all programming must be balanced and in the public interest; that no one group can own an entire station, to do with what it will.

But why should the very disparate views of a modern pluralistic society be forced to pass muster before a group of five bureaucrats? This is not at all consistent with true pluralism, and has not been found necessary in the print media.

Imagine if this "balance" doctrine were applied to the churches themselves. It would mean that each denomination would have to "balance" its program, so as to include representation of all other denominations, and even all other religions. After all, is it "fair" that the Anglicans feature only Anglican programs at their services? Shouldn't they be forced to give "equal time" to the Jews, Hindus, Catholics and Lutherans? And vice versa of course.

This doctrine is ludicrous, dangerous, and ultimately destructive to all our free institutions. For any of the organs of society—our factories, our schools, our sports arenas, our hospitals, our recreational facilities, as well as our churches—are open to the charge of specializing in one or a few things, of being "unbalanced." Must we insist on a bland sameness in all our conduct?

Hardly. Our interest in diversity may best be served by means of free competition in ideas; by allowing a veritable tower of babel of different voices—not by insisting that each and every person or institution soberly "balance" its views, so as to represent an amalgam of all possible shades of opinion on every issue.

True "balance" may best be served by allowing people to set up their own electronic soap boxes to put forth their own views. A sort of Hyde Park Corner of the airwaves.

There is no Canadian Newspaper, Magazine and Journal Commission with the responsibility to impose an artificial order on balance on the newspaper and magazine industry. Nor is one needed. And yet here we find one of Canada's most glorious examples of free-spirited and open-ended exchange of opinion. (It is more than just passing curious, however, that newspaper editorialists—and others who are usually protective of the niceties of free speech—have been among the most vociferous opponents of expanding the freedom they themselves enjoy to the electronic media.)

We must conclude, then, that the case for continuing the CRTC as the ultimate authority of the nation's airwaves is extremely weak. It is an affront to the religious people of the nation who seek to purchase broadcasting stations, and to all those who hold the rights of free speech most dear.

# Chapter 54
# The Motor Vehicle Department Derider

I got a notice the other day that it was time to renew my driver's license.

So I showed up at the motor vehicle bureaucracy within 24 h. Arriving at about 1:00 p.m. I was appalled at the gigantic line-up. "There must have been at least 40 people in the queue, waiting patiently with resignation etched deeply on their faces.

I waited for about 10 min, and would you believe it, only two people were served during this time. There were about a dozen wickets, but only three clerks were on duty. The thought that impressed itself most forcefully on my mind was that if this were a bank, a supermarket or a department store, they would have hired additional staff for the luncheon rush. With so many people working nowadays, they would be open evenings and weekends too, not just from 8:30 a.m. to 4:30 p.m. during the week. If not, they'd soon be out of business. Muttering to myself about "public servants" being a contradiction in terms, I decided to kill some time by visiting the local book stores, record shops and the beautiful gardens in the neighborhood. I could have gone back to my office, but it was about a mile away, and I didn't want to make two trips since I was on foot, because of parking difficulties in this area.

I breezed back at 2:15 p.m., after calling the office to let them know of my plight. Much to my amazement, just as I got there, I noticed that two people who were at the end of the line when I was there earlier, were just leaving. Appalling—over an hour for a simple transaction. Much to my consternation, there was still a large line-up, still waiting politely. True, there were only some 20 people now, but I must have timed it almost exactly right, because by the time I reached the head of the queue, at 3 p.m. after only 45 min of twiddling my thumbs, the line had elongated again, to its initial 40-person roughly 60-min length by my calculations.

Actually, the wait wasn't so bad. Indeed, the time passed rather quickly, because I was writing this chapter while waiting, venting my spleen as I crept forward an inch at a time.


W. E. Block, *Defending the Undefendable III*,
https://doi.org/10.1007/978-981-16-3957-9_54

"MAKES YOU WANTA THROW UP, DON'T IT?!!"

The actual form filling and picture taking took about 2 min and I was out of there before 3:05, counting myself lucky that I wouldn't have to go through this mess for another 5 years. The person right before me, however, wasn't so lucky. He forgot to bring some piece of paper or other and will have to return on another day. Nor will he be able to credit his wait today for his next visit. He'll have to do it all over again. I was fortunate. Although at the last minute I had nightmares that they would seize my notes for this column, read them, and say, "Aha, an enemy of the Motor Vehicle Branch. You'll have to come back on another day."

Too right, I really am an enemy of the present system. I realize full well that we can't let just anyone drive around on the roads, and that we need some sort of procedure to exclude dangerous drivers. But why couldn't at least the administrative part of this task be privatized (this should apply to the entire system; I wrote an entire book on that proposal), with a commission paid for each person served. Then, people would be treated like valuable customers, instead of like an annoyance, as in the post office, motor license office, and other such government-run bureaucracies.

It is a complete puzzle to me why people just wait around on these interminably long lines without objecting. Their behavior resembles nothing as much as the long queue one sees behind the Iron Curtain, only there, since the state bureaucracy runs the entire economy, this applies to just about everything under the sun, including groceries. Perhaps this is because like death and taxes, people mistakenly believe that public sector management of important services is inevitable. If there were any decency on the part of these bureaucrats, they could at the very least have supplied chairs and a number system instead of a standing queue. It does old folk no good to stand virtually still on their feet for long periods. Certainly, market forces would have led in this direction, through the profit and loss system, which is inoperable in this sector of the economy.

# Chapter 55
# The Sunday Shopper

Sunday shopping prohibitions may not rank up there with inflation, the energy crisis or the struggle over the constitution, but they are a distinct annoyance to millions of residents. And what's more, they are completely unjustified.

The usual argument on their behalf is that "Sunday is the Lord's day." This is mistaken, however, as Jews and Seventh Day Adventists celebrate Saturday and Moslems view Friday as the holy day. Moreover, there is simply no need to compel the entire society to refrain from commerce on the Sabbath just because some people, even a majority, want to celebrate this day in more quiet pursuits. Surely churchgoers can live their own way of life without imposing it upon all others?

W. E. Block, *Defending the Undefendable III*,
https://doi.org/10.1007/978-981-16-3957-9_55

Then there is the claim that without such legislation, shopkeepers and, in their turn, their employees, would be forced, if only by economic factors, to remain open on Sundays despite their own personal wishes in the matter.

There are several grounds upon which to object to the foregoing. First, this is not in keeping with the little evidence available on the subject. Far from supporting the law, most small merchants have been loud in their opposition. Secondly, while some employees may not wish to work on weekends or evenings, others may prefer to do so. Department stores usually hire additional help for the Christmas rush: there is no reason to believe they will not be able to attract adequate numbers of willing employees on Sundays should they be so disposed. Thirdly, and more basically, this is exactly what is meant by aphorisms such as "consumer sovereignty" or "the customer is always right." In a market economy, it is, and should be, the buying public that calls the tune, at least to a significant degree. Retailers who do not wish to dance to this tune are either in the wrong business or voluntarily agree to earn less profits than full service to the public would entail. A law which prohibits Sunday store opening is an attempt to protect some unwilling merchants from the needs and desires of their customers.

"MR. JOHNSON, I'M AFRAID THE OPERATION TO REMOVE THAT PART OF YOUR WIFE'S BRAIN THAT CAUSES 'COMPULSIVE SHOPPING' HAS NOT PROVEN SUCCESSFUL, SHE KEEPS ASKING FOR HER 'VISA CARD'."

The argument that it would be all but impossible to attract workers on Sundays, moreover, is fallacious. Employers pay time and a half and even double time to attract employees for the midnight to 8 a.m. shift. They could do so, if needed, for a single day of the week.

Sunday shopping laws, like many of the other commercial enactments of government, are an assault on the freedom of individuals garbed in the cloak of "the public interest." Surely the best way to determine whether people want to shop on Sunday and whether merchants want to earn the profits associated with serving the public on those occasions, is to allow people the freedom to make these choices. The Sunday Shopping Law is based on a very peculiar idea of what a consumer is: namely, a person intelligent enough to elect a government but who needs a law to tell him when he should buy his groceries.

# Chapter 56
# The Business License Rejecter

The name of a certain city in North America shall not be given, in order to save its inhabitants from embarrassment in their leadership. A ladies' wear retailer sought a license to do business. He was denied. The embattled storekeeper vowed to fight city hall. He applied to do business selling bankruptcy stock on a discount basis. But he wanted to remain in operation only for a limited time, and then move on.

The city council refused to grant permission for this, on the grounds that he would harm other stores which serve the public the entire year-round. "We have a reasonable cause for refusal," said one of these politicians. "We have a responsibility to our business community and to our residents. Businesses here have been serving the people for 12 months a year. Now this firm wants to come in at the top opportune time and take the cream of the crop and then take off."

This is a very unfortunate turn of events, and for numerous reasons.

Why should the city council make invidious comparisons between those who "serve the people" all year through and those who wish to do so just a few days or weeks per year? Cannot people "serve the public" on a part-time basis? Where is it engraved in stone that business must be conducted 365 days annually, or not at all? Why should people be prohibited from engaging in mutually beneficial trades, on however many or few days it suits them?

According to the logic (or illogic) of this city council argument, seasonal industries such as sales of ice cream from push carts should be prohibited. People should not be allowed to sell home heating fuels in the winter only, nor sell Christmas trees in the first few weeks of December alone. Churches will not be able to hold bingo games only on Friday nights, and Mardi Gras would have to be held all during the year – not on a once a year basis for a week or so. As well, this would be the end of touring symphony orchestras, traveling circuses, rock concerts, visiting lecturers and other part-time or seasonal events.

For do not those special occasion business "skim of the cream"? Why allow Santa Claus to "skim off" charity for the destitute during Christmas, when other charitable organizations "serve the people for 12 months a year"?


W. E. Block, *Defending the Undefendable III*,
https://doi.org/10.1007/978-981-16-3957-9_56

This legislative finding of the nameless city council is so perverse, it calls into question the whole idea of licensing businesses.

First of all, this practice, for whatever reason, is an infringement on human liberties. People have a right to engage in trade on any mutually agreeable basis, and a licensing requirement is an infringement on that human right.

Some pundits claim that licensing is a means of protecting the public against unscrupulous businessmen. But a certification system would do just as much to protect the public, without violating the rights of anyone to engage in business. (Under licensing, those deemed unsuitable may not practice at all; under certification, unsuitable candidates may engage in business, but cannot display the seal of approval issued by the board of certification.) In any case, the licensing scheme in this benighted city had nothing to do with protecting the consumer public. Its purpose was specifically to protect local businessmen against competition from this part-timer. (This is the way most licensing schemes work out in practice, pious platitudes about the "public good" notwithstanding.)

This specific decision must be revoked immediately, and our blind adherence to the institution of business licensing must be brought into serious question, and reconsideration.

Sometimes it is characterized as a "certification of need." The idea here is that some businesses are "needed," and others are not. In the former case, if there are no restaurants or pharmacies in a small town, then there is a "need" for them, and a new merchant will be allowed to enter the market. In the latter case, in the opinion of tin-pot economic dictators, customers are already fully served, and there is no "need" for any new entrants. One can just imagine a central planner of this ilk telling Henry Ford there is no "need" for a horseless carriage. "We already have a sufficient number of carriages with horses," he might say.

Under the free enterprise systems, the issue of whether or not there is any "need" for a new business concern to enter the field is decided automatically. There is no barrier to entry. If the newcomer can earn sufficient profits, there must have been a "need" for him. If not, then not. But there is no call for any third party to make this determination in advance by issuing a "certificate of need" or refraining from so doing.

# Chapter 57
# The Banker

Bankers are cordially hated, and all too often, not too cordially, by all those who suffer a foreclosure from this institution. Perennial "victims" of "banksters" are found in the agricultural sector of the economy.

To some farmers, especially in financially difficult times, the bank is an alien, an enemy. The banker is seen as interested in seizing his pound of flesh: in cold-bloodedly foreclosing on the farmer in trouble, and selling off his land, cattle and machinery. And, when we also consider that the banker has charged as much interest as the traffic would bear, the case against him is seemingly complete. The bankers and his minions must be opposed with all the force at the farmer's command.

This sentiment has led to interference with foreclosure on farms. Neighbors of a bankrupt farmer will gather from miles around in their tractors, and deter potential bidders from the foreclosure sale. Instead, they will bid pennies for the agricultural implements in an attempt to keep the real value of the mortgaged collateral out of the banker's hands. Afterwards, they will turn over the proceeds from a later sale at market values to the unfortunate farmer. In that way, they can at least keep the proceeds out of the grasping hands of the banks.

Governments, world-wide, have stepped in so as to ameliorate the plight of the impecunious agriculturalist. Receivership proceedings have been slowed down in order to give targets reasonable time to work out their difficulties. More radically limitations have been place on the right of banks to foreclose on farmers. Provisions have been put in place allowing the agrarian to appeal in court against any attempted foreclosure even when mortgage payments are in serious arrears. The goal is to keeping family farmers on the land. Often, these laws allow the cessation of mortgage payments at least temporarily.

Although these initiatives sound as if they were in the interest of most farmers, they are not. Nor will they benefit the consumer, nor the nation at large. What are the facts involved in this case?

Far from being the blood-suckers depicted by their detractors, a competitive banking industry is actually a great benefactor of the economy. The widow with her


W. E. Block, *Defending the Undefendable III*,
https://doi.org/10.1007/978-981-16-3957-9_57

small amount of money, the schoolchild with his savings, the businessman, those who maintain checking deposits in financial institutions, none of us are in a position to check the financial probity of borrowers. We do not have the time, nor the expertise, nor yet sufficient funds to make it worthwhile to obtain the requisite skills. Were it not for the happy intermediations by the bank community, depositors would be unable to obtain any interest income on their savings. Loans from them would be cut to a trickle.

But, if the banks are to be able to serve in this role, and pay interest to their depositors, they must ensure that their borrowers are able to repay their debts.

That is where the second great service provided by the banks to society comes in. In their search for reliable borrowers, the banks act toward the economy as does the bloodstream with regard to the body. In a healthy bio-system, the blood carries nutrients and oxygen to where they are most needed: to the stomach when digesting, to the muscles when running. In much the same way, by seeking out reliable custodians of funds, the banks promote some business ventures, discourage others.

But bankers, unlike healthy automatically operating blood cells, make mistakes. When they do so, they misallocate resources. The beauty of an open, competitive market system, however, is that the scope of banking depends on past success. Those institutions able to accurately assess the reliability of business can earn profits, grow and expand. Those unable to do so, or less able, earn less: They must contract, or, in extreme cases, close their doors.

To err, after all, is human. All creatures on this side of the Garden of Eden are subject to imperfectability. This system, then, is not flawless, but one which continually reduces error by penalizing it. This is the advantage of private enterprise banking over its complete lack, or any alternative institution.

What happens, then, when banks are not allowed to foreclose on a customer unable to repay his loans? It does not much matter whether this is due to government failure to uphold the rules of bankruptcy, or in the face of active farmer opposition. If the prohibition is general and applies to all borrowers, then the depositors are the first losers. They can no longer receive interest returns. They will be less inclined than otherwise to lend to the farmer, as intermediated by the banking sector.

But, if the prohibition is specific, and limited to farming, then the losses will be mainly confined to these two sectors. For such an enactment sends a clear message to bankers: If you lend to any other industries, your loans will be as safe as your expertise can arrange. But, if you are foolish enough to entrust your depositors' money (and thereby your own reputation) to farmers, you risk unpaid interest, and principal as well. It is as if farmers were suddenly infected with a virus of incompetence. Lending institutions would tend to avoid them, other things being equal.

The problem with this Draconian approach, of course, is that all farmers will be branded with the same tar brush: the good risks as well as the bad. It is no great loss to society if poor farmers fail to obtain loans. By definition, the money in question will be more productive if lent elsewhere. But when the most efficient agricultural enterprises are refused credits, on the grounds that, even if successful, they will still later be able to evade payments, this has several very unfortunate consequences.

Food production will be reduced, as agriculture is limited to self-finance. The value of farmland will plummet. The costs of agricultural products will rise, further impoverishing all consumers, and especially harming the poor. Imports may have to rise, causing needless and inefficient foreign dependency, and further exacerbating our international financial situation.

It is easy to see why the inefficient farmer might be tempted to violate the property rights of depositors and their agents, the banks. But the efficient farmer, the general consumer, and the overall economy will all be harmed by laws which hem in the rights of banks to protect money with which they have been entrusted.

We can generalize from the above. The same considerations apply to all sectors of the economy, not just agriculture. Also, the above is written on the assumption that the banking industry is part of the free enterprise system. If there is a "too big to fail" philosophy when it comes to banking, or if there are bailouts, then all bets are off in this regard.

# Part IX
# Sports

# Chapter 58
# The Booster

What is the case, first, in opposition to boosters who pay college student-athletes under the table? These athletes sign a contract precluding them from taking any pay whatsoever, apart from meals, defrayment of transportation costs, and other incidentals clearly specified. If they violate this bond, they are in danger of losing their eligibility status. Thus, anyone who offers them funds, surreptitiously, is guilty of suborning a contract violation. Voluntary agreements are the bedrock of a free society. If people are free to set them aside without compunction, to that degree trust, the glue that holds a commercial society together, will fray.

Now consider the argument in favor of boosters who pay college student-athletes in this under the table manner. Virtually all of these contracts with the relevant universities are invalid in the first place. Many of them are with public universities, agents of the government. Murray N. Rothbard famously stated: "if you wish to know how libertarians regard the State and any of its acts, simply think of the State as a criminal band, and all of the libertarian attitudes will logically fall into place." Are contracts with criminals valid? Of course not. Therefore the agreements the student-athletes made with their public universities should be of no legal moment. What about private universities? Most of them take massive amounts of government money, support that organization completely and thus should be viewed as in league with statists. There are only a handful of fully private universities (Grove City College, Hillsdale, Christendom College, Liberty University, Ana Maria). With those, and with regard to those only, would it be illicit for a booster to offer, and for a student-athlete to receive under the table money, contravening the contract made with this type of university.

Then there is the issue of fairness. College athletes, particularly football players, but, also, a few others such as those who inhabit the basketball court, bring millions in revenues to universities. In return they get what? A four year college education which in all too many cases is totally wasted upon them. Many are the experiences of these young men (female sports do not impact the bottom line in any such way) who cannot benefit from their classes since they are literally illiterate. So, instead of



W. E. Block, *Defending the Undefendable III*,
https://doi.org/10.1007/978-981-16-3957-9_58

normal courses, they take those in sociology, queer studies, feminist studies, black studies, and other types of grievance studies (where with but few exceptions reading and writing are not required), as well in basket weaving types of offerings, as well as in "education" where they learn how to teach people skills such playing ring-around rosy. They are all too often assigned tutors who "help" them with exams which they are not, for the most part, allowed to fail.

Is this fair to these young men? Of course not. True, they would not take on these jobs were they not the best opportunities they thought were open to them. But the authorities in charge of the rules determining these contracts are reprehensible in not paying these athletes a fair wage for a fair day's (and evening's) work. Again, if it were a private cartel treating the competitors in any such manner, the libertarian could offer no objection. However, private cartels of this sort tend to break up both from internal and external contradictions. In the former case, institutions of higher learning would be led by an "invisible hand" to compete with each other by raising the level of hidden payments. In the latter, new entrants would tend to come into the market to scoop up these young men now being "paid" far less than their contribution to scholarly revenues. But governmental restrictions prevent this from occurring.

Why are the powers that be able to keep this farce going for so long? It is because of this fetish of amateurism; that there is something underhanded about being paid to do a job. And/or, sports is not really work. We saw this for many years in the Olympics, where professional sportsmen were banned. Unhappily, this spirit is still alive and well on college campuses. Hopefully, the day will come when universities borrow a leaf from how the Olympics now treats professional athletes. Until that day, we shall have to content ourselves with rooting for the booster, who makes under the table payments to those who inhabit the playing fields of universities.

Nor can we avoid the racial element of this government interference with the free enterprise system. College football and basketball team members are disproportionately African-American. They are "paid" far less than they would otherwise obtain under laissez-faire capitalism. Exploiting young black men in this manner constitutes real, objectionable, racism.

# Chapter 59
# The NBA-NFL-MLB Eliminator

The NFL, MLB and the NBA, along with several other sports leagues, have now gone full woke. The helmets in the National Football League are now adorned with politically correct verbiage. The National Basketball Association arenas indicate that "Black Lives Matter." The uniforms of players in Major League Baseball are decorated in a similar manner. The names of black people killed by police are to be seen everywhere a ball is thrown or caught.

One difficulty with all of this is that it falsely depicts racism of the constabulary. True, African Americans constitute only some 13% of the population, and are killed by cops at a much higher rate than that, about 25%, but they commit over 50% of street crime such as homicides and robberies; this hardly indicates racism against blacks. Indeed the very opposite would appear more correct. In like manner, men proportionately come into contact with police on the street far more than women, and are killed by them to a far greater degree. Does this indicate sexism? Of course not, no more than the former statistic signifies anti-black racism.

Then there is the fact that for every African American killed by police, there is a large multiple whose lives are ended by members of the same community. Yet, black on black crime is nowhere mentioned by any of these athletes. One wonders why only some black lives matter, but not others.

Let us forget about these anomalies. Instead, let us focus on the many consumers who wish to feed their addiction for viewing sports directly into their veins, without any accompaniment at all, in any direction, from politics. How can the customer be served, if these major leagues have been made fully owned subsidiaries of left-wing politicos?

In the free society, the answer to this question would be immediate and obvious: new sports leagues would be created which focus on main-lining their product, shorn of any and all political accoutrements.

Indeed, there is precedence for this sort of thing. The American Football League operated from 1960 until 1970 (remember Joe Namath?) when it merged with its rival, the NFL. Similarly the NBA united with its competitor, the American



W. E. Block, *Defending the Undefendable III*,
https://doi.org/10.1007/978-981-16-3957-9_59

Basketball Association. The ABA's four most successful teams, the Denver Nuggets, the Indiana Pacers, the New York (later Brooklyn) Nets and the San Antonio Spurs are still functioning in the merged league.

Will this occur at present? Not too likely? Why not? It is due to government interference in the free enterprise system. How so? Various political jurisdictions subsidize the NFL and the NBA regarding their stadiums. Under a full free enterprise system, nothing of the sort would occur.

Assume that most sports fans do not at all relish having wokesterism shoved down their throats as they watch their teams at play. Then the politically correct cave-in of the owners of the football and basketball teams would bear real risks. For a new league would likely pop up and bid for this sports real estate on better than even terms, since consumer "sovereignty" would be financing them.

LeBron James and his cohorts are benefiting from sports socialism. Before we give them any credit at all for their virtue signaling, we should not forget the supine cave in of the NBA to the Chinese, in the aftermath of Houston Rockets general manager Daryl Morey's support for freedom for the Hong Kong people.

# Chapter 60
# The Olympic Drug Taker

Canada's Ben Johnson was stripped of his gold medal for the 100-metre dash in the 1988 Seoul Olympics. According to his coach, Charlie Francis, this instance of drug taking is only the tip of the sports iceberg. Numerous other Canadian athletes have been implicated in the use of anabolic steroids, and world-class athletes from several other countries have been implicated. Other high-profile Olympic drug takers include Lance Armstrong (USA), 2000, biking; Luiza Galiulina (Uzbekistan), 2012, gymnast; Marion Jones (USA), 2000, sprinter; many members of the Russian team, 2012, 2014 and 2016; Nicklas Backstrom (Sweden), 2014, hockey; Andreea Raducan (Romania), 2000, gymnast; Tyson Gay (USA), 2012, sprinter; Ross Rebagliati (Canada), 1998, snow-boarder; Johann Muhlegg (Spain), 2002, cross-country skier.

The main reaction on the part of leading sports authorities is a call for a "war" on muscle-building medications.

There are several shortcoming with this approach. For one thing, there is the matter of arbitrariness. Why is it that anabolic steroids are banned while other performance enhancing drugs such as cortisone and Xylocaine, are allowed? Even aspirin, for that matter, is a performance-enhancing drug.

For another, who gives the Olympic and sports authorities the right to ban anabolic steroids? They are widely used in many nations for patients suffering from rheumatoid arthritis and other debilitating diseases, and are available upon prescription. Ben Johnson's doctor, after all, prescribed them for him, at least according to testimony.

Eleanor Holm, a U.S. swimmer in the 1936 Olympics, is a case in point. Avery Brundage, President of the IOC at the time, banned her from competition because she had imbibed a glass of champagne at a ship's party on the trip across the Atlantic to Berlin. There are many who would question his right to have done so.

A further difficulty is that the war against these particular performance enhancing drugs seems almost as futile as the war against addictive drugs such as cocaine and heroin for the general public. Keeping pace with the development of newer and



W. E. Block, *Defending the Undefendable III*,
https://doi.org/10.1007/978-981-16-3957-9_60

better body building pharmaceuticals, and often outstripping it, is the technology necessary to disguise their use.

Whatever the shortcomings, there is a clear need to establish some sort of rules that everyone must follow. “A level playing field” is a much abused notion when applied to free trade, but when it comes to sports, it is vital. If there is no commonality to which sports participants must be held, the whole point of athletic competition vanishes. We might as well assign some people to the starting line, and others 10 yards behind or in front.

The big question is, what must be equalized? In high schools and colleges, the amount of training is subjected to egalitarian considerations, for example, team practices are limited to a specified number of weeks. This is not done in professional endeavors. In swimming there is virtually no difference in the type of equipment used, given that everyone has access to the latest in terms of swimsuit technology. In sail-boating and car racing, there are gigantic disparities. Here, the competition is as much between men as gear. Bicycle racing could equalize the apparatus by random assignments to bikes, but has chosen not to do so. Some sort of equalization must be imposed, but its dimensions are not given to us from on high.

The drug scandal stems from the fact that commonality cannot now be achieved. We can impose stricter and more frequent controls, but we can only hope that the testing mechanism will be able to overcome those which mask drug usage.

A more radical solution to the present drug scandal is the suggestion that the rules be relaxed completely, allowing everyone to take the muscle-building drug of his choice. The problem with this is that we will no longer know what the human body—unaided by drugs—is capable of; we will only see the result of the combination of such artificial stimulants plus training. (Yes, these materials may be harmful. But we're talking about adults here, and they have the right to weigh the pros and cons and decide such issues for themselves.)

A compromise is to urge the creation of two completely different sections of the Olympic Games (and all other related professional sports activities). One would be an "open" division, where medications of all kinds and varieties would be allowed. The other would be a "closed" division, open only to the drug free. Every subsequent world record would have an asterisk, or not, depending upon drug usage.

This is no panacea; no compromise ever is. We would still face the difficulty of drug users posing as drug-free athletes. But the compromise would go a long way toward resolving a most perplexing difficulty, since with two divisions there would be less incentive to cheat.

Under present institutional arrangements, the drug taker is not violating the non-aggression principle of libertarianism. Yes, he is out of step with the widely promulgated rules in this regard, and thus may properly be accused of something untoward. But we may take this one step further, and ask whether those in charge have any right to set up these rules and penalize those in defiance of them. If it is a purely 100% private affair, then yes. But as long as governments are still involved, matters are not so clear.

# Chapter 61
# The Olympic Commercializer

Up until 1984, the Olympics were noted for splendid athletic accomplishments, coupled with financial disaster. The 1976 Games in Montreal, for example, posted a monumental $1 billion deficit.

For the first time in the history of the Olympics, the 1984 event was run by private enterprise. Yes, instead of cost-plus, trough-wallowing bureaucrats, the LA Olympic games were brought to us courtesy of the marketplace. Thirty four major US corporations had underwritten the costs in return for publicity. The roll-call of honor in this regard included such stalwarts as Anheuser-Busch, Coca-Cola, ABC t.v. and radio, American Express, *Sports Illustrated*, Xerox, Levi-Strauss, Budget Rent-A-Car, General Motors, United Airlines, Canon, Kodak and Fiji Phot Film, AT&T, Pacific Bell, IBM, MacDonald's, Converse, Allied Corp., Arrowhead Puritas Waters, ARA services, Atari, Atlantic Richfield, Motorola, Sanyo, Southern Pacific, Southland, Times-Mirror, Warner Communications, Westinghouse Electric, Transamerica, Mars Inc. and First Interstate Bank of California. Their corporate names deserve to be written in gold and inscribed in the hearts and minds of all people who value private initiative, resourcefulness, and enterprise.

With this procedure the hard-earned incomes of the world's people will no longer be savaged by the tax collector in order to put on this athletic extravaganza. These events will be brought to us at a much cheaper price—due to the well-known efficiency of private enterprise compared to public. And best of all, the taxpayers will no longer be forced to underwrite these costs, at any level. That is, instead of forcing people to pay these costs through the tax system, voluntarism was used, and the necessary financing was garnered through ticket sales, sponsorship, advertising, sale of broadcast rights, etc.

But the complaints against the market principle were legion. Accusations filled the air: "buck-chasing," "the death of the Olympic spirit," "the dollar sign Olympics," "the dollar green tarnish on Olympic gold."



W. E. Block, *Defending the Undefendable III*,
https://doi.org/10.1007/978-981-16-3957-9_61

Behind most of these objections is the ideal of the amateur Olympics. This vision was held by Pierre de Coubertin, the originator of the modern Olympics who must by now be spinning in his grave. In his view, the games were not to be sullied with the gross presence of the filthy lucre of the marketplace. That would not pass the smell test. No, they were to be above all that. Holding their noses aloft at so plebian a notion, these contests were to be run by gentlemen, that is, aristocrats, who need not dirty their hands with the need to earn a living, and who could thus devote their full leisure time to the pursuit of athletic excellence. From whence, then, would spring the money necessary to finance these games? Why, from government, via compulsory taxation. That would be the "pure" way to go.

We can thus see that the objections to Olympic commercialization are rooted in upper class values. It is also easy to see that a strictly enforced philosophy amateurism, the bete noir of the patrician world view, would only make it far more difficult for the less well-off to take part in athletic competition.

Paradoxically, then, this "lusting after the buck" which is so heatedly repudiated by the press, is actually in the interest of those without too many dollars to their credit. And the insistence upon Olympic "purity" plays into the hands of the most economically fortunate (not "privileged"; that implies something illicit).

For years, too, professionals were not allowed to take part in these games. Their mere presence would sully this extravaganza. After all, there is something not really "top drawer" about having to work for a living.

On the other hand, from a strict libertarian point of view, if a bunch of upper class twits want to discriminate against those who dirty their hands with being paid (ugh) for services rendered, they are entitled to do just that. But, it comes with particular ill grace for them to cast aspersions on those of us who relish the most gifted athletes on the planet competing with one another, even if they are, horrors!, paid employees.

We seem to have a fetish for anti-commercialization in our society. If a woman goes to bed with a man and no money changes hands, this is not a crime. If this financial arrangement is made, the exact same act becomes criminal. If one person donates a kidney to the other, free of charge, he is considered a hero. But when he asks to be paid for this identical behavior, he is punished by law. Whassup with that?

# Part X
# Finance

# Chapter 62
# The Billionaire

Bernie Sanders ran in the race for Democratic standard bearer in the 2020 election; the hatred of billionaires he espoused and inculcated to a large part of the electorate still burns with a white-hot heat. This chapter is dedicated to cooling things down, at least a little bit.

Here's an important question that should be asked of all presidential candidates: do you favor billionaires or oppose them? Do you want there to be more or fewer of them at the conclusion of your term in office than at the outset should you be elected? I think this challenge will separate the sheep from the goats.

How do I, a libertarian and an economist, answer this question? My response? I dunno. It all depends on what type of billionaire we are talking about.

This question is akin to: would you like to eat this undifferentiated substance? Here, again, it all depends. If it is a poison, then, no, thank you. If it is a strawberry milkshake, then, yes, bring it on. Or, would you like to take a plane, a car, or rely upon your own 2 feet? Again, I haven't a clue. It all depends upon the distance to be traveled. For a trip of 10,000 miles, get me into the air. For 20 miles, an automobile will do just fine. For 20 feet, the distance between the couch and the fridge, hoofing it is the way to go.

My reply is crucially predicated upon how billionaires came by their vast wealth. There are several ways in which this can occur.

One, through laissez-faire capitalism. Here the billionaire earns stratospheric wealth, every penny of it, through the free enterprise system. Consider an amalgam of the following very rich people: Henry Ford, Bill Gates, Michael Milken, Oprah Winfrey, Mr. Charles Montgomery "Monty" Burns, Scrooge McDuck, Lebron James. Not these "people" themselves; rather an idealized type of them, an amalgamation of all of them. Assume these billionaires never took a cent in government subsidies. How, then, did they come by their vast wealth? They did so entirely via voluntary exchange, with not a single solitary exception.

Suppose one of these super affluent personages sold a good or service for $500. How much did the buyer value this item at the point of sale (ex ante)? We cannot tell



W. E. Block, *Defending the Undefendable III*,
https://doi.org/10.1007/978-981-16-3957-9_62

for sure, but we do know that it was a rate greater than that amount. Perhaps $600 would have been the highest price the buyer would have been willing to pay. If so, he earned $100 from the purchase, his consumer surplus. What value did the vendor place on this good? Posit that the full cost of putting it together amounted to $300. If so, he gained $200. The Marxists amongst us (are you listening, Bernie?) would call this exploitation, or out and out robbery, since the rich man profited at the expense of the poor one. What "expense"? True, based on this numbers the zillionaire seller gained $200 while the relatively poor buyer only came away with an extra $100, but these numbers could easily have been reversed. But it cannot be denied that both improved their economic positions. Of course, after the fact, ex post, one or both may have regretted his decision to engage in this commercial interaction. But in the absence of a lemon car (covered by insurance, warranties), or changing tastes, etc., this is indeed rare in the free enterprise system.

The same considerations hold true then the billionaire purchased the raw materials, or the factory, necessary to put together this particular good. In all such transactions, there would have been mutual benefit, at least ex ante.

Nor is labor an exception to this general rule. Mike Bloomberg, say, hires a technician for $100 k per year and a floor sweeper for $10 per hour. Did he expect to benefit from these two dealings? You bet your boots he did; you don't get rich by impoverishing yourself. If he didn't anticipate a profit, he would not have employed either of them. True, if he errs in this regard, he would fire the worker, but, still, he would have lost money thereby. He could not have suffered such a loss too often, and still amassed his gigantic fortune.

What about the employee? It is the same old story. Taking all things into consideration, the salary, the commuting, the working conditions, etc., all of those who labor in the salt mines of Mr. Moneybags do so because in their view, this is the best opportunity open to them. They, too, thus benefit. If not, they would not have taken on the job. If and when they no longer feel they still gain, they can quit and search for greener pastures. If you want to wax poetic about this and say they were compelled by poverty to do so, fine. Just don't deny that the employer was their benefactor, and that they were also his. Trade of any kind is mutually beneficial.

The second type of billionaire is the crony capitalist. One category thereof includes Lynden Baines Johnson, the Clintons and all other politicians whose documented life-long salaries are only a small proportion of their total holdings. Where did all the rest come from? Regulations, subsidies, gigantic bribes disguised as "speaking fees" selling influence, etc.

Then there are firms who profited not only from supplying valued products but from government subsidies, regulations, sweetheart contracts, tariffs and other hand-cuffings of competitors. These firms are usually mentioned in this category: Alliant Techsystems, Archer Daniels Midland, BAE Systems, Blackhawk Industries, Blackwater, Boeing, Chrysler, Colt, General Dynamics, General Motors, Goldman Sachs, Halliburton, KDH Defense Systems, Lenco, Lockheed-Martin, Martin-Marietta, Monsanto, Northrup-Grumman, Oshkosh Defense and Raytheon.

Yet another category of the unjustified billionaire is the kleptomaniacal socialist. For example, Idi Amin, the Marcoses from the Philippines, the Duvaliers from

Haiti. Their ill-gotten gains stem from ripping off their impoverished citizens (it appears that you can get blood out of a stone if you are sufficiently ruthless), and seizing foreign aid presumably intended for them.

Did the actions of these super wealthy cronies constitute a positive sum game as did those of the first type of billionaire? Of course not. Rather, they were indicative of zero-sum games (think poker with no house take) where the winnings of all the winners necessarily equal the losses of all the losers. More like, even, negative-sum games where social wealth of all decreases (the winners win less than the losers lose) due to the costs of these forced transactions.

Bernie and his ilk simply do not distinguish between these very, very different types of billionaires. (Interestingly, the Senator from Vermont previously inveighed against "millionaires and billionaires." Now that he has himself joined the former group – lots of book sales, he now owns three houses, he only castigates the latter.) That is a moral flaw on his part.

What is the third source of wealth other than laissez-faire capitalism and cronyism? It is inheritance. But this devolves into the former pair of categories. That is, if you have inherited billions from an honest entrepreneur, athlete, movie star or television personality, it is rightfully yours. Some critics may think you don't deserve it, but your parent certainly had the right to bestow it upon you. As for the latter, you are inheriting stolen wealth, which should indeed be taken from your parent and/or from you, after the intergenerational transfer.

Fair-weather friends of the free enterprise system such as Nobel Prize winner James Buchanan favor a 100% inheritance tax. They, too, fail to make the "fine" distinction between crony and free market capitalist billionaires. As with most taxes, those on inheritance tend to be avoided. Large birthday gifts to children are one way to avoid them. Shall we tax them too, and at 100% of income?

In the Democratic debate of 2020, then candidate Mike Bloomberg said of his fortune: "I earned this money through hard work and now I'm giving it away." I don't know about the hard work part of this statement but if he earned it all honestly, there is no reason for him to be apologetic; he is an honest market-place billionaire. There is absolutely no reason for him to apologize for that success.

He is sorry about all too many things. His stop and frisk policy while mayor of New York City saved numerous lives. And, to be sure, "black lives matter!" Of course, so do white and all other lives. As for giving it away, Bill Gates does quite a bit of that too. Yet, it is not at all clear that his good charitable works helped the human condition more than the very process through which he earned his gelt in the first place.

# Chapter 63
# The Bankrupt

This state of affairs is a tragedy from the personal point of view of people compelled to take on this role. An entrepreneur pours more than his life savings into a business. Along went his heart and soul, too. And, yet, in the event, he failed to convince enough customers to purchase his offering, and/or enough suppliers to sell factors of production to him at low enough prices, to continue in business. They say that small grocers can never fail since they always can eat their stock. But this is not true. There are lots of "mom and pop" operations that litter the pages of financial failures. Yet, despite the fact that these are personal calamities, when viewed from an entirely different perspective, they can be seen as not only neutral, but as a positive benefit.

How so? That is easy to demonstrate. Resources are limited. At any given time, there are only so much of them: land, human labor, capital goods. If no firm ever went bankrupt, from whence would spring the wherewithal to undergird new ventures? Yet, if no new operations can ever come into being, we approach something akin to economic arteriosclerosis. No, just as dead cells in the body make way for live ones, business failures spell opportunities for fresh undertakings. One simply cannot have "creative destruction" with no "destruction" e.g., bankruptcies, at all.

Then there is the issue of misallocation of resources. At one time, there was an economic need for hula hoops (you wiggle around in them; don't ask), beta maxes (an old-fashioned way of watching movies at home), non-electronic picture taking (remember the Kodak moment!?) and typewriters (these are those things, for the uninitiated, that have keyboards but no screens; how did that work, you may well ask? They used paper, of all things. Don't believe me? Go look it up. Get thee to a museum). But then, events, changing tastes, innovations, overtook these industrial offerings. People wanted something different in these and many other such cases. How could the consumer be served? By bankruptcies, of course. The firms producing these and numerous other items no longer sought by customers went to the wall. Their expenditures exceeded their receipts. Even if they tried to bail themselves out based on previous savings (loans were no longer forthcoming) there was only a limited time they could stave off the inevitable. Bankruptcy was the end result.



W. E. Block, *Defending the Undefendable III*,
https://doi.org/10.1007/978-981-16-3957-9_63

So, let us hear at least two cheers for bankruptcy. It hurts some people, to be sure. But, without it, we would achieve economic stultification, something harmful to everyone.

Should we have bankruptcy protection by law? Chapter 11, Title 11, of the United States Code, protects bankrupts. It enables firms that seek this legal protection to ward off creditors while they become reorganized. We might as well protect dead cells in the body. This is a warrant for disaster, whether we are discussing the body politic, the body economic, or the plain old human body. What about "protecting" creditors? What about protecting live cells? What about protecting economic newcomers some of whom in the future may also fail, but at least they have not yet done so? No, no, no, there is no economic sense in any such attempt to undermine the free enterprise system. Nor do such laws pass muster under the libertarian legal code. Debts must be paid, and debtors not shielded from creditors seeking what is due to them.

# Chapter 64
# The Predatory Lender

A predatory lender whose name shall not be revealed really believes in beating down the customer's door. In what may be a Guinness Book of Records—Hall of Fame advertising breakthrough, this company recently sent through the mail personalized and unsolicited checks for $1500 to tens of thousands of people all across the country.

This was not a freebie, though. Anyone who cashes in this check thereby agrees to borrow the $1500 from this firm at a significantly higher than market rate of interest! Talk of tempting people with visions of sugarplums and lemonade fountains.

And this, indeed, is what has disturbed many social commentators about the initiative—that it will place the poor in an unviable situation as they go into debt over their heads. Says one pundit, a prestigious financial columnist: "What I'm afraid of is that those in desperate financial straits may have blurred vision. I can see these people telling themselves: 'Well, the $1500 really will help with the cash flow…'. But if, by chance, they don't pay, they will be hounded by one more bill collector and possibly end up in court."

Because of sentiments such as these, there has been a widespread call for prohibition of promotional practices of this sort.


W. E. Block, *Defending the Undefendable III*,
https://doi.org/10.1007/978-981-16-3957-9_64

"I'M SORRY, JOSEPH. WE CAN'T LEND YOU THE $1200 TO BUY THAT 2ND HAND PICKUP TRUCK AND LOG SPLITTER, BUT DO YOU KNOW WHAT I'M GOING TO DO? I'M GOING TO GIVE YOU EACH A LOLLIPOP—WOULD YOU *LIKE THAT*?"

But this is entirely unjustified. Any government interference with advertising lending availabilities—even at usurious rates—would, paradoxically, hurt the poor, the very people the prohibition is expected to help.

Middle-class people, those with credit cards, established credit ratings, long histories of financial viability, have no need for a $1500 loan at such higher than market interest rates; they have far cheaper loan opportunities available to them through more traditional channels. Rather, it is the poor, who may almost be defined in terms of their lack of gilt-edged credit ratings, who are likely to take advantage of this offer.

Middle-class commentators may deplore this new added opportunity given to the poor, but they usually do so for one or two reasons. They may not realize that those less well off financially than themselves do not have as many credit avenues open to them, as are commonly enjoyed by the more affluent.

And/or they may not care. Instead, they may adopt the paternalistic attitude that "we know better than the poor what is in their own interests." This can account for all those crocodile tears shed by the middle-class pundits on behalf of their supposedly child-like financial inferiors, the poor.

So much for the practicality of prohibiting such offers.

What about deontology? Are any rights violated by offering people loans at high interest rates? None that I can think of. By the way, I am now making an offer to all readers of this book: I'll sell you this here paper clip for $1,000,000. It is a really nice paper clip. It will hold a few papers together without any difficulty. There is nothing special about this office supply; it is not made of gold or platinum or anything like that. It is just an ordinary paper clip, indistinguishable from its many "brothers and sisters." I am offering it at such a high price since I'm greedy; I can use these bucks. This offer of course is more than just a bit silly, but the question is have I violated anyone's rights in so doing (by the way, this offer is off the table for all children, senile people, etc.) Clearly, there is no rights violation involved in this offer.

But the same applies to the proposition made by the unnamed lending institution.

# Chapter 65
# The Anti-egalitarian

Open your eyes, gentle reader. Peruse that thar sunset or this beautiful flower. Visual magnificence is all around us, from a baby's smile to the rainbow.

Now, close one eye. Yes, you. Keep it closed shut just for a moment. It won't kill you. Work with me on this. Are those gorgeous visions still out there? Well, yes, even if in somewhat attenuated form. We lose a bit of depth perception with only one eye. If this were permanent, and not just an experiment I am now imposing upon you, you would have to give up all attempts to become a professional baseball player or a race-car driver. There, depth perception is all-important. But life would go on pretty much as it does with two working eyes. Our second eye is important. It is more than just merely convenient. However, we could live an otherwise normal life without the eyesight with which it furnishes us.

Now close both eyes. And keep them shut. No peeking will be tolerated. You, the curly hair headed kid in the third row, keep them tightly shut. Imagine what life would be like under the condition of no sight at all, not even faint gray images. This could ruin your entire day, to say nothing of the rest of your life. You would need a guide, or a seeing-eye dog, or a special cane, or the "kindness of strangers" more than merely upon occasion. This is not to say that blind people cannot live happy, rewarding productive lives. They can, they can. But the inconvenience of not even one good eye is not to be underestimated.

As an Austrian economist, I cannot say that the move from no eyesight to one eye is more important than a single eyed person gaining yet another, and becoming normal in this regard. All I can say is that I, along with virtually everyone else on the planet, would prefer two good eyes to one, and the latter to none. However, in my role as a non-economist I can, without fear of contradiction, make that very claim. Therefore, if we take one eye from a fully sighted person, and transfer it to a blind man, so that both come out of this little experiment with the eyesight of a single eye, when we add up the wellbeing of the two of them, there will be a gigantic increase in total happiness. The individual from whom we relieved of one eye will move to a slightly lower indifference curve, so to speak, but the formerly blind man



W. E. Block, *Defending the Undefendable III*,
https://doi.org/10.1007/978-981-16-3957-9_65

who can now see out of one eye will gain an astronomical amount of "happies." To put this in less formal terms, this will be due to the fact that the loser, here, loses far less than the beneficiary gains.

What has all this to do with egalitarianism, the subject of the present chapter? Have we wandered too far afield? No. Egalitarians are only fair-weather supporters of their own doctrine. They do not have the courage of their convictions. This being the case, there is one less reason for the rest of us to credit them with truth on insight for their position. If they were to really act on this position, they would not go prancing around, fully sighted, with two, read two, eyes. They would have long ago have donated one of them to the betterment of a blind person. If they do not act upon their supposed beliefs in this manner they do not hold them too firmly. This is a polite way of saying they are hypocrites.

Egalitarians such as Thomas Piketty (who opines that the rate of return on capital is greater than the rate of growth of the economy), John Rawls (he of the original position behind the veil) and James Buchanan (who favored a 100% tax in inheritance) call for government to forcibly take money from the rich and give it to the poor. Yet none of them has yet donated as much as even a single eye to anyone else.

Those who publicly support this philosophy of equalization, such as the intellectuals mentioned above, are undoubtedly intelligent. Evil, yes, but not stupid. Posit that their average IQ is, oh, 150. There are individuals out there with IQs of 50. Imagine for a moment what that would be like. Possibly, to employ Kurt Vonnegut's short story "Harrison Bergeron," an IQ of that level would be akin to being forced to wear a set of earplugs, that blast loud raucous sounds at you every few seconds, in terms of being able to think clearly. Suppose it were possible to transfer IQ points from those who had too many of them (150) to those who had too few (50), so that both the donor and the done end up with 100. (If Robert Nozick can concoct all sorts of weird imaginary machines, then so can I). Surely, this would be the egalitarians' dream come true. But how many intelligent egalitarians do you think would voluntarily engage in this transfer? About as many who have already given up one eye, I would imagine.

The views of most advocates of this perspective do not contemplate applying it to vision or intelligence. Rather, they limit their scope to what these characteristics make roughly possible in the first place, namely income, or wealth. But the same principles apply, or at least should, to everything. Egalitarians rely on the notion that a dollar taken from a rich man means less to him than that same amount received by a poor one. They depend upon the fallacious notion of interpersonal comparisons of utility, plus the more sensible diminishing marginal utility of money or wealth. But there is nothing in the latter that implies both the wealthy and the impoverished start at the same point or have the same characteristics throughout. In technical terms, they need not be located on the same diminishing marginal utility curve. This would undermine the conclusion of net benefits of the transfer, even if interpersonal comparisons of utility were valid. Both the man in the street and most professional economists buy into both notions, although the latter have no excuse for this fallacious belief. Further, the egalitarians are hypocritical in this dimension as well: they have far more wealth than the average. Yet, you do not see people such as Picketty, Rawls and Buchanan donating most of their money to those poorer than them.

As of the time of this writing, egalitarianism has taken hold of the body politic. Bernie Sanders and Elizabeth Warren propose a wealth tax, the sole purpose of which is to level out well-being. Estimates are that this initiative of these social justice warriors will cost multi-billionaires up to a full half of their net worth.

One problem with this greedy tax grab is that these funds have already been taxed when they accrued to wealth in the form of increments of incomes. Double taxation, anyone? Another difficulty, philosophically a more serious one, is that egalitarianism is itself dead from the neck up. First of all most intellectual and academic seekers of equality are safely ensconced in tenured positions in our institutions of higher learning. They earn, typically, in the low to mid six figures. They are now in a position to actually do something about unequal wealth and income. Do they avail themselves of this golden (pardon this expression) opportunity, by voluntarily giving away substantial portions of their possessions to the poor? To ask this is to answer it: of course not. Thus, they are hypocrites.

But why should these "progressives" limit themselves to transfers of mere money to the impoverished? Why not include, instead, or in addition, the characteristics that garner wealth in the first place? Suppose it were possible to transfer IQ points from those above the mean to those below it. This is grotesque, of course, but it is congruent with this philosophy. Want to bet that no one even those fervently espousing this perspective will acquiesce in engaging in this reallocation? They are entirely happy to redistribute OPM (other people's money), but not OPIQ, and certainly not their own.

We have barely scratched the surface of this reductio ad absurdum of ours. Intelligence is far from the only desiderata that constitutes the good life. Some of us are outstandingly beautiful. Others, let us just say, were at the end of the queue when this characteristic was being handed out. Was this fair? Of course not. One day, possibly, we will have machines capable of righting this wrong, which cries out to the heavens for redress. The attractive people do not deserve their good looks. Let us take some of it away from them, and give it to the needy in this regard. Which Hollywood leftie will be the first to volunteer to step up to the plate and make an ugly person more beautiful?

We do not need to resort to future inventions to embarrass the socialists, virtually all of whom are marching about replete with two kidneys, the usual complement. If they were true to their evil views they would donate one of them to the some 80,000 Americans who now rely on kidney dialysis machines to keep them alive.

One last shot. Recently, I participated in a half marathon race. The leaders clocked in at around one hour. But the variance was immense. Some very fit people staggered in after four hours. Is this fair? Is this conscionable? No way. Immediate transfer of running speed is requisite.

Let us hear no more about the high moral status of egalitarianism.

# Chapter 66
# The End the Fed Supporter

A pre-Covid brou-ha-ha entered into by president Trump concerns interest rates. The Federal Reserve System is raising them to inappropriate levels, in the view of Mr. Trump; he would like them to remain as low as possible, so as to pump up the economy. Specifically, he averred: "I think we have much more of a Fed problem than we have a problem with anyone else."

Members of the economics profession are divided on this matter. Some argue that pre-Covid unemployment rates were at near-record lows, and quit rates high (indicating worker confidence). There were then more help-wanted advertisements than unemployed people. Also, they maintained, it is easier to nip inflation in the bud than to wrestle it back down to the ground. This would tend to suggest higher interest rates are justified so as to cool down an economy possibly becoming overheated. All of this mitigates in favor of raising rates to historically more normal levels.

However, argue other dismal science professionals, the Fed is too keen to see an inflationary threat. Excluding food and energy, which oscillate more rapidly than other elements of it, the then consumer price index had increased by an annual rate of only 1.6%. As well, it is difficult to argue with such economic success, which has emanated at least in part from low interest rates, a precedent followed under the Obama Administration.

But whatever their views on whether small, gradual boosts in interest rates are justified, the financial soothsayers are united on one thing: the Fed operates best when it is kept independent of politics. This has been the policy of the executive branch for lo these many years. Until Donald Trump, that is, according to some commentators. The overwhelming proportion of economists maintain that the President should adopt a strict hands-off policy. Appoint its leader, and then let the Fed be the Fed.

Why are interest rates so important? Simply because they pervade the entire economy, every jot and tittle of it. Prices of steel, fuel, food, are of course important, but their scope is far more limited. Interest rates are integral to calculating present



W. E. Block, *Defending the Undefendable III*,
https://doi.org/10.1007/978-981-16-3957-9_66

discounted values, pretty much the be-all and end-all of all economic evaluations, investing, buying, selling, etc. Plus, these rates impact all other prices, including these of other such important staples of the economy.

So, should the Fed raise or lower interest rates? Mr. Trump wanted them as low as possible, so as to pump up the economy, in time for the election of 2020. This is sometimes referred to as the "political business cycle," which conforms Fed policy to the preferences of those who hold political power. Many others think the time is right for a return to normalcy, and to slow down the previous over-exuberant economy.

Let us ask a very different question: should the price of lima beans be boosted or decreased? This is a silly question: the proper answer is, allow supply and demand to set the price of this foodstuff. In that way, we can avoid shortages and surpluses. Non-market decision making for this issue smacks of central planning Soviet style.

But, contrary to the views of practically all and sundry, it is the same with interest rates. It is identical. There is no difference. Allowing the Fed, and not the supply and demand for loanable funds, the savings and investment decisions of millions of market participants based on time preferences, to determine the height of interest rates, equally reeks of central planning. The Fed, in this view, amounts to the Sovietization of an absolutely crucial aspect of our economy.

Ah, but the critic will say the Fed must set the money supply, and without its wise determinations, the economy would veer, helplessly, from vast unemployment to inflation and back again in never-ending horrendous cycles. The Fed's job is to attain price stability and the maximization of employment. However, a quick peek at the roughly one hundred years before and after the establishment of this institution in 1913 indicates that the oscillations of the business cycle were much smaller before than after. As for price stability, the dollar has lost something in the order of 95% of its value since the Fed came on stream.

Should the Fed raise or lower interest rates? Neither. It should get out of the way of the free enterprise system. Interest rates, as in the case of all prices, should be determined by the marketplace. End the Fed.

Why is this chapter included in the present book? This is due to the fact that the advocate of ending the fed is seen as a weirdo and treated with great derision. Only a few "nuts" like Dr. Ron Paul, it is thought by our betters, would even contemplate so scatter-brained an idea. And yet … Critics have not yet learned that central planning is socialism, and it creates havoc in all realms of the economy, up to and including its lifeblood, money.

# Part XI
# International

# Chapter 67
# The Water Seller

"Water, water, everywhere, but not a drop to trade." That, except perhaps for water in containers seems to be the Canadian policy on the matter.

Said one high-placed politician from that country, "We're not going to let Americans have any of our water. That's our policy." To the extent that Canadians are unified on anything, this determination would seem to apply to this one issue. A member of the opposition peppered the ruling party for assurances that large-scale diversions of fresh water not be allowed.

A Canadian environmental group released a Gallup poll which indicated that seven out of 10 Canadians don't want water, snow or ice exported to the U.S., and would be less likely to support a political party that allowed such occurrences. Water was named as the most essential natural resource in this survey, followed, distantly, by farmland and forests.

Virtual unanimity of opinion, however, hardly guarantees common sense. It may only indicate that people tend to think in the same tired ruts. And this, unfortunately, applies to the present case.

Among the disquieting elements in the present discussion is that it doesn't seem to have occurred to anyone to determine the price Canadians might be offered in return for their precious but renewable water resources. All participants act almost as if the question were one of giving this fluid away, for free. But trade is just about the opposite of that. It is not the unilateral making of a gift; it is rather, an exchange of commodities, or a sale of a resource in return for cash.

Suppose, then, that our neighbors to the north were to receive $10 per quart for their $H_2O$. Is there any Canadian who would not be deliriously happy to sell water to the U.S. on these conditions? Why, by sending us a few trillion gallons—a mere pittance in terms of the astronomical availabilities—they could all be rich beyond their wildest dreams.

Naturally, no one would rationally offer such an exalted price under today's conditions. Perhaps on the moon, or Mars, one day far in the future; not here and now. But the point still holds: crucial to a determination of whether it is in the



W. E. Block, *Defending the Undefendable III*,
https://doi.org/10.1007/978-981-16-3957-9_67

interest of Canadians to sell water is what they would be offered in return. Without knowing that, they are not in any position to accept or decline such an offer. This basis element of economics seems to have escaped the inhabitants of the "true north, strong and free." Perhaps it is too cold up there for rational thought.

What if the price offered were more reasonable? Say, one penny per barrel? Then, the advantages and disadvantages of it might be more evenly balanced. Perhaps the best result under these conditions would be to meet part of the demand in an attempt to obtain still more advantageous terms of trade.

There is a great difficulty, however, in any such scenario. Water, unlike other natural resources, is not privately owned. Rather, it is possessed on much the same basis as are commodities in the pre-prestroika Soviet Union. That is, the government owns them.

Under the inspired leadership of Vladimir Putin, the Russians are battling valiantly to overthrow almost a century-long dependence on central economic planning. Unfortunately, at the very time the Communists seem to be embracing the teachings of Adam Smith, politicians, pundits and professors in the West are urging a move in the very opposite direction. (The reactions against free trade, privatization and deregulation are cases in point.)

"...AND IN NEARBY CEDARVILLE, MOTORIST JOHN WHARTON DROVE INTO THE 'MILK KARWASH' FOR HIS WEEKLY ENRICHED, HOMOGENIZED MILK CAR WASH. UPON CLOSE INSPECTION HE FOUND IT TO BE LOW FAT SKIM MILK. THE CAR WASH OPERATOR WAS SUMMONED BEFORE A MAGISTRATE AND FINED $250."

It will not be easy to privatize water resources (I have co-authored an entire book making that case). Indeed, the very idea will appear ludicrous to many. But if

Canadians are to put water exports on a business basis, if they are to become wealthy international "drawers of water" at a time of drought, no less must be undertaken.

There seems to be some sort of magical thinking about water; and that is not limited to Canadians. It couldn't be because this substance is a liquid. Oil, wine, milk, beer, orange juice all take upon that format, and it does not seem horrendous that they are commodified. There seems to be some sort of quasi—religious opposition to putting this resource on a commercial basis. The closest analogue would appear to be widespread revulsion against buying and selling human blood. But until and unless this bias is eradicated, economic rationality will not be able to be applied in these cases.

Having bashed our neighbors to the north, it is now time to give a smackdown to us Americans. When the Japanese purchased Rockefeller Center, the howls of outrage could be heard all across our nation. "How dare this occur," was one reaction, "the U.S. is not for sale." Another, a more vicious one was, "Hey, we beat 'em fair and square in World War II; we should be taking over their country, not them over ours. USA! USA!"

These economic illiterates are making the same mistake as the economically misbegotten Canadians. (Maybe imbecility is contagious??) Both neglected to ask the price being offered!

Is the U.S. for sale? It all depends upon the price we can get! Suppose the offer was the remainder of the planet? Everyone else would have to move to our 50 states; we could take over the rest of the world. If so, even the poorest of us would end up with not acreage, but square miles of territory.

Not satisfied yet, us greedy Americans? Suppose the previous offer included a cure not only for cancer and covid but for every disease known to man? Posit that this would allow us all to live to 110. Are we now ready to sell out the land now under the control of the U.S.? Hey, there's nothing sacred about the dirt, the rivers, the lakes which now comprise our country. We'd still have the ideal of the nation, even if we all lived elsewhere in the world, and that comprised America.

Ok, ok, we've got a greedy bunch of patriots. I'll increase the offer. We all get to live forever, in the bodies we had at a time of our individual choosing (most of us will pick 25 years of age or so). In addition to owning the rest of the world, I'll toss in the Moon and Mars. Heck, the rest of the solar system too, plus the technology to make them all habitable (don't ask). Wait, I'll sweeten the deal: I'll toss in instantaneous travel to anywhere in the universe we want, and no tickets from any cop for going faster than the speed of light.

Of course all these offers reek of science fiction. I only mention them to bash the views of Canadians who won't sell water without asking the price, and Americans still sore at the Japanese for purchasing Rockefeller Center, and those who sold this real estate to them, ditto.

By the way, I assume that the sellers of this property in mid-town Manhattan valued the money they received more highly than what they had to give up. Addendum: a few years later, the Japanese owners of this valuable acreage and buildings sold it for less than they paid.

# Chapter 68
# The Illegal Immigrant

Most of the headlines made by illegal immigrants in North America these days are made in the United States. No immigration story emanating from either Canada or Mexico has ever garnered as much attention from the mass media as the story of how Zoe Baird was forced to withdraw her name from consideration to become President Bill Clinton's Attorney General after confessing to the heinous "crime" of providing decent jobs for two illegal immigrants from Peru.

But Democrats are not the only ones caught with their hands in the immigrant cookie jar. Donald Trump, scourge of illegal immigrants, has hired dozens of people from Mexico without proper papers, to work on his golf courses and other properties. At least Zoe Baird was not associated with any vendetta against undocumented workers. The same cannot be said for President Trump.

Illegal immigration is of great concern from the perspective of labor markets. Many people are on the warpath in an effort to protect Americans from the hordes of would-be immigrants who allegedly wanted their jobs.

Now, there may be many reasons for limiting immigration, but protecting scarce jobs is certainly not one of them—notwithstanding the fact that this is the rationale most commonly offered for doing so. On the contrary, the fear that there is only a certain number of jobs to go around, and that if immigrants take any of them, there will be just that many fewer available for native workers, is one of the most basic fallacies in all economics.

This "lump of labor" fallacy is easily refuted. New immigration (and also the increasing native population) brings not only additional workers, but additional consumers as well. Why else would people be willing to work, if not to engage, ultimately, in consuming more goods? Immigration authorities are especially fearful of accepting newcomers during periods of high unemployment rates. But unemployment is due to a whole host of unwise government policies (minimum wage laws, excessive union pay scales promoted by labor legislation, liberal unemployment insurance policies), that have little to do with immigration rates.



W. E. Block, *Defending the Undefendable III*,
https://doi.org/10.1007/978-981-16-3957-9_68

The U.S. could double, triple or even quadruple its acceptance of refugees without in any way increasing its unemployment rate. Instead of unemployment, new immigrants would bring with them economic buoyancy, hard work, thrift and productivity, as they always do.

Consider the following speculation. Right now, the future of Hong Kong looks uncertain. Red China has asserted her sovereignty over this island despite the agreement she made with Great Britain after the 99-year lease with that country ran out in 1997. The deal was "one country, two systems" but this has been fully abrogated. Suppose that as a result the inhabitants of Hong Kong, all five million of them, apply en masse to immigrate to the U.S. (Not that China would allow any such thing, but work with me here).

Would it be economic disaster to accept such an application? Hardly. This hypothetical Chinese presence would only enhance the American economy. They would create more job opportunities for the present population, not fewer. For these people are among the most hardworking and prosperous on the face of the Earth. They have carved a magnificent standard of living out of barren, inhospitable rock.

Because our current immigration policy would bar the possibility of accepting all these Hong Kong Chinese, it cannot be defended on economic grounds.

On the other hand, it cannot be denied, there are immigrants, and would-entrants to our country, who are murderers, rapists, arsonists, kidnappers, etc. If our economic well-being is not to be destroyed, we must have a means to separate the sheep from the goats. Private property rights is the best answer to this challenge, see below in this chapter.

"...MR. OCRAJA SAYS HE'S A LUDDITE AND IF HE'S PERMITTED TO ENTER THE COUNTRY, HE'LL SMASH JUST ENOUGH MACHINERY TO OPEN UP JOBS FOR HIMSELF AND HIS 3 BROTHERS ABRÖJA, STUMFA AND ES̈KEEJI."

So much for the economics of the situation. What about the libertarian philosophy? How does this impact the immigration situation? Does illegal immigration necessarily violate any rights that the libertarian must respect?

Consider the following. An immigrant from China, or Africa, or Mars for that matter, swoops down to earth in his helicopter (or rocket ship), and lands in a totally unoccupied stretch of land in the middle of the Rocky Mountains somewhere in Wyoming. He begins to homestead the land, puts in a crop, builds a house, digs for water, sets up a well, etc. Has he yet violated the non-aggression principle? Has he stolen anything from anyone? Has he engaged in trespass?

It is difficult in the extreme to see how he has since, remember, this is totally virgin territory we are now discussing, never before touched by human hands (or feet). Along comes Immigration and Customs Enforcement (ICE) and arrests him for this act of homesteading; e.g., illegal immigration. Who is in the right here, and who is in the wrong? It is difficult to reject the notion that the police are in error, not the undocumented immigrant.

According to some libertarians who really ought to know better, this immigrant really is trespassing, since the U.S. government is the rightful owner of this land, and holds it in trust for all American citizens. Stuff and nonsense! This entity has never "mixed its labor with this land" and thus cannot be the licit owner of the terrain. This is a more than curious argument even for a limited-government libertarian, let alone an anarcho-capitalist. Either this exceeds proper state function, or the government which claims sovereignty over these lands ought not to exist in the first place. In any case, none of the other residents of the country ever so much as visited the acreage under dispute.

But what about pragmatic considerations, apart from unemployment. Suppose a quadrillion Martians emulate this homesteader (you didn't realize that the fourth planet from the sun was so highly populated?) They are all swell people, we may assume, but if they all came here, they would overcome our beloved culture, contribute to overcrowding, and not vote in the correct manner (none of them are libertarians). Is there any way to exclude them from our country without violating their rights? And, even more so for the criminals, mentioned above, who would enter our country only to violate the rights of present inhabitants.

Fortunately, there is: privatize all land and water in the U.S., every square inch of it. Leave no stone untouched by privatization, nor drop of $H_2O$. Every molecule. Then, there would no longer be any virgin territory on which newcomers could perch, without any by-your-leave. If they did so, they would then but only then be guilty of trespass. We could then have our cake and eat it too: pick and choose who we wanted as neighbors, without committing any rights violations. With every inch of territory owned by someone, anyone who invites in foreigners would then be responsible for them if they committed a crime under the libertarian legal code.

# Chapter 69
# The Free Trader

A unilateral declaration of free trade on the part of our country is hardly at the top of the agenda of the government. But it may be of interest to examine this public policy alternative since it is the only one compatible with libertarianism.

"Fast track" negotiations sputter along at a snail's pace, or, more to the point, rarely get under way at all, lost in a tragic escalating tariff war. An end to all international trade barriers is in our national interest, but may well be out of reach no matter how desirable.

A unilateral end to all tariffs, quotas and other such interferences has at least the advantage that it could be attained without the co-operation of any other nations. Moreover, it would undoubtedly bring great benefits to this country. (To say that it will be difficult to convince Americans of the merits of such a move, however, would be the understatement of the century.)

Under a regime of this sort, our consumers would be able to avail themselves of goods at hitherto unimaginably low prices. This alone would be a magnificent spur to our standard of living, and would probably do more for the well-being of the poor than all the welfare programs on the books put together.

Further, this boon to consumers would likely spill over to our export sector. For the additional funds spent in the U.S. would eventually return here, in the form of domestic purchases. And this could not help but spur additional domestic employment opportunities.

In fact, a unilaterally-declared end to trade barriers is such a good idea that it makes sense to adopt this policy right away, and forget all about negotiations. This holds true except for one small point: better even than a unilateral declaration would be a mutual agreement between all countries to fully open our common borders to commerce.

We can, in effect, gain a smaller amount right now under unilateralism, or wait it out and possibly attain a greater amount later on, if the negotiations succeed, through mutual agreement.

Given this situation, two questions present themselves for analysis.



W. E. Block, *Defending the Undefendable III*,
https://doi.org/10.1007/978-981-16-3957-9_69

First is the question of whether a "bird in the hand" is worth more than "two in the bush." Economic theory alone cannot answer this, because we do not know the size of the immediate (unilateral) payoff, the larger size of the later (negotiated gain), nor the rate of discount through which one may be meaningfully compared with the other.

"NO, THERE'S NOTHING WRONG WITH BARTERING, SHEILA, BUT WHAT ARE YOU GONNA DO WITH 1200 BOARD FEET OF TONGUE AND GROOVED OAK FLOORING?"

Secondly, we must ask whether seizing the "bird in the hand" will increase or decrease the likelihood of our ever capturing the second, which is still lurking "in the bush." That is, will a unilateral declaration of free trade enhance or retard the chances of every other country agreeing to end their own trade restrictions?

According to one theory, if we go it alone, we can shame all other nations into following suit. If we blaze the path toward free enterprise, we can expose their otherwise hypocritical allegiance to the marketplace, and thus force them into a golden era of mutual free trade.

According to another, it is impossible to embarrass them. Commercial relations between countries are a matter of pure brute bargaining power, in this view. If we throw away our chips (their access to our markets), they will just laugh at our hope or expectation that they will throw away their chips (our access to their markets).

Unfortunately, again, there is nothing in the realm of economics that can provide a definitive answer to this puzzle. Nevertheless, the "dismal science" may be of some use.

For one thing, it clearly exposes and categorizes our ignorance. This helps us to know where and how we must seek additional information. For another, it indicates that there may well come a time when the certain but smaller benefits of unilateralism will start to outweigh the larger but ever-receding gains of waiting for a negotiated settlement of completely open commercial borders world-wide.

This, it must readily be admitted, amounts to saying that were we ever fully convinced that all others under no conceivable circumstances would negotiate a free-trade agreement with us, we should then declare our borders open to their commercial incursions. It appears uncomfortably close to advocating that we turn the other cheek, trade-wise.

Yet, for all of the superficial implausibility of the idea, it is sound public policy. American industry would benefit from stepped-up exports, from the ability to increase specialization, to join in a partially open international division of labor, and from the added economies of scale that this would make possible. The domestic consumer, too, would gain from a unilateral dismemberment of trade barriers.

It may seem unlikely, but it's comforting to know that our economic lives are not fully in the hands of the rest of the world. It would be vastly preferable to be able to negotiate full free trade with all of them (that is, we all agree to end quotas, all tariffs and other such barriers). But we would benefit from a unilateral declaration of open borders even if everyone else failed to follow our inspired lead.

# Chapter 70
# The Car Warrior

What are "car wars?" One aspect is a vehicle inspection slowdown of imported Toyotas and Hondas. This is not a tariff, charging a tax on these vehicles, nor a quota, an arbitrary limitation of supply. In effect, it constitutes, merely, a tossing of sand into the mechanism of free trade: it just slows matters down.

Most people think the primary victims were the Japanese exporters. After all, this snails' pace hurts the manufacturers of these automobiles.

But in reality, such trade restrictions also harm the consumer. It is the auto buyer who was restricted from purchasing any of those thousands of cars which piled up on the docks.

These trade interferences, moreover, are an implicit subsidy to domestic auto manufacturers. If fewer of the more highly preferred Japanese vehicles are purchased, the local consumer would have a more limited set of alternatives – and be encouraged to patronize the less efficient local product. But where is the case for supporting inefficient domestic enterprise? Nowhere, that's where.

And these subsidies have a price. The benefits received by the American automobile industry, and by their powerful and highly organized unions, must be paid – by taxing other indigenous industries. A commercial "weak sister" is strengthened – by weakening numerous more viable enterprises. Such a policy renders our other industries less able to compete on a world-wide basis. It will imply future balance of payments difficulties, for those who worry about that sort of thing, not I, not I. (I have a horrid balance of payment with WalMart; I patronize them regularly, they have never once purchased any of my services. In contrast, I have a very good balance of payment with my employer, Loyola University; apart from a few meals at the cafeteria, I have it all over them money transaction wise. Isn't this silly!)

Such slowdowns also distort our industrial structure.

This policy does not encourage us to concentrate on those things for which our talents, abilities and natural resource endowments give us a comparative advantage. Instead, government tends to artificially reduce our enjoyment of those things which can be more cheaply and more efficiently manufactured abroad. As programs of this



W. E. Block, *Defending the Undefendable III*,
https://doi.org/10.1007/978-981-16-3957-9_70

sort become more fully entrenched in our economy, our industrial structure becomes more and more like an edifice built on sand.

What of the claim that the Japanese, too, maintain restrictive practices, and that therefore a slow-down is justified as a means of wringing trade concessions from them?

To be sure, the Japanese also engage in tariff and non-tariff barriers to trade. Their complaints about our economic nationalism thus come with particular ill grace. The land of the rising sun restricts the importation of autos, steel, computers and other items too numerous to mention.

But this is all beside the point, as far as our economic welfare is concerned. To refuse to embrace free trade until and unless other nations also do, is to cut one's nose off to spite one's face. It is like a child who craves friendship refusing to play with other children unless they make the first overture. Now surely the child in question will benefit if other children initiate a connection. But if they do not, he will still be better off if he continues to be forthcoming. If he does not, he loses out.

In like manner, we would benefit if the Japanese fully embraced a policy of free trade. But if they persist in their error, there is no justification for us to emulate them. We would still be better off by remaining fully open to trade. Two men are in a wooden rowboat. One of them, a real moron, shoots a hole through the bottom, and water starts seeping in. Should the other, in retaliation, shoot another hole in the boat, just to get even?

For trade, like friendship, benefits both parties, otherwise it would not take place. None of us would be willing to give up several bushels of wheat for a car if he didn't value the latter more than the former.

No, the true car warrior opposes this outbreak of economic fallaciousness.

# Chapter 71
# The Foreign Aid Denigrator

This chapter is dedicated to Lord Peter Bauer, who has done more than anyone else to critically analyze this phenomenon.

It a good time to review foreign aid policy. Heck, it is always a good time to do that, as long as this wasteful and unproductive program continues to plague both donors and recipients.

At first blush, aid to underdeveloped countries (this is a far more accurate characterization of these nations than "developing" in that some of them are actually retrogressing) seem noble, humanitarian, and serendipitously, in our own nation interest as well. After all, aid to the less fortunate nations surely must save people from starvation, encourage the development of primitive economies, increase our exports and enhance freedom by forestalling the spread of communism.

There is much evidence, however, showing aid programs to be questionable means toward these worthy ends. Further, there are strong indications that private trade and investment, currently shackled and hampered by tariff and import barriers in the Western industrial countries, may be more efficacious than intergovernmental transfers of funds (this is a neutral and far more accurate characterization of these policies; "aid," in contrast, implies that the recipients actually gain, a claim that must be rejected).

Food grants are a major part of foreign aid. Agricultural products are obviously basic, because the malnutrition which unfortunately prevails in many less developed countries is one of the blocks to economic betterment. But placing humanitarian requirement in cases of actual famine aside, even this sort of aid is fraught with danger: massive gifts can take the profit incentive out of local agriculture; with fewer farmers and less land under cultivation, this can paradoxically worsen, not improve, the long-term prospects of food production and hence safety from future starvation.

Capital grants are likewise destructive to long-term productivity. Although the ancient Egyptian pyramids were an extraordinary instance of capital accumulation, they resulted in no economic gain in the basic sense of contributing to the well-being of the great masses of people at the time. Indeed, the very opposite was the case.



W. E. Block, *Defending the Undefendable III*,
https://doi.org/10.1007/978-981-16-3957-9_71

Even more wasteful are the modern equivalents of such monument-building made possible by foreign aid: the steel mills in Egypt, the modern chemical plants in India, the tractors given to aboriginal peoples who cannot operate them, the automobile assembly plants scattered widely throughout the Third World (which are the result of protective tariffs on automobile imports as well).

These are wasteful because the products fabricated in this highly technological manner actually cost the underdeveloped countries more to manufacture themselves than they could have paid by importing the finished product from more developed countries.

Monuments are the first of the three "M's" of so called foreign aid. The second is Mercedes. These are the vehicles driven around in by the recipients, usually dictators, of the poor recipient countries. More generally, this stands for the vast wealth they garner from the donors. The third "M" is "machine guns" and we all know what they are used for: to cement the dictatorial power of the leaders of these nations.

Many people deduce from the fact that the rich countries have much capital and the poor ones little that what is required is vast capital infusions. But this wet-sidewalks-cause-rain reasoning points to almost the exact opposite of what is really needed. Capital, in and of itself, does not create wealth. It is rather the result of a process of economic development that also includes, as complementary factors, such things as the willingness to work, the skill and education of the labor force, and relatively free and private markets protected by a stable code of law so that locals are incentivized to save and foreigners to invest, without the fear of nationalization - expropriation.

"DUE TO INFLATION, MY COUNTRY DESPERATELY NEEDS A SUBSTANTIAL INCREASE IN FOREIGN AID, MR. AMBASSADOR. OUR 5 YEAR PLAN FOR MY APOTHEOSIS IS RUNNING 80% OVER ORIGINAL ESTIMATES."

One indication of the importance of these other phenomena is the fact that a large proportion of the very limited capital generated in the poor countries is actually invested in the more advanced nations, where private property rights are far more secure.

Then there is foreign "aid" in the form of technological and other education. But the difficulty is that in the absence of such facilities as fully equipped laboratories, libraries, computer centers, and without the mutual support of thousands of other similarly educated scientists and technologists, such assistance cannot be efficiently utilized. And the proof can be seen in the immigration patterns of the educated classes in the Third World: a "reverse brain drain," toward the more advanced countries. Another problem is that all too often this kind of knowledge transfer comes replete with first-world craziness: political correctness, feminism, queer studies "insights," labor unionism, radical environmentalism and all the rest now plaguing donor nations.

Foreign "aid" of whatever variety—food, capital, technology or outright cash grants—moreover set up a welfare-like dependency status on the recipient country. In much the same manner as domestic welfare programs sap the economic ambition, vitality and progress of their local clients, so do programs on international levels have similar effects.

If "foreign aid" is unlikely to help the recipient, can it at least help the donor? (Note: the focus here is on economic, not military aid, which must be justified on entirely different grounds.) Pragmatic consideration would seem to support his view. For one thing, patron nations require that significant proportions of the bilateral disbursements be spent on domestic goods and services.

But behind the bookkeeping, legerdemain, this amounts only to a free gift of goods and services to other countries, with no offsetting returns. No one is foolish enough to suppose that West German reparations to Israel actually benefitted the economic self-interest of West Germany—even though much of it took the form of exporting domestic items. Nor does the defendant in a civil case rejoice in his newfound wealth when he is forced by a court decision to compensate the plaintiff—even if in the form of goods he himself produces.

Will transfers of funds to other countries at least make it more likely that they will choose the path of democracy and market institutions rather than fall into the communist ambit? Unfortunately, not only will Western foreign aid not attain this end—it is likely to undermine it, and instead to encourage socialism and totalitarianism in the Third World.

First of all, these payments are made traditionally in the form of government-to-government grants. This strengthens the role of the public vs the private sector in the underdeveloped countries. But political freedom is a delicate and precious flower, it cannot live where the bulk of economic activity is carried on in the public sector.

Second, foreign "aid" has been given to countries that have made explicitly socialist avowals in their centralized economic plans—and our largesse has in no small degree shielded them from the repercussions of such policies and allowed them to continue unchecked down this path. For example, we find in the five-year plan of India, a country that continues to receive strong support, the view that planning should take place with a view to the establishment of a socialistic pattern of society where the principal means of production are under social ownership or control.

Of far greater benefit to the nations of both North and South is a policy of free trade and unregulated international flows of capital. This will greatly benefit the benefactors' standard of living, as we can purchase many goods such as clothing from the less developed world for far less than it costs to make them ourselves. But also of great importance, such policies will truly lead to Third World economic development—and to higher integration with our own economy.

How, then, to account for the decision of a nation whose leaders loudly proclaim their interest in economic development for the poor countries and yet remain steadfast in their determination to maintain protective tariffs, quotas and other impediments to economic intercourse with the Third World? Hypocrisy anyone?

# Chapter 72
# The Dumper

The complaint heard far and wide, and bitterly, is that foreign exporters are "dumping" products on us, selling them at prices below their own costs, let alone ours, and thus ruining domestic producers as customers flock to these artificially cheap foreign products.

As can be expected, this concatenation of events is alleged to have adverse effects on the local economy, at least as a first approximation.

True, concedes the critic of the dumper, this flood of low priced products will benefit the domestic consumer. But, he will maintain, this is only true in the short run. For in the long run when most or all of the home manufacturers and farmers have been driven to the wall, the large scale dumpers will be able to charge whatever astronomical prices they wish.

And the anti-free trade answer to this challenge? It is to slap an extra duty on dumped imports so that our fellow citizens can compete more effectively against these evil foreigner dumpers.

One problem with this response is that such additional punitive duties would be reciprocated by the other country. And then the "victimized" nation would retaliate. This tit for tat tariff escalation can end in only one way: with a radical reduction in trade and a ruination of the international division of labor.

But there is more to be said about this harebrained scenario, and interventionist tariff response—much more.



W. E. Block, *Defending the Undefendable III*,
https://doi.org/10.1007/978-981-16-3957-9_72

"...RELAX, RELAX! I'M PUTTING A TARIFF ON HIS FISH!"

First of all, this alleged dumping is not really dumping at all. If foreign producers can bring a product to the local market for, say, $10 and it costs domestic manufacturers $11 to create, this shows only that these other people are more efficient.

For dumping to be proven, it is not enough to show that entrepreneurs outside our border can produce a good more cheaply than their local counterparts; it must be shown that they sell in markets at prices below those charged in the U.S. or at prices below actual costs. And this is rarely demonstrated.

But this is a relatively unimportant point which skirts the real issue. And that is: There is nothing wrong with "dumping," even if it were shown to actually exist.

The very phrase "dumping" is a misnomer, and misleading. The word evokes a vision of foreigners flying a fleet of B52s filled with potatoes, or cars, 50,000 feet in the air and then "dumping" them on helpless citizens scurrying around seeking a fallout shelter. That's what this phrase means, etymologically, right? To "dump" is to let loose something from high above. And, since it is claimed to be harmful, it must be something along these lines.

Nothing, let me assure the scared reader, could be further from the truth. Far from bombing our residents with potatoes or forcing this vegetable down the unwilling throats of the citizenry, or compelling us to drive their underpriced cars, they are offering us "a deal we can't refuse." It is a voluntary trade which benefits both parties, otherwise it would not—it could not—take place. Rather, this entire brou-ha-ha consists of domestic producers complaining about more efficient foreign competition.

"NOW HERE'S MY PLAN, KRRYRAK. WE'LL SELL THE EARTH PEOPLE OUR MIRACLE METAL OKMINIUM FOR 100 TRILLION DOLLARS, AND THEN DO YOU KNOW WHAT WE'LL DO? WE'LL BRING THE 100 TRILLION DOLLARS BACK TO TVIK AND BURN IT, FOREVER DESTROYING THE WORLD'S ECONOMY—HA, HA, HA, HA, HA!!!"

As to the claim that the outsiders are hoping to drive local producers out of business, so as to raise prices through the roof, this is a scare tactic, a basic fallacy in economics used only in a self-serving manner by inefficient domestic producers.

Large successful businesses do not attain or retain dominant market shares by raising prices. They are achieved in the first place by price cutting (relative to quality), and this is how they are retained. A high price, in contrast, is like a bleeding fish in the ocean: predators come to attack, lured in by the specter of great profits. When (and if) the interlopers make inroads to indigenous markets, the last thing they will do is arbitrarily raise prices. This would only encourage others from further afield to enter the market as competitors.

As well, the most efficient, cost-conscious firms would still likely remain in operation in such a scenario. Protected by low transport costs, they would be able to pick off their newly higher-priced opponents and begin to raise their market shares once again.

In any case, if consumers fear that present low prices will lead to vastly higher ones later on, they, or their agents, the wholesalers, can buy futures and thereby protect themselves against such eventuality. They don't need market critics to ride to their rescue—armed to the teeth with the coercive power of the state.

But there is an even more basic economic point at issue here. If the foreigners were really selling at below-cost prices or for less than they could receive elsewhere, they would be in effect presenting a gift to the local inhabitants. The amount of the gift would be equivalent to the difference between the actual sale price and the greater amount that could have been attained elsewhere (or the difference between the price sold to the locals and the supposedly lower cost of production).

"I ASSURE YOU, MR. NAGUCHI, WE HAVE WAYS OF FORCING JAPANESE MANUFACTURERS TO BUILD PLANTS IN OUR COUNTRY!"

It would still be a puzzle as to why the greedy, capitalist pig exporters had so suddenly been overcome with charitable instincts. But we could concentrate our attention on the old adage: "Don't look a gift horse in the mouth!"

John D. Rockefeller was accused of internal "dumping." His company, Standard Oil supposedly sold this product at below cost prices, in an attempt to drive competitors out of business. When they were gone, he would unconscionably jack up prices and exploit consumers. Stuff and nonsense. The competitors could suspend operations, leave on a skeleton crew just to make sure they could quickly reopen then the "exploiter" raised prices through the roof, and in the meantime buy up that company's oil and store it. No, John D.'s success was due to the fact that he was a low cost refiner, not due to this cockamamie scheme.

Here is another example. In the aftermath of World War II, Germany paid reparations to Israel. Some of this took the form of money, others were paid in goods and services. In other words, the Germans "dumped" items on the Israelis. Did the former undermine the economy of the latter? Of course not. Had this occurred, the new country in the Middle East would just have refused the largesse forthcoming to them from the nation in Europe.

Every time a storekeeper offers a bargain, or a "loss leader," they may be with equal rationality accused of "dumping" their products on us the hapless consumers. You've heard the joke, "Please, take my wife?" Well, in like manner, we can say: "Please 'dump' on us!"

The manufacturer's authorised representative in the EU is Springer Nature Customer Service Centre GmbH, Europaplatz 3, 69115 Heidelberg, Germany. If you have any concerns regarding our products, please contact ProductSafety@springernature.com

Printed and bound by CPI Group (UK) Ltd, Croydon, CR0 4YY
30/09/2026
02225325-0012